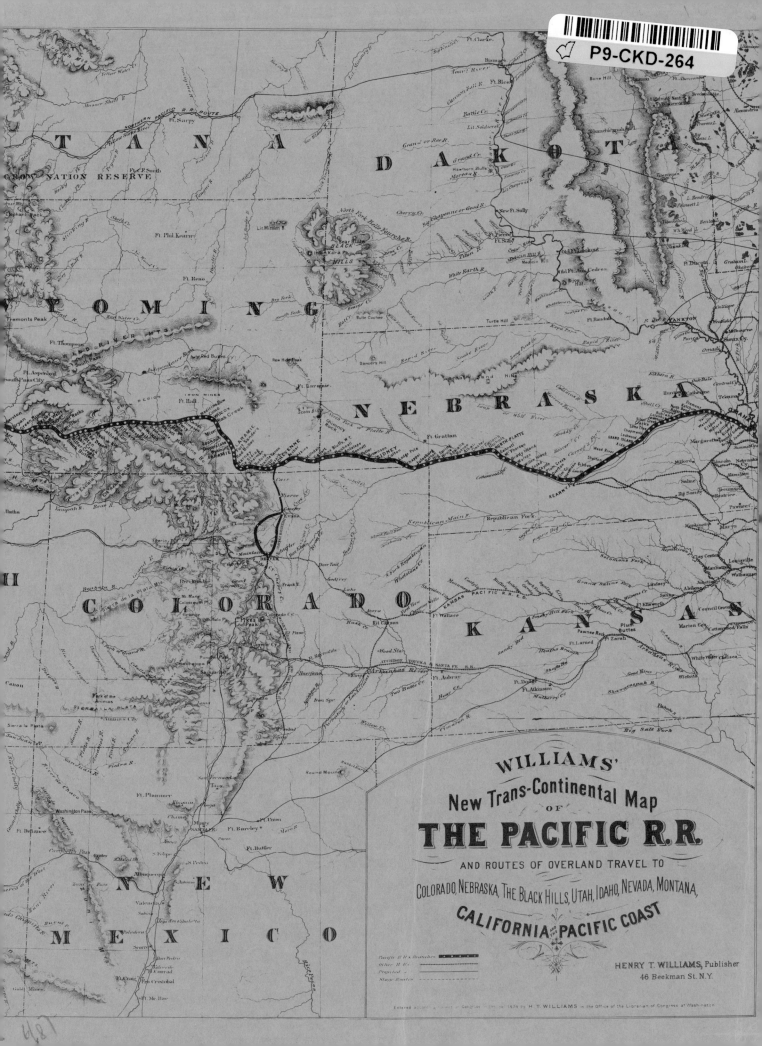

WILLIAMS'
New Trans-Continental Map
OF
THE PACIFIC R.R.
AND ROUTES OF OVERLAND TRAVEL TO
COLORADO, NEBRASKA, THE BLACK HILLS, UTAH, IDAHO, NEVADA, MONTANA,
CALIFORNIA AND THE PACIFIC COAST

HENRY T. WILLIAMS, Publisher
46 Beekman St. N.Y.

IRON HORSES
TO
PROMONTORY

IRON HORSES
TO
PROMONTORY

Gerald M. Best

GOLDEN SPIKE EDITION

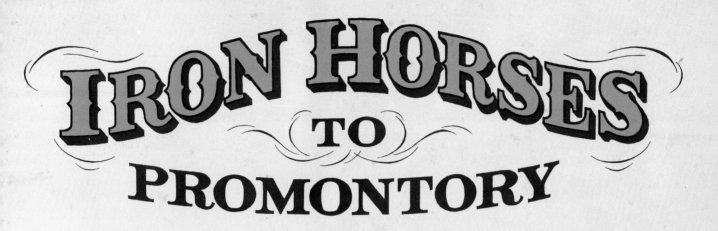

Golden West Books

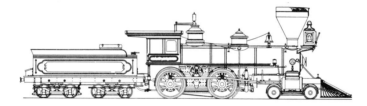

TITLE PAGE ILLUSTRATION

The Union Pacific roundhouse and shops at Laramie, Wyoming, under construction since May, 1868, had just been completed when Andrew J. Russell exposed this beautiful 10x13-inch collodion plate of locomotive No. 80 about to take water. Along the North Platte, windmills supplied engine water to the Union Pacific for nearly 40 years. — AMERICAN GEOGRAPHICAL SOCIETY

Golden West Books

P.O. BOX 8136 • SAN MARINO, CALIFORNIA • 91108

Table of Contents

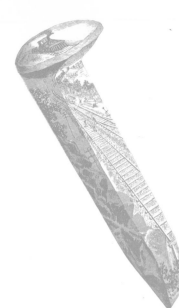

Preface

THE ACCEPTED historical definition of the Transcontinental Railroad is the combination of the Union Pacific Railroad from Council Bluffs, Iowa, to Promontory, Utah, and the Central Pacific Railroad from Promontory to Sacramento, California, with an extension to Oakland a few months later. The Central Pacific was incorporated in California on June 28, 1861, and could do nothing towards building a line east from Sacramento, its starting point, until laws could be passed by Congress which would subsidize at least a part of the construction costs.

The Enabling Act by which the Union Pacific Railroad was created was signed by President Lincoln on July 1, 1862, and under the provisions of this Act, the Central Pacific would receive the same subsidy of government bonds and land grants as the Union Pacific, for each mile of track accepted by a government commission. The Union Pacific Railroad Company was organized in Chicago, Illinois, on September 2, 1862. Ground was broken in Omaha, Nebraska Territory, in December 1863, with a small amount of grading done shortly afterwards, but it was not until the end of the Civil War in 1865 that actual tracklaying on the Union Pacific began.

Ground was broken for the start of the Central Pacific at Sacramento on January 8, 1863, long before the similar event in Omaha. Due to the tremendous difficulties of building a railroad from sea level to an altitude of over 7,000 feet at the summit of the Sierra Nevada, most members of Congress thought the Central Pacific would be lucky to meet

the Union Pacific at the eastern California border.

Over a dozen books about the construction of the two railroads have been published in the past 40 years, with three major works since 1950. As one Union Pacific official said to the writer recently, "Every last one of them except Sabin's book ends with the driving of the Golden Spike, which was only the beginning for the thousands of men who operated the two railroads after through train service was established."

Various papers have appeared in historical society bulletins on the subject of the motive power of the two railroads. An all-time roster of the Union Pacific was published a few years ago, the engine lists being grouped by types instead of in sequence, making it very difficult for anyone to reconstruct the original roster. The Central Pacific engines were listed in Railway & Locomotive Historical Society Bulletin No. 94 in 1956, but the locomotives were listed by classes and required a search by any interested historian to reconstruct the Central Pacific roster. Several papers were presented by the late David L. Joslyn of Sacramento on the history of the early Central Pacific locomotives, with biographies of the early day motive power officials. Much new information has come to light in recent years, and all this is included in the rosters of the two railroads at the end of the text. The Central Pacific roster extends to 1891, as this was the year all locomotives of the railroads controlled by the Southern Pacific were renumbered into one common system. The Central Pacific bought a total of 283 locomotives between the beginning in 1863 and the 1891 renumbering, although the highest road number ever used was No. 250. The difference was caused by the sale or scrapping of 33 locomotives. Not counted are the locomotives of subsidiary roads of the Central Pacific, which are described in the text.

The Union Pacific roster ends July 1, 1885, when a general renumbering of the main line and all subsidiary railroads occurred. At the time of this event, the Union Pacific owned 225 locomotives; also six small switch engines called "Ponies." It had acquired 300 locomotives from the start in 1864 to the renumbering of 1885, but 75 had been sold, transferred to subsidiary lines or scrapped. The Centennial of the driving of the Golden Spike will be held on May 10, 1969, at Promontory, Utah. For the benefit of the locomotive hobbyists who will be working on models of the two locomotives which headed the trains of the Union Pacific and the Central Pacific on that date, as well as the host of aficionados of the steam locomotive everywhere, this book was prepared. The complex and often devious ways in which the money to build both railroads was raised and the complicated corporate details have been skipped. Instead, the text concentrates on what most historians to date have given brief and sometimes highly inaccurate mention — the locomotives and rolling stock, their operation, and the highlights of the first few years of operation of the two railroads.

The story of the Central Pacific locomotives perhaps seems more glamorous than that of the Union Pacific power, for prior to May 1869, all of the former were brought by ship around Cape Horn from eastern ports. To the writer's knowledge, no detailed study has ever been made of the length of time required to deliver a locomotive from a factory on the east coast to the Central Pacific as a working locomotive. The information is in the various great libraries in California, such as the Huntington Library in San Marino, the California State Library in Sacramento, and the manuscripts and papers at Stanford University in Palo Alto. To dig it all out has required a great deal of reading and an enormous amount of time, which most railroad historians do not have during library hours. Fortunately, the hobby of train and locomotive watching was picked up by the reporters for the newspapers in many cities through which the two railroads passed, and though some of their observations were inaccurate, others, like those of the reporter for the *Sacramento Union* in particular, were not only accurate but elaborate. He fell in love with the locomotives, he became a pioneer Pullman car name collector and haunted the Sacramento station for

months after the trains were running through to Omaha on the chance of seeing another new Pullman car or something unusual coming in from the east. All this in the face of open hostility on the part of the owners of the *Sacramento Union* to the Central Pacific from its very beginning.

It would have been easy to write what the late Lucius Beebe termed a "nuts and bolts" tome, and to fill it with technical details quite intelligible to locomotive enthusiasts but of little interest to the general public, many of whom like to read books about locomotives if there is enough human interest accompanying the story. As many readers may not have any of the books written about the construction of the two railroads, all of which are out of print, short sketches of the progress of each railroad are included from time to time throughout the narration of the locomotives. For anyone interested in the complete history of both railroads, many excellent books are available in the public libraries.

The following libraries, foundations and individuals were of great help in furnishing pictures for use in this book;

The American Geographical Society, New York.

The Huntington Library, San Marino, California.

The State Library of California, Sacramento, California.

The DeGolyer Foundation Library, Dallas, Texas.

The Railway & Locomotive Historical Society, Charles E. Fisher, president, Boston, Massachusetts.

Donald Duke, San Marino, California.

Richard Prince, Green River, Wyoming.

Guy L. Dunscomb, Modesto, California.

Richard B. Jackson, Beverly Hills, California.

To the Huntington Library and the State Library at Sacramento go my thanks and appreciation for the use of their files of early California newspapers.

To the Public Relations staff of the Union Pacific Railroad at Los Angeles, and to that of the Southern Pacific Company at San Francisco go my thanks for the use of photographs from their collections. Most of all, my deep appreciation goes to Roy E. Appleman, Chief, Branch of Park History Studies, National Park Service, Washington, D. C. for having suggested the need for this type of book on a special phase of building the transcontinental railroad.

GERALD M. BEST,
Beverly Hills, California.

In 1868 this Central Pacific construction tra[in] carrying supplies to the advancing railhea[d] pauses in rugged Humboldt Canyon, Nevad[a] for a stereograph portrait. Note the new[ly] laid, unballasted track and minimum excav[a]tion. — HUNTINGTON LIBRARY, SAN MARIN[O], CALIFORNIA

THE CENTRAL PACIFIC

THE Central Pacific Railroad Company was incorporated in the State of California at Sacramento June 28, 1861, following the remarkable survey made by engineer Theodore D. Judah of a route over the Sierra Nevada as the first section of a transcontinental railroad. His route was considered not only feasible but could be constructed with a minimum of tunnels and rock excavation work as compared with previous surveys. Judah's only mistake was underestimating the snowfall near the summit of the Sierra, an error which was later to cost the railroad a fortune in building snowsheds and snow fighting equipment.

The new company was headed by Leland Stanford, Governor of California, and the Directors were businessmen of Sacramento and vicinity who had confidence that Judah's proposed railroad could be built if the U. S. Government could be persuaded to finance a part of it. The financial bigwigs of San Francisco would have nothing to do with this wild scheme, and as a result, the organizers of the Central Pacific were the following gentlemen: Governor Leland Stanford; James Bailey, a jeweler; Charles Marsh, gold mine owner of Nevada City; Lewis A. Booth, a Sacramento grocer;

Collis P. Huntington and Mark Hopkins, owners of the Huntington & Hopkins hardware store in Sacramento; Charles Crocker, drygoods merchant; and Theodore D. Judah, civil engineer.

Judah was sent to Washington in October 1861, to serve as a lobbyist representing the Central Pacific Railroad. Largely through his efforts, Congress passed the Enabling Act which President Lincoln signed into law on July 1, 1862. The Act authorized the construction of a railroad from the Missouri River to the Sacramento River, with loans of $16,000 a mile in government bonds for the level sections of the line and as high as $48,000 per mile on a graduated scale depending on the amount of work involved in crossing the Rocky Mountains and the Sierra Nevada. In addition, grants to the railroad of a strip of land 400 feet wide and alternate sections of land north and south of this strip were included. The two companies specified in the Act were the Union Pacific Railroad, to build west from a point later fixed at Council Bluffs, Iowa, and the Central Pacific Railroad, as previously outlined, to build east from Sacramento to a meeting point first set at the California-Nevada border, later amended to permit the Central Pacific to build 150 miles east through Nevada, and finally to continue

9

The station and shops of the Sacramento Valley Railroad at Folsom. These facilities later served the California Central and the Sacramento, Placer & Nevada railroads. — GERALD M. BEST COLLECTION

The Folsom shops and yard of the Sacramento Valley as they appeared in this 1859 scene. — R. B. JACKSON COLLECTION

Theodore D. Judah stands by the *L. L. Robinson's* tender, a New Jersey built locomotive which had a colorful career on the Sacramento Valley line. — GERALD M. BEST COLLECTION

The *Pioneer*, built by the Globe Locomotive Works in 1849, was the first locomotive west of the Rocky Mountains. Originally named *Elephant*, it became *C. K. Garrison* for 15 years, and renamed *Pioneer* when this photo was made in 1870. — GERALD M. BEST COLLECTION

building east until it met the rails of the Union Pacific.

At the time the Central Pacific was organized, Sacramento already had a railroad, the Sacramento Valley Railroad, incorporated August 16, 1852, and completed to Folsom, 22.9 miles, on January 1, 1856. Its ultimate goal was a crossing of the Sierra to the mines of the Comstock Lode at Virginia City, Nevada. According to the State Railroad Commission reports, it was built to a gauge of five feet, three and one-half inches, but newspaper accounts, historical articles and much other data indicate a gauge of five feet. Its motive power consisted of four 4-4-0 type locomotives, two from the Boston Locomotive Works, earlier known as Hinkley & Drury, and two secondhand engines acquired from Garrison & Company, contractors in San Francisco. Another five foot gauge railroad, the California Central, was built north from Folsom to Lincoln, 18.5 miles, in 1858-1861 as part of a plan to build a railroad to Marysville and points north of there in the Sacramento Valley. For obvious reasons the Sacramento Valley Railroad owners opposed the Central Pacific from the beginning. They controlled the Virginia City-San Francisco traffic; their trains met the steamers coming up the river from San Francisco to Sacramento and carried passengers, express and mail bound for the Nevada mines to Folsom, where

the Pioneer Company stages were waiting. Any railroad paralleling theirs and headed for Nevada would be a threat to their existence.

The men who formed the directorate of the Central Pacific were quite frank with Judah in stating that their first objective was to build the railroad quickly to a point far enough east of Sacramento to rob the Sacramento Valley Railroad of its traffic, by means of a new wagon road built along the line of Judah's survey. That the wagon road would be privately owned by Huntington and his associates meant that the Central Pacific would earn nothing from the wagon road profits other than its share for carrying freight and passengers between the railhead and Sacramento. To Judah, this meant the abandonment of building a railroad to meet the Union Pacific and the surrender of his ideas to the business of making money by hauling passengers and supplies to and from the Nevada mines. Judah was supported in his attitude by director Bailey and opposed by all the other directors, resulting in a showdown a few months later. The ground breaking ceremonies for the Central Pacific were held on the Sacramento River levee in Sacramento on January 8, 1863. Charles Crocker resigned his directorate to become General Superintendent of Construction, a job vastly different from selling drygoods to the housewives of Sacramento.

11

At the time of this ceremony, the Central Pacific owned not a single length of rail, no locomotives, rolling stock, or the tools needed for grading the line. Since there were no locomotive builders in California with the capability to produce anything larger than a tiny industrial engine, all locomotives and rolling stock for the two existing railroads near Sacramento had been purchased on the Atlantic seaboard and brought around Cape Horn by vessel between 1855 and 1861. The Central Pacific would have to emulate these roads by purchasing everything needed on the east coast except crossties and the lumber for buildings, car bodies, etc. The Enabling Act prohibited the importing of rails or rolling stock from Europe.

After the Enabling Act had been passed, Huntington instructed Judah to order rails, track hardware, locomotives and rolling stock sufficient to build and operate at least 50 miles of railroad, which had to be completed within two years of the start of construction to qualify for government bonds. With the Civil War well into its second year, there was a tremendous military demand for railroad material of all kinds, due to the loss of much rolling stock captured by the Confederates. Judah was able to place orders for only four of the six locomotives Huntington told him to buy, and

these sold for prices at least 50 per cent above the going price for locomotives two years earlier. He bought one from Richard Norris & Son in Philadelphia at a cost of $13,688 and three from William Mason in Taunton, Massachusetts, at a total cost of $50,374. As the passenger and freight car bodies would be built in Sacramento, Judah bought the trucks and metal parts for the cars in the East. The orders which he placed for wrought-iron rail specified a weight of 56 pounds per yard, the weight being later increased to 66 pounds for all rail used in the mountains, especially in snow districts. Wrought-iron chairs were used to tie the rail ends together, but proved to be unsatisfactory after several years use, and the line east of Truckee used fish plates bolted together at the rail joints. A large supply of spikes, switch stands, frogs, and the tools needed for tracklaying was also ordered.

Judah returned to Sacramento, arriving shortly after the ground breaking ceremony. Huntington went to New York in February 1863, established an office there, spending most of his time in Washington on the political affairs of the company which will not be covered in this story. He did take time out to go over to Paterson, New Jersey, shortly before returning home, to look at two locomotives which had been offered for sale by the firm of Dan-

The *Governor Stanford*, first Central Pacific locomotive, was photographed on a construction train shortly after going into service in 1863. Headlights were not used during the early months of construction, since no trains were run at night. — GERALD M. BEST COLLECTION

The *C. P. Huntington* No. 3 on an excursion train in 1864. Ordered for use on construction trains, it proved too light and served for many years on short local passenger runs. — GERALD M. BEST COLLECTION. (BELOW) The *T. D. Judah* No. 4 on a local train in Oakland. Note the backup headlight and pilot on the rear of the tender. — GERALD M. BEST COLLECTION

forth, Cooke & Company. These were light locomotives with a single pair of drivers, intended primarily for hauling several passenger cars on level track. Huntington was in a hurry, Danforth, Cooke & Company could not promise two heavy locomotives for him immediately, so he bought the two light engines for $20,148 and they were soon on the high seas enroute to California via Cape Horn.

On one of Huntington's trips from New York to Washington that year, he stopped off in Philadelphia to call at the Baldwin Locomotive Works, the largest builder in the country in terms of production capacity. It is not known what transpired between Huntington and the Baldwin management, but Huntington was quoted on his return to California to the effect that his company would never buy a Baldwin locomotive as long as he had anything to say about it. Except for three Baldwins inherited from the Western Pacific Railroad of California a few years later, not a single Baldwin ran on the Central Pacific. It was not until 1902, after the Central Pacific had long since become a part of the Southern Pacific and that railroad was con-

trolled by E. H. Harriman, that new Baldwin locomotives were purchased.

The sailing vessel *Young America* left New York on June 1, 1863, with the locomotive *Governor Stanford* No. 1 from the Richard Norris Works in Philadelphia, a few freight car trucks and a quantity of rail. Thomas Norrell, John H. White, Jr., and other historians specializing in the history of Richard Norris & Sons and their locomotives seem in agreement that the *Governor Stanford* was built in November or December 1862. What delayed the departure of this engine for California is a matter of speculation at this late date. The ship which brought it to San Francisco made the voyage around the Horn in 112 days, arriving on September 22, 1863. The freight bill on the locomotive came to $2,282. The steamer *S. C. Grant* and several others were on the high seas with more rail, but when all their cargo had arrived in Sacramento there was enough rail for only four miles of track.

While this material was still enroute, the quarrel between Judah and Bailey on one side and the group headed by Huntington on the other reached

The Sacramento Valley Railroad track along the top of the levee near R street in Sacramento, looking north. Many river steamers tied up along this levee during the years the Central Pacific was under construction. — GERALD M. BEST COLLECTION

its peak. Huntington set a price on the shares held by his group and told Judah and Bailey to buy them out or sell their shares and get out of the company. In September 1863, Judah and Bailey sold their shares to Charles Crocker for $20,000. Unable to raise money in San Francisco or Sacramento to buy out the betrayers of his beloved transcontinental railroad, Judah sailed for New York via the Isthmus of Panama in October 1863, for the express purpose of obtaining financing in the East to buy out Huntington's group. Judah contracted yellow fever while crossing Panama and died in New York City on November 2, 1863, just a week after the first rail had been laid in Sacramento. Judah's obsession with building the transcontinental railroad, regardless of whether or not it paid at least part of its way during construction, proved to be his undoing. In spite of Judah's untimely demise, when Governor Stanford commissioned an artist to paint the scene of the joining of the rails at Promontory, Utah, he requested the artist to include Judah, though he had been dead for over five years. Also painted into the assemblage were Crocker, Huntington and several others who were not present at the ceremonies.

The locomotive *Governor Stanford* was transferred to the river schooner *Artful Dodger,* and arrived in Sacramento on October 6, 1863. It came in knocked-down form, such items as the cab, pilot, smokestack, headlight, engine and tender trucks and cab fittings being crated separately. The boiler, tender tank and frame, and the chassis were all in separate crates. These were brought to Front and K Streets, where a temporary building had been erected. On October 20, the work of assembling the locomotive began under the supervision of engineer W. M. Davis. Parts requiring the services of a machine shop were taken across the levee to the

shop of Goss & Lambard, who also had small brass and iron foundries, the best in the city. The first rails were laid at the corner of Front and I Streets on October 26, and by November 6, the rails had reached 10th and I Streets on the north levee. On that day, a fire was built in the boiler of the *Governor Stanford* and after Davis was satisfied that the locomotive would run when it was placed on the rails, he notified Crocker that he was ready to test the engine. On November 9, a connection was made between the track on which the engine had been assembled and the main line. On the following day the officers of the road then invited a few citizens including State officials and local bankers to have a ride on the engine to the end of track and return.

Thus, on November 10, 1863, the *Governor Stanford* was again fired up, and to quote the *Sacramento Union,* "Steam was finally let on and after several trials the engine passed onto the permanent track and moved slowly forward. The invited guests took their positions alongside the track, ready to jump on board; but before the locomotive halted, the tender, which constituted the only accommodation for passengers, was crowded to its capacity with men and boys, who climbed on two or three deep while it was still in motion. The engine moved slowly east as far as 4th Street with the design on the part of engineer Cash of returning to Front Street for the expectant passengers. It was found, however, that the engine was not in running order and that some of her valves, pumps, etc., required overhauling. She returned to the starting point and for the time being, the trip was abandoned."

Champagne and other refreshments which had been placed in the cab for the officials were retrieved and though a cannon was fired 35 times in

14

honor of the first run of the locomotive, it was a premature event. Davis and Cash went to work on the *Governor Stanford* and by evening all the defects were remedied. On November 11, the following day, an official excursion was made from Front and I Streets to the railhead at 22nd Street, but it was preceded by several round trips made by Cash to be sure the engine was right, the tender being crowded with freeloaders each time. When the official excursion party reached the railhead, champagne was opened and for an hour the officials toasted their first ride on the Central Pacific. To quote the *Union*, toasts included — "To the *Governor Stanford* — may her boiler never, like the glass of Father Gallagher at present, become empty." Also, "To the *Governor Stanford* — may she hold out in service until there is a Governor Stanford, Jr. ready to take her place." Little did engineer Cash or the others present on this occasion dream that the engine would still be in existence 106 years later, though her boiler is very, very empty.

Through November, tracklaying continued east of Sacramento until the rails reached the American River bridge, which was almost completed. Car building began in that month, in new shops erected near 6th and H Streets, Huntington engaging the services of Benjamin Welch, former Superintendent of Shops of the Sacramento Valley Railroad, to supervise the work. Soon a number of platform car bodies had been built and mounted on the trucks brought from the East. Today we call them "flat cars" or "flats," the word "platform" having fallen into disuse within a few years. On the 1st of

December there were 16 vessels enroute from the East with iron rails for the Central Pacific — one had been out of New York for six months. The first to arrive was the *Thatcher Magoun*, which made the trip in 135 days. An enginehouse was built between the blacksmith and carshop buildings in anticipation of the arrival of the other five locomotives which had been ordered. By the middle of January 1864, an additional 20 platform cars were built and rushed into service. An excursion was held on January 19, 1864, several of the platform cars being equipped with benches for the passengers. The party was taken to the railhead 12 miles east of Sacramento, where the *Governor Stanford* was turned on a temporary turntable. The road's only locomotive was a very much overworked machine during these days, such things as a boiler-wash and light repairs being done at night.

On February 9, 1864, the ship *Electric Spark* 128 days out of Boston arrived in San Francisco with one locomotive, material for six passenger cars, and other supplies. A total of 1,200 tons of rail arrived that same day, and was soon trans-shipped aboard river schooners and barges. On February 18, the boiler of the locomotive *Pacific* No. 2, the first of the Mason engines, arrived in Sacramento on the schooner *William*, and on the 25th the rest of the locomotive and the passenger car parts arrived. The following day the parts for two passenger, two baggage, and 16 platform cars arrived in San Francisco and the log jam was broken.

On March 21, 1864, the *Governor Stanford* hauled the first two completed passenger cars, filled with officials and their guests. It ran to the

The first bridge on the CP crossed the American River 4 miles east of Sacramento.
Fire destroyed this double Howe Truss in 1870, and an iron structure replaced it.

The *Atlantic* No. 5 built by William Mason in 1863, hauled the first passenger train into Colfax. This locomotive also brought the CP train from Sacramento to Newcastle in the great train race with the Sacramento Valley Railroad in 1864. — GERALD M. BEST COLLECTION

In the scene above, the *Conness* No. 6 hauls one of the first passenger trains between Roseville and Newcastle, as it nears Jenny Lind station. — COLLEGE OF THE PACIFIC

The trial trip of the *Conness* March 16, 1865. The locomotive stands on Arcade Creek trestle with its tender and cab filled to overflowing with guests. — GERALD M. BEST COLLECTION

end of the line and back, so the locomotive was not only the first to run on the road, but the first to haul a passenger train. The first ten passenger cars on the Central Pacific were flat roofed, without ventilating clerestories, resembling their counterparts on the Sacramento Valley Railroad, from where car builder Welch had come. On March 23, the *Sacramento Union* in a dispatch from San Francisco stated that on March 12 the ship *Mary Robinson* had arrived in San Francisco with the locomotives *C. P. Huntington* and the *T. D. Judah*, while the ship *Success* brought material for two passenger cars, 15 box cars and 35 platform cars, besides more rail. Several historians believe the above two locomotives made the journey on the *Success*, but unless the reporter in San Francisco, who sent the dispatch got his ships mixed, it would seem the *Mary Robinson* brought the locomotives. The engine *Pacific* No. 2, turned out by William Mason in September 1863, made its first run on March 25, 1864, and on the same day the *Governor Stanford* brought into Sacramento a train of three cars of granite rock from Brigham's Quarries, the first revenue freight carried by the Central Pacific.

Six days after they came through the Golden Gate, the two Danforth, Cooke locomotives arrived in Sacramento on the steamer *Pet*. Work of assembling them began two days later. On April 9, 1864, the *T. D. Judah* No. 4 made its trial trip and was immediately set to work on the line. This engine had a separate tender, with a two-wheel trailer under the cab, giving it more fuel and water capacity than the *C. P. Huntington* No. 3, which was tested on April 15. The latter had its water and fuel compartment in back of the cab, mounted on the engine frame and supported by a four-wheel truck, making the engine a 4-2-4 tank-back type. Ironically, the day the *C. P. Huntington* went into service the supply of crossties was exhausted and all track construction was halted for over a week.

The *Governor Stanford* hauled the first revenue passenger train on the Central Pacific on April 15, 1864, from Sacramento to Roseville and return, covering the 18 miles in 39 minutes each way. At this time it was announced that the California Central tracks, which crossed the Central Pacific at Roseville and extended from Folsom to Lincoln, a few miles north of Roseville, would be narrowed from five feet to standard gauge, and that as soon as this was done, the Central Pacific would operate the trains of that road. Another Mason locomotive, the *Atlantic* No. 5 arrived in Sacramento on the schooner *Clara* on May 26, 140 days out of Boston. It was a 4-4-0, exactly like the *Pacific* No. 2, and

was tried out and certified for service on June 21, making a run to the railhead at Newcastle the following day. The sixth locomotive, the *Conness* No. 6, a 4-6-0 designed for freight service and weighing 35 tons, arrived from the East after a 190-day voyage around the Horn during which the sailing vessel had been driven back twice by severe storms. The boiler arrived in Sacramento on November 28, 1864, but a month passed before the rest of the parts were delivered. Named the *Arctic* when it left the factory, the name was changed to *Conness* as soon as it arrived in Sacramento, in honor of California Senator John Conness. The locomotive seemed enormous in the eyes of the Sacramentans, who saw it when it made its first run on March 16, 1865, and a great crowd assembled to see the engine leave on its trial trip, its tender loaded with officials and their friends as it steamed out to Arcade Creek trestle and back. Its rating was 319 tons up a 2.2 per cent grade, so it easily handled a train of six passenger cars loaded with excursionists to Newcastle and return, ten days after it went into service.

The *Conness* No. 6 completed the group of locomotives ordered by Judah and Huntington, and except for an unexpected addition from California, no more locomotives were purchased for over a year, during which time all the money the company could raise was expended on advancing the railhead towards Colfax, the goal which would provide the company with 50 miles of completed railroad and would qualify it for further issues of government bonds. At this time the company hired J. H. Graves as Master of Machinery, he having had considerable experience in the shops of several eastern railroads.

During all the building activity of the Central Pacific in that year, the owners of the Sacramento Valley Railroad had not remained idle. They conceived the idea of building a new river port to be called Freeport, a few miles down the river from Sacramento, and to connect it with the Sacramento Valley Railroad by means of a new railroad from the Freeport wharf to the town of Perkins, nine miles distant. The traffic to and from Virginia City and San Francisco would then use the river steamers to Freeport, the railroad to Perkins and Folsom, and the stages over the Sierra to the Nevada mines. The Freeport Railroad was organized in 1863, rails and a locomotive were ordered in the east, and in the spring of 1864 the Placerville & Sacramento Railroad was organized to build from Folsom to Placerville, 38 miles, shortening the stage journey to Virginia City by that distance.

The *Atlantic* with a westbound passenger train from Newcastle, crosses Dry Creek bridge a mile west of Junction, later called Roseville. — COLLEGE OF THE PACIFIC

18

The first Central Pacific public time-table. In early day railroading, the schedules were posted on bulletin boards in the stations. — SOUTHERN PACIFIC

CENTRAL PACIFIC RAILROAD.
NO. 1, TIME CARD NO. 1.
To take effect Monday June 6th, 1864, at 5 A. M.

TRAINS EASTWARD.			STATIONS.		TRAINS WESTWARD.	
Frt and Pass No 3	Frt and Pass No 2	Pass & Mail No 1.		Frt and Pass No 1	Pass & Mail No 2	Frt and Pass No 3.
5 P M leave	1 P M leave	6-15 A M, l	Sacramento.	8.45 A M arr	12 M arr.	6.40 P M ar.
5.50 5.55 } mt frt	2·15	3.55	18 Junction.	18 3	11.20	5.55 5.50 } mt. Ft
6.09	2·38	7·05	22 Rocklin.	4 7.40	11,07	5.37
6.22	2·55	7.15 meet F.	25 Pino.	3 7.15 mt pass	10.56	5.25
6.40	3.30 P M arr	7.30 A M arr	31 Newcastle.	6 3.45 A M, L	10.30 A M, L	5 P M, L

Trains No. 2 and 3 east, and 1 and 3 west, daily, except Sunday.
Trains No. 1 east and 2 west, daily.

LELAND STANFORD, President.

The roundhouse at Rocklin, with the *Majestic* No. 45 on the turntable, was the service point for helper engines after it was completed in 1865. — GERALD M. BEST COLLECTION

The *Humboldt* No. 10 with a construction train of rails and ties, crosses the trestle at Newcastle. — HUNTINGTON LIBRARY, SAN MARINO, CALIFORNIA

The railroad scene at Sacramento in the mid-1860's, with the Sacramento Valley Railroad station and freight house in the center. The Central Pacific station is just up the street. The city water pumping station is the large building in the distance. — SOUTHERN PACIFIC

Looking down Front Street in Sacramento in a reverse view to the scene above. The Central Pacific station is on the right, while the Sacramento Valley station is down the street. — RICHARD B. JACKSON COLLECTION

The Freeport Railroad locomotive arrived in Sacramento on May 28, 1864, on the steamer *Harriet K.* With the unlikely name of *Nebraska*, it was a Danforth, Cooke 4-2-2 like the *T. D. Judah*, with separate tender. It was set up by the Sacramento Valley Railroad and made its first trip to Folsom on July 6, 1864, going into service immediately on the construction train which provided the rails and ties for the Freeport Railroad.

Work was pushed on the line from Folsom towards Placerville, being completed to Latrobe, 13 miles from Folsom in August 1864. The Freeport Railroad, its warehouse and wharf were finished by then, and train service to Freeport began on August 19, 1864. Two days later, an event which had been prearranged by Charles Crocker and the owners of the Pioneer Stage Lines attracted more attention than a championship horse race. It was to be a test to see which route from San Francisco to Virginia City was the faster; via river steamer to Freeport, rail to Latrobe, and stage coach to Virginia City, or via the same steamer to Sacramento, the Central Pacific to the railhead at Newcastle, and their stage coach line to Virginia City. The steamer *Chrysopolis* left San Francisco on the morning of August 21 with 43 passengers bound for Virginia City, plus a quantity of late San Francisco newspapers. The *Chrysopolis* docked at Freeport at 11:12 p.m., discharged 38 of the 43 passengers bound for Virginia City, besides several large packages of late San Francisco newspapers, and left immediately for Sacramento. At 11:15 the locomotive *G. F. Bragg*, formerly the *Nebraska* and renamed in honor of the Freeport Railroad's principal stockholder, left Freeport with one coach and

For years the river steamer *Yosemite* met Central Pacific trains at this dock, a short distance from the Pacific Railroad Depot on Front Street. — ROBERT WEINSTEIN

made a fast run through Folsom to Latrobe, 38 miles in 90 minutes. There the passengers boarded several stages and were quickly on their way to Virginia City.

In the meantime, the *Chrysopolis* steamed up the river to Sacramento with the other five passengers bound for Virginia City. At the Central Pacific station they were joined by three Sacramentans, one of whom was Charles Crocker. The Central Pacific train, hauled by the engine *Atlantic,* with James Campbell as engineer, left Sacramento at 12:04 a.m. on August 22 and made the fastest run to Newcastle since the railhead reached there — 31 miles in 42 minutes. There the party boarded one of Crocker's new stage coaches and proceeded over the Sierra via Donner Pass and Truckee, through heavy rain and what at times seemed almost impassable mud. Had they known the Pioneer stages were having the same trouble, they need not have worried. The Central Pacific stage arrived in Virginia City to the cheers of a large crowd gathered along the main street, at 1:05 p.m., just 13 hours and one minute from Sacramento. The Pioneer stages arrived at 10 p.m., or 22 hours, 29 minutes from Freeport. Boiled down to hard statistics, it was nine hours faster to go via Sacramento

and the Central Pacific's rail-stage route than the Freeport-Latrobe rail-stage line.

This defeat did not cause the Sacramento Valley Railroad owners to raise the white flag. They continued the Placerville & Sacramento Railroad to Shingle Springs, reaching there June 14, 1865, and eliminating another eleven miles from the stage ride. The California Central Railroad, in a bad way financially, sold out to the Central Pacific on November 10, 1864, its owner, Sam Brannan, accepting $120,000 in Central Pacific stock for the railroad and its rolling stock. The latter included four locomotives, all built by Richard Norris in 1860 and a number of passenger and freight cars. The Central Pacific operated the trains from Folsom to Lincoln through 1864-65, but it was obvious that the road had been acquired as part of a plan to build north through the Sacramento River valley to Marysville and Redding.

The Central Pacific reached Auburn, 36 miles from Sacramento, on May 11, 1865, and Clipper Gap, seven miles east of Auburn, on June 10. The railhead continued to advance through the lower reaches of the Sierra that summer, and on August 16, 1865, the Sacramento Valley Railroad sold out to Huntington and his associates. Construction of

Strobridge's portable turntable in use by the *Conness* at end of track near Auburn. Just one of the many novel features of Central Pacific's construction. — HUNTINGTON LIBRARY, SAN MARINO, CALIFORNIA

Train activity at Auburn depot shortly after it was opened to traffic in May 1865. Auburn became the hub of stagecoach traffic to the mining towns of Nevada County. — HUNTINGTON LIBRARY, SAN MARINO, CALIFORNIA

the Placerville & Sacramento Railroad had already ceased when the railhead reached Shingle Springs; the Freeport Railroad had been closed down due to lack of business, and the Central Pacific rail-stage route to the Nevada mines had become the main artery for passenger and freight traffic. Before the year was up, the gauge of both the California Central and the line of the Sacramento Valley from Sacramento through Folsom to Shingle Springs had been narrowed to standard, and work on changing the gauge of the engines of both roads was begun at the Folsom shops. The Freeport Railroad remained unused until November 1866, when a strange feat was performed by first narrowing the gauge from five feet to standard so that locomotives could run over it; then after the warehouse was dismantled and shipped in sections to Sacramento, the rails were pulled up and the railroad abandoned. The locomotive *G. F. Bragg* became Sacramento Valley No. 5 and Freeport's bid as a principal river port was lost forever.

The Central Pacific received an unexpected dividend as the result of the abandonment of the Placerville & Sacramento Railroad's plans to build beyond Shingle Springs. The road had ordered two locomotives from the San Francisco firm of H. J. Booth & Company, successors to the Union Iron Works, which had begun locomotive building early in 1865. In July 1865, when one locomotive had been completed, the order was cancelled. Booth offered the engine to the Central Pacific at a reasonable price, and a deal was made. Thus, with little fanfare, Central Pacific No. 7, the *A. A. Sargent*, came up the river on a barge, fully assembled and already tested on the rails of the San Francisco & San Jose Railroad. A 28-ton 4-4-0, the Booth engine was first class in every respect, and one would think that the Central Pacific would have ordered more like it when they began buying locomotives again. Perhaps it was because of the constant refusal of the bankers in San Francisco to take the plans of a group of Sacramento merchants seriously that caused Huntington to give his patronage to other builders; in any event, No. 7 was the only Booth engine purchased by the Central Pacific.

The year 1865 marked the first use of Chinese laborers by Crocker in grading east of Newcastle. He had been unable to find enough local labor to do the work, and over the opposition of almost everyone connected with the enterprise, including his new assistant, Charles Strobridge, he hired a few unemployed Chinese left stranded in the various mining towns. He found them as good or better than the average white laborer, though at first the whites refused to work within sight of them. When the supply of available Chinese was exhausted, Crocker sent an agent to China and soon the men he hired there began coming into San Francisco by the thousands, until near the end of construction he had 10,000 of them working on the line. They proved their worth in many ways; they were sober, industrious and clannish, keeping to themselves and causing no trouble for Strobridge. By their example they shamed the local laborers into doing a full day's work and in time they earned the respect of everyone connected with the enterprise.

In the late spring of 1865, the railhead of the Central Pacific was approaching Colfax, 54 miles from Sacramento, and grading had been partly completed for many miles east of there. With the Civil War over, the demand for locomotives by the military had not only ceased but they were selling rather than buying. The locomotive builders of the east could accept orders and promise deliveries. Six freight locomotives of the mogul or 2-6-0 type, and two ten-wheel freight engines were ordered from the Paterson factory which had built the *C. P. Huntington* and the *T. D. Judah*. With Cooke having left the company, the name of the firm became the Danforth Locomotive & Machine Works. Four additional locomotives were ordered from William Mason, three freight engines of the 4-6-0 type the same as the *Conness* and one 4-4-0 for passenger service.

On March 1, 1866, the Danforth moguls *Nevada* and *Utah* were landed at Sacramento, and at the end of the month a third mogul named *Winnemucca* was unloaded from the schooner *Star of the Union*. The engine's name was promptly changed to *Humboldt*, thereby robbing the Chief of the Piute tribe of a chance to see his name on a locomotive. By July 1866, four of the Danforth moguls and two of the Mason engines had arrived. The *Sacramento Union* reported that the *Oneonta* and *Washoe*, both Danforth moguls, had left New York on the ship *Haze* on April 10, 1866, the Danforth 4-6-0 *Piute* sailed on the *Intrepid* April 19, its mate the *Carson* on the vessel *Washington* April 19, and the Mason tenwheelers *Owyhee* and *Idaho* on the ship *Revenue* out of Boston on March 9. Over 100 cars of all types were now in use on the Central Pacific, and 100 more were on order. After building the bodies of the first ten passenger cars at Sacramento, 16 complete coaches were ordered from the Wason Manufacturing Company of Springfield, Massachussets, and the last of the twelve new locomotives, the *Washoe*, was placed in service November 15, 1866, at which time the railhead was at Cisco, 92 miles

The *A. A. Sargent* No. 7 at Sacramento in 1866. This locomotive was the only Booth & Company engine to run on the Central Pacific. — GERALD M. BEST COLLECTION

During the construction era, the *Nevada* No. 8 was photographed at Dutch Flat. It was the only Mogul type locomotive not rebuilt to a 4-4-0 by the Central Pacific. — GERALD M. BEST COLLECTION

The *Oneonta* No. 14 at Cisco when the town was bursting with construction activity. The locomotive was named after C. P. Huntington's home town in New York State. — GERALD M. BEST COLLECTION

23

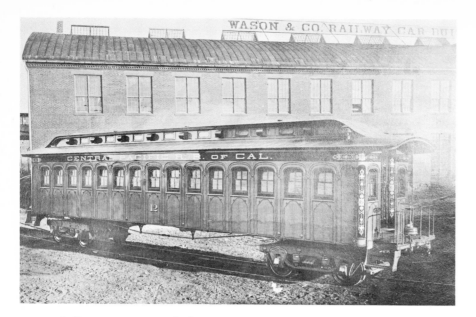

east of Sacramento, and the wagon road to Virginia City was getting shorter and shorter.

In June 1866, the Central Pacific signed a contract with the firm of McKay & Aldus of Boston, a company then but two years old, its owners anxious to become an established major builder of locomotives. At prices which were well under those asked by contemporary builders, McKay & Aldus agreed to deliver 25 passenger locomotives of the 4-4-0 type and 17 4-6-0 freight locomotives. Orders were also placed with Richard Norris in Philadelphia for ten locomotives of various types, and four from the New Jersey Locomotive Works, later known as the Grant Locomotive Works. The price paid by the Central Pacific for the McKay & Aldus locomotives was less than their cost and the company entered bankruptcy in 1868, closing its doors for good.

In October 1866, the first bucker snowplow was turned out of the Sacramento Shops to fight the plague of drifting snows in the high Sierra, and on February 5, 1867, the first McKay & Aldus locomotive, the *Amazon* No. 20, a ten-wheeler weighing two tons more than previously received engines of that type, was unloaded from the propellor driven steamer *Commodore*. Locomotives arrived all through 1867 and what a strange lot they were. Two 0-6-0 switch engines named *Samson* and *Goliah*, their water tanks mounted on the sides of the boiler, enormous cabs perched on top of the engine almost in the style of a Ross Winans camelback, were placed in yard service. Two handsome passenger engines, the *Gold Run* and the *Antelope*, arrived from McKay & Aldus, and by the end of the year there were 29 engines on the line in addition to those of the Sacramento Valley and the California Central.

Bloomer Cut was a temporary world wonder, 800 feet long and 65 feet maximum depth, cut through a ridge of conglomerate rock between the towns of Auburn and Newcastle. — HUNTINGTON LIBRARY, SAN MARINO, CALIFORNIA

On September 24, 1867, the locomotives and rolling stock of the California Central were brought into Sacramento and pooled with the Central Pacific's equipment. California Central No. 1 (Richard Norris, 1860), and named the *Harry Wilson* was shopped at Sacramento, renamed the *Oronoco* and became Sacramento Valley No. 6. The other three California Central locomotives vanished from the records and no further information as to their disposal can be found. The 8.2 mile section of the California Central from Folsom to Roseville was

abandoned late in 1866 when the bridge across the American River at Folsom was found to be unsafe and was condemned. Five years later the bridge collapsed into the river in the middle of the night with a roar which could be heard for miles around. The part of the California Central north of Roseville to Lincoln was extended under the name of the Yuba Railroad and in effect was the first link of the railroad soon to be called the California & Oregon Railroad, completed within a few years to Redding.

California Central's *Lincoln* poses with its train on the great bridge and trestle at the American River crossing north of Folsom (town in background). — SOUTHERN PACIFIC

At the end of 1867 the Central Pacific cracked the barrier of the summit of the Sierra by opening Summit tunnel. A special train of officials and guests, hauled by the locomotives *Idaho* and *Tamaroo*, left Sacramento on December 7, for an inspection of the tunnel and the complex of snowsheds and short tunnels east of there, on the grade down the face of the mountain overlooking Donner Lake. Having already laid many miles of track east of the Summit, it was now possible to bring trainloads of supplies direct from the Sacramento docks to the railhead. Four locomotives, a number of platform cars, and great quantities of rail had been hauled over the wagon road, past the summit, and down to the Truckee valley, permitting extension of the line beyond Truckee, 120 miles east of Sacramento, before the summit line was opened.

Though it was not until May 1, 1868, that Central Pacific rails reached Reno, Nevada, where the Truckee River left its canyon and flowed through almost desert-like flat country, the force of over 10,000 Chinese and white laborers advanced the railhead to Wadsworth, Nevada, 35 miles east of Reno reaching it on July 9, 1868. Here the great race across the Nevada desert began, with the ob-

The west end of Summit Tunnel, altitude 7,042 feet, before it was holed through in the fall of 1867. — HUNTINGTON LIBRARY, SAN MARINO, CALIFORNIA (BELOW) The railhead at Cisco, with temporary turntable and enginehouse, and the ill-fated *Idaho* in the foreground. — RICHARD B. JACKSON COLLECTION

The great curved trestle at Secret Town was the largest structure of its type on the railroad. In this remarkable photograph, which shows the Chinese laborers bringing a never-ending supply of dirt from the mountainside, the trestle is being filled in to eliminate the fire hazard and avoid replacement of the aging timbers. — SOUTHERN PACIFIC

jective of beating the Union Pacific at least to Ogden, the heart of Utah Territory. As measured by the survey lines, this was over 550 miles away, and at that time the Union Pacific railhead was at Benton, Wyoming, only 337 miles from Ogden. For the accomplishment of this goal, Charles Crocker's men would have to average at least two miles of track laid each day. All of this meant a large increase in the number of locomotives, platform cars and other rolling stock to keep the crews supplied.

The locomotives ordered for this work in 1867 began to arrive early in 1868. In San Francisco, a special transfer wharf had been built. On one side

the ships from the East would unload their cargo; on the other, the river steamers, sailing ships, and barges towed by tugs awaited their loads. Crated locomotive parts were unloaded and moved across the wharf with little delay, reducing the time lost at San Francisco to a small fraction of what it had been five years earlier. At Sacramento, a special wharf was equipped to handle the crated locomotives and cars. Locomotive parts were loaded on platform cars for transport to the assembly shop or, in the case of complete cars, placed on the rails at the wharf and hauled to the shops on their own wheels. The original roundhouse becoming too

One of the new Wason-built coaches appears at the end of a passenger train near Summit, in the view above. (RIGHT) The *Arctic* No. 11 brings passenger service to the railhead in Dixie Cut, near Blue Canyon. — BOTH HUNTINGTON LIBRARY, SAN MARINO, CALIFORNIA

small, the Central Pacific completed a new 29-stall roundhouse in the fall of 1868, with shop buildings for all branches of locomotive and car repairs adjacent. These were north of the station, in what had been an old river slough, now solid ground built up with rock and cobble stones from nearby quarries.

On September 28, 1868, the reporter for the *Sacramento Union* noted that the locomotive *U. S. Grant* No. 81, built by Danforth and destined to be a favorite with the passengers on the trains it hauled, was tested on Front Street, while in the shop were its mates, the *Phil Sheridan* No. 80, and the *Terrible* No. 73, the latter a ten-wheel freight engine. The *Gazelle* No. 84, the first of a large order of Schenectady-built 4-4-0s of which the *Jupiter* No. 60 was the most famous, was also being set up. On November 8, 1868, the company had 75 locomotives in service and 50 more either being assembled in Sacramento with more in San Francisco awaiting transfer to river ships, or enroute on the high seas.

The *Goliah* No. 27, hauling a construction train, was described by reporters as having a cab as big as a house. — GERALD M. BEST COLLECTION (**BELOW**) Like the *Goliah*, the *Ajax* No. 32 was designed as a yard engine, but converted to a 4-4-0. — R. B. JACKSON COLLECTION

The *Mono* No. 23 passes through Lost Camp Spur cut. This scene shows the heavy excavation, all done without the aid of machines. — HUNTINGTON LIBRARY, SAN MARINO, CALIFORNIA

The first Long Ravine bridge, 120 feet high, was made of three Howe truss sections. The wagon road at the lower right was later used by the Nevada County Narrow Gauge Railroad. — HUNTINGTON LIBRARY, SAN MARINO, CALIFORNIA. At the right, the west approach to the Long Ravine bridge was a curved trestle, later filled in when the bridge was replaced with a steel structure. — WARD KIMBALL COLLECTION

Cape Horn

After crossing Long Ravine, it became necessary for the Central Pacific to turn to the right along the perimeter of a granite mountain, blasting the right-of-way out of the rock, to create a shelf on which the track could be laid. This line made a sharp left turn into the gorge of the American River, at a point which became known as Cape Horn, 2,500 feet above the river. Here it was necessary to reinforce the shelf with a stone wall, and this spot soon became a view point, where all passenger trains stopped for ten minutes so that passengers might view the abyss. Here, too, in 1876, the Emperor Dom Pedro of Brazil was left behind when his train inadvertently left before he had regained his car. When the second track was laid across the mountains, a tunnel was holed through which bypassed the Cape Horn line, which is now used as the eastbound track.

The *Auburn* No. 22 stands on the shelf at Cape Horn, at its narrowest point, with the American River in the distance. (BELOW) The *Colossus* No. 44, as it was photographed at the west end of the curve at Cape Horn. Long Ravine may be seen in the background.
— BOTH GERALD M. BEST COLLECTION

Excursions to Cape Horn before completion of the railroad were frequent. The *Nevada* No. 8 with a train of sightseers viewing the landscape. — DeGolyer Foundation Library

A double-header freight with 4-6-0 locomotives descends Cape Horn into Long Ravine on a 2.2% grade, westbound toward Sacramento. — Huntington Library, San Marino, California

Four locomotives came from an unexpected source. In 1864, the Globe Locomotive Works of Boston, owned by John Souther, had closed down and four 4-4-0s still unsold were purchased by the Oregon Central Railroad, then projected to build south from Portland, Oregon. These locomotives reached San Francisco in 1866 and were stored on the dock for two years, since the Oregon Central had not yet begun construction. On July 24, 1868, Charles Crocker telegraphed S. G. Elliott in Portland, offering to buy the locomotives for cash or for replacement later. He even offered Elliott a tank switcher for track laying if they needed it, as he had a surplus of them. The owners set a price of $15,750 each plus freight charges from the East, which Crocker accepted, though remarking that the price was very high. At the end of August 1868, two of the locomotives arrived in Sacramento, were set up there and placed in service. They retained their Oregon Central names, a fact which was duly noted by a Reno newspaper when the locomotive *Umpqua* passed through there.

The fastest time any vessel carrying locomotives from the East made on the voyage around the Horn was 90 days, the slowest was 270 days, and the average was 150 days. Historian Sabin remarked that two locomotives were carried across the Isthmus of Panama to speed up their delivery, but the exorbitant freight charges across the Isthmus resulted in a total cost averaging $37,000 each for the two engines when they were ready for service. The time saved was not worth the extra cost, and no further engines were shipped via Panama. Ten

Before Summit Tunnel was opened, a nine car excursion train stops on a curve near Emigrant Gap. The flat roofed coaches were all built at Sacramento in 1864. — HUNTINGTON LIBRARY, SAN MARINO, CALIFORNIA

The *Hercules* No. 13 ready to leave Cisco with a westbound freight in 1868 after the line was open to Truckee. — GERALD M. BEST COLLECTION

CENTRAL PACIFIC RAILROAD.
TIME TABLE No. 22.
TAKES EFFECT MONDAY, FEB. 18, 1867, AT 5 O'CLOCK, A. M.

STATIONS.	TRAINS GOING EAST.			Dist. from Sac.	STATIONS.	Dist. from Cisco.	TRAINS GOING WEST.			STATIONS.
	No. 5 Way Freight	No. 3 Through Fg't	No. 1 Passenger.				No. 2 Passenger.	No. 4 Through Fg't	No. 6 Way Freight	
Sacramento.	2.15	6.40	6.30		Sacramento	92	12.55	5.35	7.30	Sacramento.
Arcade.	2.55	7.25	6.55	7	Arcade.	85	12.32	4.55	6.55	Arcade.
Antelope.				15	Antelope.	77				Antelope.
Junction.	3.55	8.25	7.18 7.23	18	Junction.	74	12.05 11.52	3.55	5.45	Junction.
Rocklin.	4.20	8.53	7.45	22	Rocklin.	70	11.40	3.30	5.15	Rocklin.
Pino.	4.45	9.15	7.55	25	Pino.	67	11.30	3.10	4.45	Pino.
Newcastle.	5.35	10.00	8.15	31	Newcastle.	61	11.10	2.30	4.00	Newcastle.
Auburn.	6.20	10.45 10.55	8.39	36	Auburn.	55	10.55	1.55	3.20	Auburn.
Clipper Gap.	7.10	11.40	8.56	43	Clipper Gap.	49	10.30	1.05		Clipper Gap.
N. E. Mills.	7.50	12.25	9.16	43	N. E. Mills.	43	10.10	12.25		N. E. Mills.
Colfax.	8.30	12.55 1.10	9.30 9.35	54	Colfax.	38	9.50 9.30	11.55 11.20	1.15 1.05	Colfax.
Gold Run.	9.45	2.20	10.15	64	Gold Run.	28	8.47	10.15 10.05	2.00	Gold Run.
Dutch Flat.	10.15	3.40	10.27	67	Dutch Flat.	25	8.35	9.45	1.59	Dutch Flat.
Alta.	10.50	2.55	10.55	69	Alta.	23	8.25	9.30	1.15	Alta.
Shady Run.		3.25	10.55	73	Shady Run.	19	8.05	9.00		Shady Run.
Blue Cañon.		4.00	11.20	78	Blue Cañon.	14	7.40	8.25		Blue Cañon.
Emig't Gap.		4.40	11.50	84	Emig't Gap.	8	7.10	7.45		Emig't Gap.
Cisco.		5.30	12.30	92	Cisco.		6.30	6.45		Cisco.

All Trains run Daily, Sundays Excepted.

Employes will destroy all previous Time Cards, and note carefully the alterations in Rules 5, 7, 13, 18, 19, 21 and 24.

C. CROCKER, Superintendent.

When the Central Pacific was open for business to Cisco, it took six hours for passenger trains to make the 92 mile run. All trains were secondary to running construction trains, but the schedule was a lot faster than stagecoaches over the wagon road. — RICHARD B. JACKSON COLLECTION

Donner Summit

In the 17 miles from Blue Canyon to Summit Tunnel, and for ten miles east of the summit, drifting snow in the winter made it necessary to build wooden sheds over almost the entire line. Construction of these sheds had to be rushed in the summer of 1868 in order to keep the line open during the following winter, and it was not until recent years that improved snow fighting methods enabled the railroad to eliminate all but four miles of the sheds.

At the left, a completed section of snowshed west of Donner Summit in 1869. — CALIFORNIA STATE LIBRARY (BELOW) A double-tracked section of the sheds under construction in the summer of 1868. — SOUTHERN PACIFIC

Donner Lake and Pass from a rugged vantage point above Summit Tunnel. The snowsheds at the right cover the exposed sections of track between tunnels. The wagon road may be seen in the left corner of the view. — HUNTINGTON LIBRARY, SAN MARINO, CALIFORNIA

An early view of the sheds on the mountainside south of Donner Lake. Sloping barriers were built at every exposed point to divert falling snow and rocks. — GERALD M. BEST COLLECTION

Truckee

When the Central Pacific rails reached the bend of the Truckee River below Donner Lake, the stage hostelry and saloon called Coburn's Station was soon transformed into a busy railroad town. It was an engine changing point for all trains, and a helper station, for one or more helpers were needed on each westbound train which climbed the face of the mountain above Donner Lake to the summit. A fire in 1868 destroyed most of the town, and when it was rebuilt, it was renamed Truckee.

Coburn's Station early in 1868, with two trains on the main line, and two helpers on the siding.
— COLLEGE OF THE PACIFIC

The Truckee wrecking train, in the view above, was usually powered by the *Goliah* which also served as a fire engine. — GUY L. DUNSCOMB COLLECTION At the right, looking east at Coburn's station in 1868, with passenger train activity at the station and a construction train bound for the "front" waiting on the siding. — RICHARD B. JACKSON COLLECTION (BELOW) Truckee was so cold in winter that all of the buildings, including the circular water tank house on the right had to be heated. Water barrels on the roof of each building were vital necessities for extinguishing small fires started on the shingle roofs by sparks from locomotives. — GERALD M. BEST COLLECTION

The *Pacific* No. 2 crosses Little Truckee River with a trainload of ties, just 128 miles from Sacramento. — RICHARD B. JACKSON COLLECTION (BELOW) Construction train in Truckee River Canyon, the orphaned section of the railroad, before Summit Tunnel was completed. — HUNTINGTON LIBRARY, SAN MARINO, CALIFORNIA

days were spent in the transfer at San Francisco, two days or more for the journey to Sacramento, several days ensued before the crated locomotive parts arrived at the roundhouse, and two weeks passed before the finished locomotives were tested. This all added up to a time lapse of six months between the date the engine was turned out of the factory and the time it was placed in service. One locomotive, the *Saturn* No. 69, a McKay & Aldus 4-6-0 delivered to the Boston docks in April 1868, had the misfortune to be aboard a sailing ship which was dismasted in a great storm near Cape Horn and was towed into Valparaiso, Chile, for repairs. Eight months were lost due to this accident, and the *Saturn* was finally tested in Sacramento on August 12, 1869, three months after completion of the transcontinental railroad. Central Pacific's *Peoquop* No. 68, delivered to the Boston docks with the *Saturn*, was loaded on another ship and was in service on the Central Pacific in November 1868, holding to the six month average.

The business of testing new locomotives intrigued many more people than the reporter for the *Sacramento Union* and part of the psychology of this fascination seems to have been the combina-

Reno, the nearest point on the Central Pacific to the Comstock mines, soon became a thriving city. In the view above, looking west from the station, the C.P. fire engine No. 46 stands near the junction of the newly completed Virginia & Truckee Railroad. (BELOW) Looking east, a V&T engine with tender piled high with wood, is ready for the trip to Virginia City. — BOTH HUNTINGTON LIBRARY, SAN MARINO, CALIFORNIA

tion of the names of the locomotives and the colorful paint schemes of the different locomotive builders. Usually there were 50 or more interested spectators at a locomotive test; the *U. S. Grant* No. 81 brought out a horde of Grant supporters as the word got around. General Grant had been nominated by the Republicans for President earlier in 1868, and as he was very popular in Sacramento, the locomotive bearing his name received special attention. Imagine the dismay of Grant's supporters when, on December 19, 1868, after Grant had been elected, the locomotive named for him met with an accident at the entrance of a snowshed near Summit, resulting in everything on the top of the engine from the headlight to the roof of the cab being knocked off by lumber which had been left sticking down below the top of the shed by a careless workman. The *U. S. Grant* was brought to Sacramento and was soon back in service as good as ever.

There were frequent accidents to work trains and their locomotives; this was to be expected, with the track still imperfectly ballasted, rocks constantly falling down the slopes of the cuts through the hills and the trainmen frequently disregarding the rules of safety in their inexperience. There were rear end collisions; the *J. R. Moores* No. 125, former Oregon Central, and the *Mohave* No. 37 met head-on near Winnemucca in March 1869. A report in the same month stated that the *Deerhound* No. 132 was brought back to Sacramento in a "badly demoralized" condition due to rolling upside-down into the mud at the bottom of a ditch. The *Klamath* No. 31 blew up and was destroyed near Elko, Nevada, March 30, 1869, following the fatal boiler explosion of *Yuba* No. 25 the previous year. Engine crews were learning the hard way that the water level had to be above the crown sheet at all times. The *Piute* No. 18 was nearly

The earliest Central Pacific wreck photograph known, shows the Tule, Nevada, head-on wreck of March 1, 1869. — GERALD M. BEST COLLECTION

39

Two loaded construction trains wait on the siding in Truckee River Canyon at one of the few locations spacious enough to permit a double track. — GERALD M. BEST COLLECTION

The Truckee River ended in a vast swamp called Truckee Meadows, east of Wadsworth, where this train paused for photographer Hart in 1868 — GERALD M. BEST COLLECTION

The only quality photograph of one of the former Oregon Central engines built by the Globe Locomotive Works, shows No. 124 at Mill City, Nevada, with a mixed train carrying four second-class coaches filled with immigrants on the tail end. — GERALD M. BEST COLLECTION

melted down by the fire which destroyed the Truckee roundhouse in April 1869; the *Pluto* No. 59 had to be completely rebuilt at Sacramento after a wreck near the railhead at Toano, Nevada, and the *Utah* No. 9 overturned there a few days later, killing the fireman. The *Montana* No. 24 and the *Arctic* No. 11 met head-on in the middle of Summit Tunnel, badly injuring the crews and tying up the railroad for many hours. That there were no more accidents in the last year of construction is nothing short of a miracle, and even more surprising was the fact that the Central Pacific had no passenger train accidents, though the newspapers were filled with tales of great disasters on the railroads of the eastern seaboard. To give the reader some idea of the traffic handled by the Central Pacific in the years 1865-1868, gross earnings were approximately $5,000,000 and after deducting operating expenses, nearly $2,000,000 was available for construction expenses.

All through 1868 the hordes of graders and track-layers worked eastward across Nevada, while groups of Mormon workers hired by President Leland Stanford after a visit to Salt Lake City, began grading from Ogden westward along the survey line for a meeting with Crocker's eastbound forces.

Brown's Station, 235 miles from Sacramento, reached in August 1868, was no paragon of beauty. Stations in the Nevada desert were hastily built. — RICHARD B. JACKSON COLLECTION (BELOW) Water was one principal commodity shipped from Winnemucca, pictured here in 1868 shortly after construction was completed to this point. — GERALD M. BEST COLLECTION

Carlin, Nevada, was reached by the tracklayers in December 1868, and soon became a division point with shops and roundhouse. This view, looking west towards the Humboldt range, was made by photographer Hart, probably on May 6, 1869. On the end of the train in the center are the two cars of Governor Stanford's special train enroute to Promontory for the Golden Spike ceremony. — DeGOLYER FOUNDATION LIBRARY

A construction train stands below Powder Bluff, at the west end of 10-Mile Canyon, 20 miles west of Carlin. — RICHARD B. JACKSON COLLECTION

Engine No. 46, former *Unicorn*, a McKay & Aldus 10-wheeler converted to a 4-4-0 fire engine, is decorated for 4th of July at the Sacramento roundhouse in the mid-1870s. — DeGolyer Foundation Library

The new 29-stall Sacramento roundhouse, completed in November 1868, was landscaped by the planting of hundreds of eucalyptus trees from Australia. In time they became a nuisance and were removed. — Gerald M. Best Collection

On August 17, 1868, the Central Pacific was furnishing daily passenger service from Brown's Station, 235 miles east of Sacramento, to the latter city, with the end of track nearly a hundred miles east of there. By the end of 1868 the railhead was at Osino, ten miles east of Elko and 478 miles from Sacramento. Winter snows caused little delay to Crocker's men, and they continued their daily progress east while the Union Pacific was fighting severe snowstorms west of Wahsatch.

Saturday, March 20, 1869, was a special day at the Sacramento roundhouse although the men charged with testing locomotives did not know it at the time. For on that day the locomotive *Jupiter* No. 60, built by the Schenectady Locomotive Works in September 1868, was tested along with the *Heron* No. 114 from Danforth, the *Rambler* No. 104 from Rogers and the *Mercury* No. 127 from McKay & Aldus. The *Jupiter* was to make history at Promontory, Utah, less than two months later. Another locomotive which was in the news at this time was Sacramento Valley Railroad No. 1, the *Sacramento*, which had been borrowed by Charles Crocker in 1866 when he needed a hoisting engine

during construction of the Summit tunnel. It had been disassembled, moved by wagon road from the railhead to the tunnel, and was there set up to be the motive power for a large cable drum and elevator. Upon completion of this job, historians have left this locomotive at Summit, but such was not the case. The *Sacramento Union* for May 3, 1869, states — "The locomotive *Sacramento*, the first locomotive in the State, laid up a long time since it was brought down from Summit tunnel where it had been used as a hoisting engine, is now out of the shop and is being put to work hauling trains of cobble stones from Brighton (the end of the Western Pacific Railroad)." This same item said that the Sacramento Valley locomotive *Pioneer* had also been completely overhauled and was back in service on Western Pacific work trains. The sale of the bankrupt McKay & Aldus plant at auction for $250,000, the closing of the Richard Norris Works in Philadelphia and the J. A. Norris factory in Lancaster, Pennsylvania, due to bankruptcy were also announced.

At the time the *Jupiter* was being placed in service, the Central Pacific had purchased a very im-

43

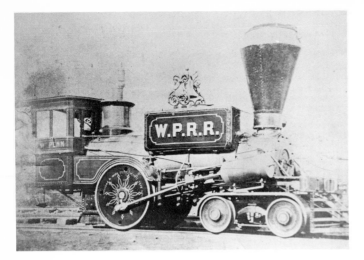

Stevens-built San Francisco & Alameda *J. G. Kellogg* became C.P. No. 176. — GERALD M. BEST COLLECTION

Stevens built the *Liberty* in 1863 for the San Francisco & Oakland. — GERALD M. BEST COLLECTION

portant link in their system, the Western Pacific Railroad of California. This line was organized December 13, 1862, to build a railroad from San Jose, the projected terminus of the San Francisco & San Jose Railroad, to Sacramento via Niles, Livermore and Stockton. It was headed by Timothy Dane and Peter Donahue, principal officers of the San Francisco & San Jose; Donahue also was the prime mover in building the San Francisco & North Pacific. Construction began in San Jose in January 1865, and reached Niles in 1866. A total of ten locomotives were purchased in the East and shipped to California during those years. The available money for the enterprise was used up long before the Western Pacific was completed and it was turned over to the Contract & Finance Company, a Central Pacific subsidiary, which proposed not only to complete the railroad but extend it from Niles to Oakland.

The Sacramento newspapers reported on October 23, 1867, that the Central Pacific now owned both the Western Pacific and the Lincoln & Marysville Railroad, the latter extending north from the Cali-

fornia Central's terminal at Lincoln. The legal purchase date was much later in the case of the Western Pacific, but it is interesting to note a small paragraph in the *Union* dated July 30, 1868. "Two locomotives were brought up on the steamer *Moulton* from San Francisco. One is 30 tons weight, the other the smallest ever brought to this city. They are in running order, having been used on the San Francisco & San Jose. The locomotives were landed with considerable difficulty, as they were complete machines and it was necessary to erect temporary tracks to get them ashore. The large locomotive is the *Merced.*" The *Merced* made its trial run on August 21, 1868, hauling a passenger train to Wadsworth, Nevada. It was a 4-4-0 built by J. A. Norris in Lancaster, Pennsylvania, in 1864, and was one of four of this type built for the Western Pacific Railroad. In addition, there were three Baldwins and two from Mason, all 4-4-0s.

The other engine which was brought to Sacramento with the *Merced* was easily identified by an article in the *Union* on October 17, 1868. "The little locomotive *William Penn,* which was brought up

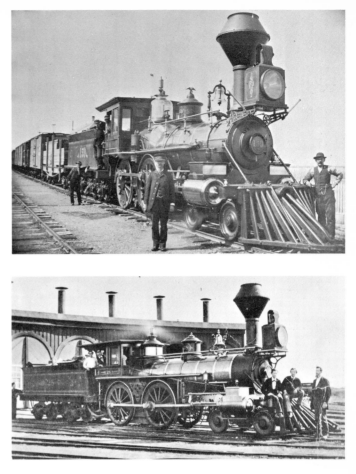

Above, the Wadsworth roundhouse and shops, with the locomotive *Driver* No. 95. — RICHARD B. JACKSON COLLECTION (RIGHT) Central Pacific No. 159 arrived from Schenectady after the road was completed. — GERALD M. BEST COLLECTION

In 1869, Piute Indians inspect the *Champion* No. 50, at Argenta, Nevada. — GERALD M. BEST COLLECTION

No. 28, formerly *Gold Run*, after names were removed from cab panels. — GERALD M. BEST

from San Francisco several months since and used as a switching locomotive on the Central Pacific and Sacramento Valley tracks, has been overhauled at the shops. The unsightly water tank on the boiler has been removed and a neat little tender constructed at the shops. The engine is much improved in appearance." The *William Penn* had a long and colorful history. Built by William Norris of Philadelphia in 1835 for the Philadelphia & Columbia Railroad, it was soon taken over by the Pennsylvania Railroad. The locomotive was leased by the Pennsylvania to the Strasburg Railroad, a four-mile shortline connecting the town of Strasburg with the Pennsylvania Railroad. In 1863, the Strasburg Railroad bought a new locomotive and since the Pennsylvania did not want the *William Penn,* the J. A. Norris factory in Lancaster rebuilt it to a 2-4-0 tank engine and sold it to the Western Pacific.

The Central Pacific must have had stock control of the Western Pacific in 1868, for otherwise the former would not have taken an active part in building the line which left the Central Pacific main line at Brighton and in furnishing locomo-

tives and rolling stock for the tracklaying crews. Purchase of the Western Pacific was completed May 15, 1869, with the railheads at Liberty, 30 miles south of Brighton, and east of Livermore on the Niles-Stockton section. In order to gain entrance to Oakland quickly, the Central Pacific bought the San Francisco & Oakland Railroad and the San Francisco & Alameda Railroad, two suburban lines with ferry service to San Francisco from their east bay terminals. Work on the Western Pacific was rushed during the summer of 1869, the two sections meeting on opposite sides of the San Joaquin River west of Stockton a few days before the bridge was completed. On September 8, the locomotive *San Mateo* brought the first through train from Alameda Pier to Sacramento over the new 135 mile line, which would now permit Central Pacific trains to run through to Alameda, a short ferry ride from San Francisco. The two suburban railroads had not connected with each other, necessitating a tie line which the Western Pacific built in October 1869, after which the through trains from Sacramento went to Oakland Pier.

45

Returning to that day in March 1869, when the *Jupiter* was placed in service, the work of locomotive assembly continued at a feverish pace, in addition to much needed repairs for those locomotives wrecked or worn out. The *Oronoco*, California Central's first engine, after being wrecked and the back of its boiler blown out in a derailment on the Sacramento Valley Railroad in 1868, was repaired and sent back to work, only to be wrecked again at Cochran's Station on the Placerville & Sacramento Railroad. When it was turned out of the shop February 20, 1869, it became Central Pacific's *Oronoco* No. 93.

During the first three months of 1869, Crocker's forces advanced the railhead across the Peoquop Mountains, reached the Nevada-Utah border and arrived at the west side of Great Salt Lake Desert at Lucin early in April. Almost every day that month, a new locomotive either arrived in Sacramento from the San Francisco docks, or was placed in service. When the pieces of the exploded locomotive *Klamath* No. 31 reached Sacramento, it was decided not to rebuild the engine. The Western Pacific's *Mariposa* took its place as second No. 31. Though rebuilt several times since then, this engine spent its last days on the Stockton Terminal & East-ern Railroad and is now in Traveltown, Los Angeles.

On April 9, 1869, the meeting point of the two railroads had been settled by Huntington and Durant and ratified by Congress. This place, Promontory, was 53 miles west of Ogden and in the hills north of Great Salt Lake. On April 26, the Central Pacific rails were within 16 miles of this meeting point, and at this time Charles Crocker decided to beat the Union Pacific's record of eight and one-half miles of track laid in one day. Most of April 26 was spent in laying plans for what was to take place the next day, and early on the morning of the 27th, the great effort began. After two miles of track had been laid in two hours, the locomotive hauling a train of empty platform cars back from the railhead derailed, blocking the line, and the event was postponed until the 28th. Once again the signal was given shortly after daybreak. The effort commenced with the unloading of a 16 car train heavily laden with rails, spikes, bolts, and fishplates. Teams of horses by the hundreds already hauled the crossties and dumped them in piles along the ten-mile section which was to be completed that day, and all was in readiness for the tracklayers. Swarms of Chinese laborers unloaded the first train, then rails and supplies were loaded on small, 4-wheel flat cars called "trucks" which could be hauled by horses, and the rails began moving to the railhead. There the crew of rail carriers waited with foreman George Coley, rail carriers Thomas Dailey, George Elliot, Patrick Joyce, Michael Kennedy, Edward

U. S. Government Commissioners, protected from the cold by buffalo robes, sit on the *Falcon*'s pilot during an inspection trip. — SOUTHERN PACIFIC

Killeen, Fred McNamara, Michael Shay, Michael Sullivan, and two relief men, William Cartin and Peter Egan, who substituted for any of the eight rail carriers whenever they needed time out for personal reasons.

Standing alert and eager to begin, the two groups of four rail carriers each picked up a rail weighing 560 pounds and measuring 30 feet in length, carrying it on the double to the spot where it was to be laid, and setting it down on the ties. The eight men would then rush back to the rail car for two more rails, while the track gauge men lined up the first pair. Following the gauge men were gangs to spike down the rails, bolt them together with the fish plates, and with pikes straighten out the track as soon as they could find it vacant for a few seconds. As fast as one truck was emptied, it was removed from the rails and another brought forward. Train after train of rails and supplies were unloaded that morning, and when lunch was called, over six miles of track had been laid and spiked down. Standing by during this fantastic display of coordination were officials from the Union Pacific, including Vice President Durant and General Dodge, who hoped to see a fiasco but stayed to marvel and admire. At seven o'clock in the evening, Superintendent Strobridge called a halt to the day's work, with the railhead just ten miles and 56 feet east of where it had been the previous evening.

To quote historian Sabin, those eight tracklayers and two relief men carried on that day in a period of 12 hours, with only an hour rest, a total of 1,970,000 pounds of deadweight, figuring 88 tons of rail per mile of track. Between breakfast and lunch, they laid nearly a mile of track an hour, up a grade of 66 feet per mile. At lunchtime Crocker offered relief to any of the track layers who had had enough, but to a man they spurned such an idea. Crocker ordered the timekeeper to enter four days pay in the time book for each man in the track laying crew, and this they accepted with pleasure. Those who visit the location of this historic epic in human effort at the Golden Spike National Historic Site in 1969 and in the years thereafter should remember this great day, when they see the sign a few miles west of Promontory, proclaiming that ten miles of track were laid from the west to this spot in one day on April 28, 1869.

On May 1, 1869, two days after the record breaking day, the remaining 3.6 miles of track had been laid to the designated meeting point at Promontory. On that day the official date for the joining of the two railroads was set for Saturday, May 8. On May 5, a special train consisting of the locomo-

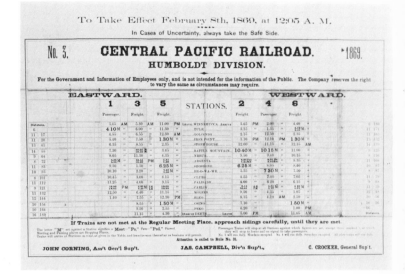

Humboldt Division employees timetable showed three scheduled trains. — RICHARD B. JACKSON COLLECTION

Strobridge in the dark suit, stands in the center of a flat car at Rozel after the record breaking tracklaying feat. — SOUTHERN PACIFIC (BELOW) The sign at milepost 108 marked the east end of the 10 miles of track laid in one day. It is now in the Daughters of the Utah Pioneers Museum in Salt Lake. — UTAH STATE HISTORICAL SOCIETY

tive *Antelope* No. 29, McKay & Aldus built 4-4-0, and two cars backed into the Sacramento station early in the morning to await its distinguished passengers. The train was made up of a "subsistence car" or "tender," and President Stanford's business car. The "tender" looked like an ordinary baggage car externally, but the interior was divided up into a large number of compartments — one lined with zinc and surrounded with ice, for meat; several for vegetables; one with a wire door for fowls; large tanks of fresh water; bins full of ice, lockers for liquor, wine and champagne, and several sleeping berths for the crew. It had been built in the Sacramento shops a month earlier to serve as a supply car for any of the business cars which were to be away from home base for a long time. Leland Stanford's private car with a combination dining compartment and office at one end could accommodate ten passengers with sleeping quarters.

Stanford's invited guests included California Chief Justice Sanderson, Governor Safford of Arizona, three government commissioners and a few of Stanford's friends, one of whom was Dr. J. D. B. Stillman of Sacramento. Running as a second section of the regular 6:30 a.m. passenger train, the *Antelope,* cleaned and polished to a high degree for the occasion, hauled the train over the Sierra and it was intended to keep the engine on the train all the way to Promontory. All went well until after the train had passed Truckee and was rolling down the Truckee River valley towards Reno. At a point in a fairly deep cut just before the track entered a

tunnel, a group of Chinese laborers were cutting trees on the mountainside, and having seen the regular train pass, thought they had plenty of time to roll a trimmed log down the mountain to a point near the railroad. They lost control of the log, it rolled down the steep bank into the railroad cut and came to rest close to one of the rails. The log was over 50 feet long and over three feet in diameter at one end; when the *Antelope* and its train came around the curve and the engineer saw the obstruction, it was too late to stop. Dr. W. H. Harkness, Editor of the *Sacramento Press* was riding on the pilot, all wrapped up in a buffalo robe and enjoying the spectacular view. Seeing the inevitable crash, Harkness jumped to the ground, and fortunately escaped with a few bruises. The *Antelope* lost its pilot, one side of the engine and the steps of the cars were somewhat damaged, though not enough to prevent the train from continuing on to Reno, where a telegram was sent to Wadsworth to hold the regular train until the special arrived.

At Wadsworth, normally an engine-changing point, the special's two cars were attached to the rear of the regular train, which was hauled by the *Jupiter* No. 60, in its sixth week of service. The

The *Antelope* No. 29, which did not reach Promontory in 1869 due to unfortunate circumstances, was later leased to the Virginia & Truckee Railroad and is shown below at the Carson City enginehouse in 1872. — JOHN B. HUNGERFORD COLLECTION

Jupiter was on the augmented train to the end of its run at Elko, where most of the passengers left for the White Pine mining country. When the special train left Elko, it consisted of the *Jupiter*, water car No. 1543 filled with water for the locomotive, and the two cars belonging to Governor Stanford's party. The special arrived at Promontory on the evening of the 7th, and it was fully expected that the driving of the golden spikes would take place the next morning, but word was received that the Union Pacific special train would be delayed due to storm damage to the track east of Ogden, so the date was postponed until May 10.

The following day the party was invited to inspect the Union Pacific line east as far as Weber

The *Jupiter* No. 60 with Governor Stanford's special train at Monument Point on May 9, 1869. Among the men on top of the hill in back of the train is the cook from Stanford's car, who shot a bag of quail for dinner that day. — CALIFORNIA STATE LIBRARY

Canyon, and a special train consisting of U. P. No. 117 and a caboose coach made two trips to Taylor's Mills Station. On Sunday, May 9, the *Jupiter* returned Governor Stanford's train some distance west, so the guests could inspect the shore of Great

Governor Stanford's train on a siding at Promontory on the morning of May 10, 1869, just hours before the golden spike event. — GERALD M. BEST COLLECTION

Members of Stanford's party at Taylor's Mills station on May 8, 1869, where they had come from Promontory on an inspection tour of the Union Pacific. — RICHARD B. JACKSON COLLECTION

49

Salt Lake near Monument Point. Photographer A. A. Hart of Sacramento was with the party and his stereoscopic views include one classic picture which shows the *Jupiter* and train passing a train of covered wagons bound towards the west, marking the beginning of a new era and the end of the old.

On Monday, May 10, early in the morning, the *Jupiter* brought the Stanford special train to the west end of a siding which was largely occupied by the boarding cars of Strobridge's construction gang. The east end of this siding joined the main track about 200 feet west of the site selected for joining the rails, and at the time the Stanford special arrived, Strobridge's special train hauled by the locomotive *Whirlwind* occupied the end of the main line. As the time for the arrival of the Union Pacific special approached, Strobridge's train pulled west to clear the siding, and the Stanford train proceeded east to a point a few yards from the end of track. Promontory is situated in a level circular valley, about three miles in diameter, surrounded by mountains and lying roughly 700 feet above the Great Salt Lake. The meeting point of the two railroads was near the east end of this valley. At 10 a.m. the Union Pacific train came in sight headed by locomotive No. 119, an 1868 Rogers-built 4-4-0, hauling a four car train. Closely following the special were four trainloads of officers and men of the 21st regiment of the U. S. Army, on their way to duty at the Presidio in San Francisco. Photographs taken by Sedgwick at the time of the ceremony show these trains very clearly, lined up in a row behind Durant's special train.

Photographer Hart made this famous photo of Stanford's special at Monument Point, as a California bound wagon train passes westbound. In the center, Monument Point appears almost as an island. ROBERT WEINSTEIN COLLECTION

Strobridge's special train stands at the end of track at Promontory early on the morning of May 10, 1869. AMERICAN GEOGRAPHICAL SOCIETY

Photographer Sedgwick captured this view of Promontory with his wetplate camera on the morning of May 10, 1869. A siding had already been built, the Central Pacific rails were in place and all was ready for the Union Pacific crew to lay the last two rails. — AMERICAN GEOGRAPHICAL SOCIETY

Close-up of a portion of the above scene. On the right is the Strobridge special with the locomotive *Whirlwind* No. 62, and behind the train of boarding cars on the siding is Governor Stanford's special train headed by the *Jupiter* No. 60. — AMERICAN GEOGRAPHICAL SOCIETY

On the Union Pacific special were Vice President Thomas C. Durant, Chief Engineer Major General Grenville M. Dodge, Colonel Silas Seymour, Superintendent Samuel B. Reed, Directors Sidney Dillon and John Duff, and the Casement brothers, contractors who had constructed most of the Union Pacific. Bishop John Sharp of the Church of Jesus Christ of Latter Day Saints was also there, and Mayor Lorin Farr of Ogden represented Brigham Young at the ceremony. To detail all that went on that morning at Promontory would take many pages, but suffice it to say that there was much wrangling among the officials of both railroads before Stanford and Durant settled the matter of who would drive the golden spike by agreeing to take the two golden spikes which were available and each would drive one. The track crews brought the rails of the two roads to a meeting, and a special laurel tie with holes already drilled for the four spikes was placed at the junction of the rails.

The hand-hewn Union Pacific ties have been laid to within 10 feet of the Central Pacific track. Many of the spectators are not railroad men, but Mormon farmers who have come to witness the joining of the rails. — AMERICAN GEOGRAPHICAL SOCIETY

51

The Union Pacific special train having arrived, the workmen install the laurel tie into which the gold and silver spikes will be set. — AMERICAN GEOGRAPHICAL SOCIETY

At the moment of the invocation, photographer Russell set up his camera on the cab roof of Union Pacific No. 119 and made this picture. His assistant, S. J. Sedgwick was on the cab roof of Central Pacific's *Jupiter* No. 60. — AMERICAN GEOGRAPHICAL SOCIETY

Sedgwick's photograph of the group at the invocation (BELOW) shows the soldiers at parade rest, and most of the bystanders with their hats off. The Union Pacific siding is plainly visible at the right. The enlargement of a portion of Sedgwick's classic view is shown on the right. Andrew J. Russell may be seen standing on the cab roof of U.P. No. 119 with his camera and tripod in plain view. Smokestacks of four locomotives can be counted in back of Durant's special train. — AMERICAN GEOGRAPHICAL SOCIETY

The officials of both railroads, their guests and a company of United States infantry standing at attention assembled at the meeting point, the employees involved in the tracklaying at the junction forming a background for this group. After an invocation, a spike from Arizona ribbed with iron, clad in silver, and crowned with gold and a silver spike from Nevada were dropped into the holes in the last tie, on the inside edge of the rails. Durant of the Union Pacific placed a gold spike in the hole on the outside edge of one rail, and Governor Stanford dropped the engraved gold spike from David Hewes into the last empty hole in the tie. The Governor then hit an iron spike already partly driven into the next tie, with a silver plated maul which formed one side of the telegraph circuit, the spike forming the ground connection. After ceremonial tapping of the spike, the telegraph operator sent out the word East and West — "It is done!" The laurel tie and its four spikes were then removed and replaced by an ordinary tie and iron spikes.

At Sacramento, 23 locomotives which had been lined up on the levee blew their whistles for 15 minutes. Parades were held in San Francisco, Sacramento and Salt Lake City, as well as a more quiet celebration in Washington. After the ceremony, the two locomotives moved slowly forward until their pilots touched, the engine crews came to the meeting point to shake hands, and later crossed bottles of champagne, which by then was flowing freely. Several pictures were made by photographers Hart, Russell, Savage and Sedgwick, after which the officials of both roads retired to Governor Stanford's car for lunch. During the period after the meal when the group exchanged experiences of the construction days, Strobridge brought in the Chinese boss of all his tracklaying gangs and introduced him to the group, who gave the man a standing ovation in honor of the outstanding performance by his countrymen. A visit was made later by the Stanford party to Durant's private car, and as a gesture of farewell before the trains departed, each train crossed the junction point, then left for the East and West.

"It is done!" This reproduction of a contact print from the original wet-plate made by Andrew J. Russell shows engineers Booth of the *Jupiter* and Bradford of No. 119 ready to touch champagne bottles, while the two chief engineers of the railroads, Montague of the Central Pacific on the left, and General Dodge of the Union Pacific on the right, shake hands. — AMERICAN GEOGRAPHICAL SOCIETY

During the actual spike driving ceremony, photographer Sedgwick was unable to take a close-up due to the limitations of his camera, but the principal actors in the affair can be seen huddled in a close circle. The telegraph operator and his assistant have the best seats in the house as they watch from the telegraph pole. (BELOW) After the spike driving ceremony and the posing of many pictures, the crowd pushed in for a closer look at the spikes and laurel tie. — BOTH AMERICAN GEOGRAPHICAL SOCIETY

Russell's most famous picture of the golden spike ceremony, probably taken after the spikes had been inserted in the holes drilled in the laurel tie. — AMERICAN GEOGRAPHICAL SOCIETY

Several years after the ceremony, Governor Stanford commissioned an artist to reproduce the scene depicted in Russell's photograph. It now hangs in the California State Capitol in Sacramento, and painted into the picture are many men who were not at the ceremony, including T. D. Judah, deceased for six years. — WARD KIMBALL COLLECTION

After the ceremony, the dignitaries adjourned to Governor Stanford's car for lunch. By this time the crowd of spectators had nearly vanished, leaving an uncluttered landscape for photographer Hart. — HUNTINGTON LIBRARY, SAN MARINO, CALIFORNIA

THE GOLDEN SPIKE

On the head of the last spike was inscribed the legend "The Last Spike." On one side, "The Pacific Railroad; Ground Broken January 8, 1863; completed May 8, 1869." Another side, "May God continue the unity of our Country as this Railroad unites the two great Oceans of the world." On the third side, "Presented by David Hewes, San Francisco," and on the fourth side, the names of the company officers. The engraver used the date of May 8, 1869 as the completion date. This was changed to May 10 at the last moment. The original spike is the property of Stanford University.

After the ceremony, while officials were having lunch, photographer Andrew J. Russell posed some of the surveyors and minor railroad officials alongside the two locomotives. This picture provided valuable historical data on the lettering and gold leaf decoration of the *Jupiter's* tender. — AMERICAN GEOGRAPHICAL SOCIETY

The band of the 21st regiment of U.S. Infantry posed alongside No. 119 for photographer Hart. This picture has been of great value to model builders seeking all the measurements of the locomotive. — COLLEGE OF THE PACIFIC

Hart photographed the rest of the 21st regiment's band in front of the *Jupiter*. At the time both band photos were being made, the engines were located on the Central Pacific side of the junction. — SOUTHERN PACIFIC

A rare Central Pacific annual pass for 1869, signed by Judge E. B. Crocker, who at that time was a director of the Central Pacific. — GOLDEN WEST COLLECTION

Central Pacific's *Jupiter* had earned its place in history on that day, by chance and not by choice. That the *Jupiter's* owners had no sentiment whatsoever about the locomotive is seen in its later history. It soon lost its name and became just plain No. 60, served the road past the 1891 renumbering of locomotives and received No. 1195. It was reboilered at Sacramento in 1893 and was immediately sold to the Gila Valley, Globe & Northern Railroad, then under construction north from Bowie, Arizona, on the Southern Pacific, to Globe and Miami, copper mining towns north of Bowie. As G.V.G. & N. No. 1, the old *Jupiter* worked out its days and was cut up for scrap at Globe in 1901. The late Seth Arkills of Globe, first the fireman and then the engineer of No. 1, told the writer after he had retired in 1936 that everyone in Globe knew that the "One-spot" was the old *Jupiter*: that it was an historic engine and that it had been at Promontory in 1869. Arkills had developed an affection for No. 1 which caused him to have several photographs made of it on different trains which it hauled — the only photographic record of the last days of the *Jupiter*. Arkills even wrote a letter of protest to Superintendent A. M. Beal, asking that the engine be preserved at Globe alongside the station. The letter accomplished nothing, for the Southern Pacific had control of the road by then, the locomotive was worth over a thousand dollars as scrap, and sentiment played no part in their thinking. If Arkills had bought it, assuming he had that kind of money in those days, had placed it in his backyard and willed it to his children, it would be worth $150,000 today.

After the joining of the rails at Promontory, Governor Stanford and his party arrived back in Sacramento on May 12, his train hauling two brand new coaches built by the Wason Manufacturing Company of Springfield, Massachusetts, and hence the first passenger coaches to make a through trip from New England to the Pacific coast. The five companies of infantry of the 21st Regiment passed through Sacramento the following day and a total of 19 locomotives returned from the "front" for much needed repairs. On May 24, rail history was again made by the arrival of Rogers-built locomotives *Success* No. 156 and *Excelsior* No. 157, which arrived in Sacramento after a 24-day trip across the continent from Paterson, New Jersey, the first locomotives to cross the continent by rail although not under their own power. They were accompanied by George Sebrier, an Erie Railway locomotive engineer acting as a runner. Six locomotives from the Schenectady Works came directly by rail in June

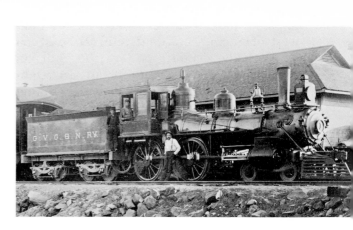

The former *Jupiter* as Gila Valley, Globe & Northern No. 1, standing in the station at Globe, Arizona, in 1898. (**BELOW**) Central Pacific No. 155, built by Rhode Island in 1868, was the last locomotive to arrive by sea, in November 1869. — BOTH GERALD M. BEST COLLECTION

and August, and these comprised the last new locomotives ordered by the Central Pacific at that time. A few stragglers came in by sea, the last being three 4-4-0s from the Rhode Island Works, Nos. 153 to 155, built in December 1868, and placed in service in November 1869.

The rambling reporter for the *Sacramento Union* who gave us so many priceless bits of information about the motive power, lost some of his interest in locomotives after the completion of the railroad, and became fascinated with Pullman cars instead. On June 16, 1869, he saw the Pullman Palace Sleeping Cars *Ogden* and *Pennsylvania* roll into the Sacramento station, the first Pullmans to cross the continent. They brought a party of Easterners who could easily claim to be the first to stage a rail enthusiast excursion across the United States, for such had been their purpose. They were not interested in going down the river to San Francisco, toured the completed part of the California Pacific Railroad west of Sacramento, and returned East on June 18. With the sleeping cars was the Pullman Commissary Car *International,* which also established a "first" as the Central Pacific had no dining cars, preferring to feed their passengers at meal stations enroute. On July 1, the first two of the Central Pacific's Silver Palace Sleeping Cars arrived from Harlan & Hollingsworth in Wilmington, Delaware. These were cars "G" and "H," the cars having neither names nor numbers. Later, when the alphabet had been filled to the letter "U," the cars were numbered beginning with No. 1. By 1878 there were 41 Silver Palace Cars, these being the total of company owned cars. The Central Pacific handled Pullmans for special parties, and the Pullman *Rawlins* arrived on July 2, followed by a return visit of the *Ogden* and *Pennsylvania.* The same train brought the Silver Palace Sleeping Car "D," equipped with a rotunda or observation parlor at one end, built by Jackson & Sharp, also of Wilmington, Delaware. When Charles Crocker returned from the East after a conference with Union Pacific officials and the formation of a regular daily train schedule from Omaha to Sacramento, he did not change to a Silver Palace Sleeping Car at Promontory. He rode in state in the Pullman *Wahsatch* from Chicago to Sacramento, the car returning empty to Ogden.

The 15th of July marked the arrival of a distinguished group of visitors on a special train, consisting of the Pullmans *Summit* and *Promontory* (Note

At Oakland Wharf in 1869 the Pullman Palace Car Company's car *Young America,* dining car forerunner. — RICHARD B. JACKSON COLLECTION

Central Pacific's Silver Palace Sleeping Car "C" at the Jackson & Sharp factory. — GERALD M. BEST COLLECTION (BELOW) Pullman Drawing Room and Sleeping Car *Woodstock* one of first to reach Pacific coast. — SOUTHERN PACIFIC

In the above scene, the station at Promontory in the late summer of 1869. A train of Union Pacific fruit cars has just arrived, and a Central Pacific engine is ready to take the train west. (BELOW) An enlargement of the above illustration, showing the Central Pacific yards. Note the flag is still flying at the spot where the golden spike ceremony took place. — BOTH AMERICAN GEOGRAPHICAL SOCIETY

Promontory station and eating house, with the same Union Pacific fruit cars as shown in above view. — AMERICAN GEOGRAPHICAL SOCIETY

how quick the Pullman Company was to name their new cars after places on the transcontinental line), and the dining car *Young America*. The passengers were the Chicago Chamber of Commerce members and their wives. After a visit to Sacramento, they boarded a river steamer for San Francisco, spent a few days there, and returned home in their private Pullmans which had been held at Sacramento. They were the first of many groups which rode the new railroad, using the Chicago & North Western from Chicago to Council Bluffs, a ferry across the river to Omaha, and the two new railroads west from there. New passenger coaches for the Central Pacific began arriving direct by rail from such builders as Gilbert & Bush of Troy, New York, Barney, Smith & Company of Dayton, Ohio, and more from the Wason Manufacturing Company. By the end of 1870 the Central Pacific owned 116 first class coaches, 56 emigrant cars, 21 sleeping cars and a large assortment of baggage, mail and express cars. As the host of settlers rode the rails west to California, emigrant cars with flat roofs and the minimum of amenities for the passengers provided many a foreigner with a hot, dusty ride, but at a very low fare.

One of the early through passengers from Omaha to Sacramento was W. F. Rae, an Englishman who published the story of his trip in the summer of 1869, in his book *Westward By Rail*. He rode in Pullman cars from Omaha to Promontory, where he transferred to a Central Pacific "Silver Palace" sleeping car. Rae stated that the best part of the car was its name; he found the service inferior to that provided by the Pullman Company and the accommodations less luxurious. It is obvious he fell into

Ogden terminal of the Central Pacific in the mid-1870's. The station building is on the left, and was replaced in 1890 by a new and larger station which was destroyed by fire in 1923. The present Ogden Union Station was built at that time. — UTAH STATE HISTORICAL SOCIETY

the hands of a disgruntled porter, who also acted as conductor of the sleeping cars, whereas the Pullmans had a separate conductor who was extremely courteous and efficient. On the other hand, Daniel L. Harris, special Commissioner appointed by President Grant to investigate the affairs of the Union Pacific and Central Pacific, had this to say in his diary entry of July 27, 1869 — "Bedtime in one of the finest sleeping cars built at Wilmington, finds us rising out of the Salt Lake Basin."

On September 16, 1869, a Central Pacific group headed by C. P. Huntington and Charles Crocker met with Oliver Ames and other Union Pacific officers at Promontory, then adjourned to meet the next day in Uintah, seven miles east of Ogden. The idea of selling the 53 miles of the Union Pacific's line from Ogden to Promontory already had been accepted by both the railroads and the government commissioners. Both groups were in agreement that Promontory was not the place to build roundhouses, shops and a town for the employees of both roads. Ogden, soon to be connected with Salt Lake City by the Utah Central, was the ideal place. The only reason for the meeting of the officials was to set the purchase price. The Union Pacific demanded over four million dollars, which Hunting-

Oakland Terminal

The western terminal of the Central Pacific had its very beginning in 1863 when the San Francisco & Oakland Railroad opened a railroad along 7th Street in Oakland to the edge of San Francisco Bay, where a long, single-tracked trestle known as the Oakland Mole reached water deep enough to accommodate side-wheel ferry boats. At first it was only a commuters' railroad, but became the key link in the Central Pacific's projected terminal in the East Bay opposite San Francisco. Taken over by the Central Pacific in 1869, it was rapidly expanded to accommodate both passenger and freight trains. A commodious station with ferry slips was built and for 85 years or until the elimination of ferry service, Oakland Terminal handled all through passenger trains, and a considerable amount of freight traffic which used Long Wharf, just south of the passenger terminal. Besides the ferry slips, accommodations were provided at Oakland Wharf for several ocean-going ships, but this service was eliminated as the wharf expanded in width and was gradually filled in.

Busy Oakland Wharf about 1870, with a 7th Street Commute train coming in on the right, passing a sailing ship as it pulls into the ferry terminal on the left. — RICHARD B. JACKSON COLLECTION (BELOW) The *White Eagle* No. 116 with a passenger train at Oakland Wharf shortly after the San Francisco & Oakland R.R. was purchased and connected with the Western Pacific's line to Sacramento. No. 116 also served as a fire engine for the wharf which rested on wooden pilings extending over a mile into the Bay. — SOUTHERN PACIFIC

A Central Pacific train with seven Pullman sleeping cars pauses for the photographer on the trestle leading to Oakland Wharf. The gleaming exterior of polished mahogany explains the origin of the railroader's term "varnish" for the luxury in passenger train equipment. — SOUTHERN PACIFIC

A local train has just pulled in to the wharf and detrained its passengers. It now nears the end of the wharf, will cross over and back to the yard. Goat Island in San Francisco Bay may be seen in the distance. — SOUTHERN PACIFIC

A former Western Pacific locomotive built by Norris-Lancaster brings a passenger train to the newly enlarged Oakland Wharf. The wharf extension was so new when placed in operation, the flooring had not been installed when photographed. — CALIFORNIA STATE LIBRARY

Central Pacific's *Gold Run* No. 28 stands on a siding near Ogden station, all wooded up for a run. A corner of the station may be seen on the left just behind the coach lettered "Central Pacific R.R. of Cal." — RICHARD B. JACKSON COLLECTION

— First Fruit Train to Leave California —

Brand new Rogers built No. 183 heads up what is labelled on the photo as the first fruit train to leave California. This is doubtful, as fruit trains were running as early as 1869, and No. 183 was not built until 1872. It was probably the very first complete train of fruit cars built by Central Pacific. — GERALD M. BEST COLLECTION

ton stated was twice what it was worth. He left the bargaining table and told reporters that within ten days the Central Pacific would commence laying rails on their own grade, long since completed, from Promontory to Ogden. To avoid this useless duplication of track, the government commissioners interceded, persuaded Huntington to delay plans for further tracklaying, and suggested a price of three million dollars in government bonds, worth about $2,700,000 on the market, for 47 miles of the Union Pacific's track, with a lease on the remaining six miles into Ogden. The latter section was sold to the Central Pacific a few years later. Both railroads agreed to this compromise and on November 22, 1869, the sale was announced in the press. Ogden became the end of the Central Pacific's Salt Lake Division officially on March 1, 1870, by which time a roundhouse, station, and shops had been completed a short distance west of the Union Pacific station. Most of the facilities at Promontory were removed and the town which had been built there the year before was soon deserted. Promontory became a whistle stop — an object of curiosity for the tourists. All that remained there in early 1968 was the monument, erected to commemorate the joining of the rails, standing alone in a deserted field.

While the officials of the two railroads were meeting in Uintah, they agreed to jointly operate a through, solid sleeping car train on a weekly basis from Omaha to Alameda Pier. Called the Atlantic & Pacific Express, the first train left Omaha on October 19, 1869, and consisted of a baggage car, the Pullman dining car *Elk Horn Club*, the drawing room Pullman *Orleans* and the Pullmans *Wahsatch* and *San Francisco*. The *Orleans* had already been to San Francisco in September for exhibit at the Mechanics Institute Fair and was the most luxurious sleeping car to reach the Pacific Coast at that time. The new train made only service stops for water or change of locomotives and ran from Omaha to Sacramento in less than 79 hours. The first train was brought into Sacramento by the locomotive *Phil Sheridan* No. 80, with engineer R. C. Reynolds at the throttle, a large crowd turning out to see the new train arrive. There were few passengers, for the connecting train from Chicago had been delayed and the Union Pacific did not wait for it. The run to Alameda Pier and the ferry ride to San Francisco was accomplished in five hours, and on the following day the train returned to Omaha.

Due to lack of patronage, no doubt because the vacation season was over, the Atlantic & Pacific Ex-

Shortly after the Central Pacific was completed, car No. 81, the first car built by the San Francisco & Oakland Railway was converted into an open observation car, and was used during the summer from Sacramento to Summit and return. — RICHARD B. JACKSON COLLECTION

A double-header mixed train with the *Peoquop* No. 68 on the head-end, the victim of the first case of engine-napping in California, stands in front of the Colfax station. — GERALD M. BEST COLLECTION

Central Pacific *Mikado* No. 65 takes on water from an enclosed tank at Stockton shortly after the line was opened to Oakland. — COLLEGE OF THE PACIFIC

A Pullman hotel car in the yards at Oakland in 1871. This was the equivalent of a luxury private car, with both sleeping accommodations and a kitchen to serve a limited group of passengers. — HUNTINGTON LIBRARY, SAN MARINO, CALIFORNIA

press was discontinued during the first week of January 1870, and a weekly through dining car and Pullman from Omaha were attached to the regular daily train. While the Express was running, it brought the first shipment of Chesapeake Bay oysters to the hotels and restaurants of San Francisco, a refrigerator carload of them coming through Sacramento on November 3, 1869. History was also made that month by the first shipment by train of California wine to eastern markets. As an experiment, the Central Pacific rented the Pullman dining car *International* for three months early in 1870 and it made a daily run on the through passenger train from Sacramento to Oakland Pier and return. It was sent back to the Pullman Company for lack of patronage. The Pullman car name collector for the *Sacramento Union* noted the arrival of many new Pullmans during the first half of 1870; the *Algoma, Omaha, Winona, Woodstock, Minnesota, Laramie, America, Riverside, Cambria, Huron, Sarnia, Kenwood, Gem, Sacramento* and the dining car *Cosmopolitan* were listed. George M. Pullman in person arrived in Sacramento on May 2, 1870, in the new Pullman *Westminster* for the announced purpose of conferring with the Central Pacific management in an effort to restore the Atlantic & Pacific Express. The Union Pacific was willing, but the Central Pacific considered the Pullman rental charges excessive and refused to cooperate.

The Chicago, Rock Island & Pacific sent their beautiful new sleeping car *San Francisco* with 30 excursionists from Chicago, through to San Francisco late in May 1870, the car being exhibited there for several days in the vain hope of interesting the Central Pacific in through service via the Rock Island from Chicago to Oakland. With the arrival of more Silver Palace Sleeping Cars, the

Central Pacific dealt the death blow to through sleeping car service from Omaha, and on July 6, 1870, the last Pullman car left Sacramento for the East. There were special tour parties from the East coming through in solid Pullman trains after this date, but they had to pay the Central Pacific an extra charge besides the railroad fare. Thereafter, and for many years, passengers bound for the Pacific Coast or vice versa had to change trains at Omaha and Ogden, and ate their meals west of Ogden at meal stations, a test of the gustatorial stamina of the passengers, for the Central Pacific restaurants were not noted for their gourmet menus.

On November 14, 1869, the Central Pacific had its first bad passenger train accident. Its luck was bound to run out some time, and the wreck was serious enough to make headlines in the newspapers throughout the country. Western Pacific trains began running through to Oakland Pier via the new tie-line on November 4, 1869, and Alameda Junction, formerly called Simpsons on the San Francisco & Alameda Railroad became an important station, with a switch tender always on duty there. On the morning of the wreck there was a heavy fog at the junction and train No. 16, the Sunday local from Melrose to Alameda was late. So was the eastbound Western Pacific express from Oakland to Sacramento. Neither train having arrived at the junction on time, the switch tender retired to a nearby eating house for breakfast. Hearing a gravel train pass through the junction on its way to Alameda, he assumed it was the Alameda local, for he did not bother to turn his head and look. A few minutes later the Western Pacific express, headed by the locomotive *Sonoma* No. 173 whistled for the junction and came to a full stop there. The switchman left his coffee, set the switch for the Sacramento-bound train and gave it a sig-nal to proceed. A mile and a half south of the junction the Western Pacific train collided head-on with the Alameda local, which came out of the fog without warning to either engine crew. The local consisted of the engine *Atherton* No. 177 and six well-filled coaches. The first two cars of each train were telescoped, 15 persons including both engine crews were killed and nearly a hundred passengers and crewmen were injured.

This calamity must have placed all the Western Pacific officials on edge, for on the 17th when the Atlantic & Pacific Express was being backed off Oakland Pier, a misplaced switch caused the train to back into some standing cars, badly damaging a Silver Palace sleeper, the Pullman *Sacramento* and a coach. Master Mechanic Mills was so angry he knocked out the switchman with one blow and was haled into court for assault and battery. On the 22nd the eastbound express was derailed at San Leandro by a broken switch and the locomotive *Lark* was ditched, though the passenger cars remained on the rails. On the same day, the pieces of the two engines from the wreck near Alameda Junction were brought into Sacramento on four flat cars, a great crowd assembling at the shops to view the damage and walk away with souvenirs. The climax of the Central Pacific's troubles that day was the stealing of the locomotive *Peoquop* by William Duffy, an inebriated bystander near the shops, who ran the locomotive five miles east of Sacramento before the engine died from lack of steam. Duffy was soon lodged in jail, the judge giving him 60 days for locomotive stealing, a new crime in the annals of California but not the last incident of this type.

November 4, 1870, was a bad day for the Central Pacific. Up on the hill, an eastbound freight hauled by the locomotives *Buffalo* and *White Bear* had

San Francisco & Alameda R.R. *F. D. Atherton*, standing by the Alameda roundhouse which was wrecked in the great earthquake of October 21, 1868. A few months later the engine was destroyed in a wreck at Alameda Junction. — GERALD M. BEST COLLECTION

69

Casualties in another wreck on the Hill are being returned to Sacramento for repairs and rebuilding. The tenders seem to have suffered the most damage. — GERALD M. BEST COLLECTION

The result of a misunderstanding of train orders almost reduced these two Central Pacific 10-wheelers to scrap. — GERALD M. BEST COLLECTION

been waiting on a siding at Shady Run for a westbound freight. Their orders were to wait a half hour and if the freight did not arrive, to proceed east to Blue Canyon. When the waiting time was up, they pulled out on the main and were running along with open throttles a mile west of Blue Canyon when the westbound freight, headed by the engine *Growler,* suddenly appeared around a curve, running at an excessive rate of speed. There was no time to apply brakes or reverse engines, and the trains met head-on. The force of the collision drove the *Buffalo* on top of the *Growler,* which had turned on its side after the impact, and the *White Bear* reared up in the air and settled on top of the *Buffalo.* Half a dozen cars of each train were scattered like dominoes on each side of the track, and it was a miracle that only the fireman of the *Buffalo* was killed. All the other crewmen survived though seriously injured. Excepting the head-on collision inside Summit tunnel during construction days in 1869, this was the first of its kind in the mountains; there had been derailments, particularly during snow blockades, but never anything like this. The cause of the wreck was a misunderstanding of train orders by the crew of the westbound freight.

Held at Colfax until the track could be cleared, eastbound express No. 1 from Oakland to Ogden was allowed to proceed at 6 p.m. About 1:30 a.m. it made its regular stop at Verdi, Nevada, ten miles west of Reno. Soon after leaving that place, a man jumped down from the tender into the engine cab and pointed two pistols at the astonished engine crew, ordering them to stop the train at once. Five passengers riding in the first coach left by the front door as soon as the train stopped. One of them disconnected the coach from the express car, all five mounted the open back platform of the car after signalling the bandit on the engine to proceed, and the engine and express car disappeared to the east in the darkness. Bursting in on the unarmed express agent, the robbers tied him up, opened a safe and robbed it of $41,600 in gold coin, several thousands in currency, a sack of gold dust and a few silver dollars. Engineer H. S. Small was forced to continue to within two miles of Reno where the men left the train. He then backed the train to Verdi. The conductor was waiting there with the passenger coaches; everyone was ignorant of what had taken place as the telegraph wires had been cut. The train then proceeded to Reno where the sheriff was notified. The money stolen was a payroll for Virginia City, and great excitement prevailed there as the news got around.

Sheriff Kincaid, aided by Wells Fargo agents and by a lack of finesse on the part of the robbers, had all six men in custody within a week and had recovered all but the currency, gold dust and a few of the coins. Over $10,000 in gold coins were recovered from an outhouse back of a hotel where one of the bandits had stayed. His actions aroused the suspicions of the landlady and after he had left, a small amount of placer mining in the little building "out back" produced a fortune. While the robbers were awaiting trial, two Reno lawyers who were defending one of the men who had been caught at Corinne, Utah, boarded a train and went to Corinne, renting horses there. Riding out into the country to a certain tree, they dug up a bag with 36 ounces of gold dust, $2,000 in greenbacks and a few silver and gold coins. They were so engrossed in their task that they never noticed two men ride up and sit patiently waiting until they had finished. The men were Wells Fargo agents who had seen the lawyers board the train and had ridden in another car on the same train to Corinne. The robbers were all convicted and served time in the Nevada penitentiary, but the two lawyers got off with small fines. This was the first train robbery on the Central Pacific, and thereafter when any large amount of negotiable funds in bills or gold coins was shipped by express, an armed Wells Fargo guard rode the train. The word must have reached the East Coast, for two weeks later a Baltimore & Ohio express car loaded with five million dollars in new greenbacks came out from Washington to San Francisco with twelve soldiers armed with rifles and pistols living inside the car with the money. The car returned East several days later with an even greater sum in old bills being returned to Washington for cancellation, and the soldiers were still on duty. This B. & O. car made a monthly round trip thereafter with money for the San Francisco mint.

Another approach to the robbing of express-mail cars was tried on the night of January 20, 1871.

The holdup of the Central Pacific express car at Verdi attracted the attention of weekly journals such as *Harpers*, *Leslies* and the *Police Gazette*. Each line drawing presented the artist's idea of an event he never witnessed, with the inevitable distortion of the facts.

When the eastbound express made a meal stop at Alta, 51 miles west of Truckee, all the passengers and the two clerks in the mail car went into the restaurant, while the engine crew busied themselves filling the tender with water and oiling around. Two men then broke the lock on the blind side of the mail compartment, the door was opened, and two sacks containing the registered mail from San Francisco and Sacramento were taken. The robbery was not discovered until the clerks returned to the car. The Sheriff in Truckee was notified, the whole area was patrolled, and on the following day most of the loot was discovered hidden under a board sidewalk in Truckee. Two suspects were arrested. One named Wyth tried to commit suicide twice and was eventually tried in Federal court in San Francisco and convicted. This incident resulted in the building of four new mail-express cars at the Sacramento Shops, with double doors and the inside of the car lined with boiler plate. The partition between the express and mail compartments was also armored. Fearing an attempt to rob the pay car, Central Pacific officials had a new six-wheel truck beauty turned out of the shops. It was lined inside with boiler plate and almost resembled a modern Brink's truck in its equipment. No further trouble with robbers was experienced. For many years the pay car was hauled by engine No. 96, the engine and car being the first to be equipped with Westinghouse air brakes.

After the Central Pacific reached Truckee, the proposed line was laid out in divisions, and sites were picked where yards, a roundhouse and machine shops could be built. It was realized that helpers would be required from Rocklin, 23 miles east of Sacramento to the summit of the Sierra, and from Truckee in a westerly direction to the summit. Also from Wells, Nevada, to the summit of the Peoquop mountains eastbound, and from Toano, Nevada, for westbound trains. At Rocklin a 29-stall roundhouse of granite was erected, and from this roundhouse engines going north on the old California Central line to Lincoln and its extension to Marysville and Redding were based. At Summit Station, inside the snowsheds, there was a turntable and several stalls for helper engines. The permanently assigned fire engine for the snowshed fire train remained there throughout the fire season. In later years the installation was moved over a mile west to Norden, the point at which the second track, built many years later, branched off to the south and tunnelled through the mountain, saving miles of sharp curves and exposed snowshed-covered track for eastbound trains.

Alta station, scene of the theft of registered mail sacks from the mail car in 1871. — RICHARD B. JACKSON COLLECTION

Central Pacific *Clipper* No. 96, which hauled the pay car for many years, was the first engine on the road to have air brakes. — GERALD B. BEST COLLECTION

For years, a balloon track was used at Truckee to turn helper engines or strings of engines with a bucker snowplow at the front. — GUY DUNSCOMB

The line from Sacramento to Oakland was naturally called the Western Division, and a roundhouse with repair shops was enlarged from the old San Francisco & Oakland installation; also there were similar facilities at Alameda. The Sacramento Division ended at Truckee, where a 16-stall roundhouse was hastily built even before Summit tunnel was completed. This roundhouse was destroyed by fire early in 1869, and was replaced by a 24-stall granite structure with a high conical roof. The interior was protected against the heavy snows and cold of the winters by tight fitting entrance and exit doors, a dozen coal stoves in the building keeping the maintenance crews warm. The first section of the Truckee Division extended to Wadsworth, Nevada, 189 miles east of Sacramento; a 16-stall roundhouse and a machine shop were built there.

The second section of the Truckee Division continued to Winnemucca, Nevada, 324 miles from San Francisco where a 16-stall roundhouse with light repair facilities was built. From Winnemucca to Carlin, Nevada, composed the first section of the Humboldt Division, and at Carlin, 445 miles from Sacramento, a 16-stall roundhouse and large repair shops were erected. This section was called the Shoshone Division from March 15, 1869, until the railroad made Ogden its eastern terminal, and the Humboldt Division during that time extended only from Carlin to Toano. When the two divisions were combined, the latter became the second section of the Humboldt Division. Toano, Nevada, 561 miles from Sacramento was at the base of the east slopes of the Peoquop range and was selected as the site for a 14-stall roundhouse and small shop, helper en-

The Truckee roundhouse, built of enduring granite, was the only completely round roundhouse on the Central Pacific. — RICHARD B. JACKSON COLLECTION

Digging out the Truckee roundhouse after a heavy snowstorm. The shed on the left sheltered Pullman sleeping cars which ended their run at Truckee, while the passengers took the narrow gauge to Lake Tahoe. — SOUTHERN PACIFIC

73

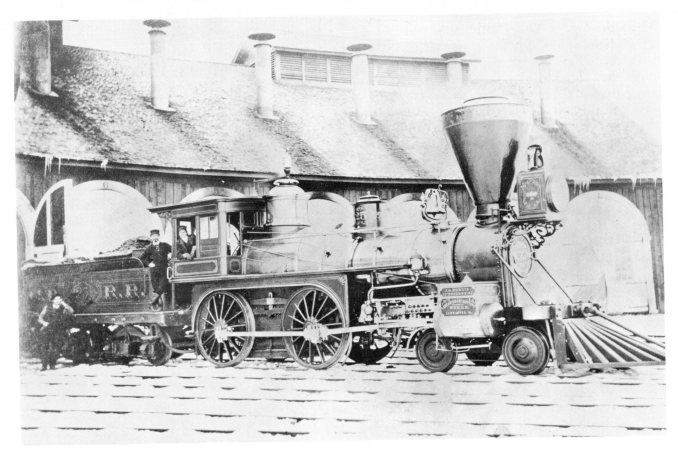

gines running on all trains east or west between Toano and Wells, on the west side of the Peoquops. As these mountains proved to be almost as troublesome as the Sierra in time of heavy winter snows, a bucker snowplow was based at Toano for years.

The Salt Lake Division started at Toano, passing through Terrace, Utah, at the end of a descent of 1,351 feet in 59 miles. Terrace was the end of the first section of the Salt Lake Division, a 14-stall roundhouse and small shop being built there as soon as the rails reached that point. It was the last roundhouse built before the rails were joined at Promontory. After May 10, 1869, and until the sale of the Union Pacific track from Promontory to Ogden, all trains of both roads terminated their runs at Promontory. Central Pacific locomotives were turned around there and went back to Terrace for service. A station, restaurant and other facilities were built at the Promontory interchange, on Union Pacific property east of the "golden spike" site.

Though out of context with the story, it is interesting to note that long after the Central Pacific had become a part of the Harriman-controlled Southern Pacific, the Ogden-Lucin cutoff, completed November 26, 1903, crossed Great Salt Lake on a trestle with a new line east and west of the lake, saving 44 miles in distance and providing a water level track 102 miles long. Service on the old line was reduced to one mixed train per day. The roundhouse and shops at Terrace were abandoned and salvageable material removed elsewhere. The old line was retained at the request of the U. S. Government as protection in case the trestle across the lake should burn, but with the building of the Western Pacific Railway south of the lake and the eventual filling in of the trestle with rock, the need for the old line disappeared and it was abandoned in 1942. All the track was removed soon afterwards because of its value as scrap for wartime use, though the Southern Pacific retained title to the 400 foot right-of-way. Recently the section from Rozel to Blue Creek was donated to the U. S. Government. Promontory has become a Golden Spike National Historic Site and after the completion of a visitor center building there, will be the scene of the Centennial of the Golden Spike on May 10, 1969.

While the Ogden-Lucin cutoff was being built, many sections of the old line west of Lucin were relocated; the grades were reduced by tunnels through the ridges and deep excavations with high fills in between. Toano was eliminated as a helper station and the facilities were moved westward to Wells some years prior to the Harriman improvements. The Wadsworth roundhouse and shops were eliminated in December 1904, and a new engine terminal and shops were built four miles east of Reno, where the new town of Sparks became the end of the Sacramento Division and the start of the Salt Lake Division on June 19, 1904. The old Humboldt and Truckee Divisions were consolidated at this time. Rocklin roundhouse was torn down in 1908, and helper engines for the eastbound main line trains were serviced at a new roundhouse at Roseville, five miles west. A small roundhouse at Colfax remained until the end of steam.

Through all this change, the terminal at Carlin remained in use and engines were changed there after the run from Ogden until the advent of the 4-8-2 and 4-8-4 types made this change unnecessary. The Truckee and Wells roundhouses retained their importance as helper stations until steam locomotives were eliminated.

To completely outline the history of the western part of the Central Pacific and the changes made in the route from Sacramento to San Francisco in the first two years of the transcontinental railroad's operation, it is necessary to include the California Pacific Railroad. This road was built from South Vallejo on San Francisco Bay, 26 miles north of San Francisco, to the west bank of the Sacramento River opposite the Central Pacific station in Sacramento between December 1866 and June 1869. Branches were also built from a junction near Vallejo to Calistoga, 38 miles, and from Davis Junction, 13 miles west of Sacramento to Marysville, 43 miles. Its owners were a group of San Franciscans headed by John P. Jackson, and their intention was to compete with the Central Pacific for the Sacramento-San Francisco traffic by offering much faster service. To cross the river at Sacramento, the Sacramento & Yolo Bridge Company was organized to build a combination wagon and railroad bridge, the California Pacific to pay rental for the privilege of crossing it. While this bridge was under construction in the winter of 1869-1870 the Central Pacific opposed the California Pacific's every move. The latter built tracks from the end of the nearly completed bridge to a point where they wished to cross the Central Pacific main line and continue to a station east of that point. As fast as the California Pacific inserted crossing frogs in the C. P. track, the latter's crews removed them, forcing the California Pacific to obtain an injunction to stop the obstructionistic tactics of the Central Pacific. The bridge was tested on January 15, 1870, by running the California Pacific's locomotive *Sacramento* over it. After some weeks of legal sparring, both railroads agreed to let the courts decide the issue. The crossing frogs were replaced and on January 29, 1870, the California Pacific's first passenger train,

The complicated lattice work of the Sacramento & Yolo bridge, across which the California Pacific trains entered Sacramento, with the swing section at the left. All is in contrast to the new construction of the Central Pacific landing in the foreground, as preparations are made for transcontinental trains to use the bridge. — HUNTINGTON LIBRARY, SAN MARINO, CALIFORNIA

California Pacific *London* No. 13, at the William Mason factory in Taunton, Massachusetts. — CHARLES E. FISHER COLLECTION

California Pacific *D. C. Haskins* No. 11, near Hornbrook, California, during the construction of the Oregon & California. — GERALD M. BEST COLLECTION

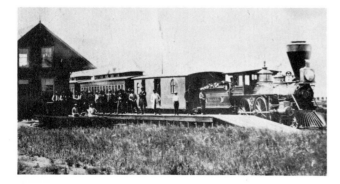

California Pacific's *Vallejo* No. 5 with a gothic-windowed baggage car, at the head of the Knight's Landing train at Woodland in 1871. — GERALD M. BEST COLLECTION

headed by the *J. M. Ryder,* inaugurated a daily service between Sacramento and South Vallejo wharf

In July 1870, the courts ruled that the California Pacific should pay the Central Pacific the outrageous sum of $360,680 for the privilege of crossing the latter's tracks. The decision was appealed and a study was made by the Railroad Commission during the rest of the year. The California Pacific built a fine new covered station in Sacramento, purchased nine deluxe passenger coaches with six-wheel trucks from the Ohio Falls Car Company, and built new baggage and smoking cars to go with these coaches. Four handsome new 4-4-0 locomotives from Mason were ordered, and by early 1871, Sacramentans were commenting on the contrast between the dusty and worn looking cars on the Central Pacific trains arriving from the East and the handsome trains of the California Pacific. The local trade from Sacramento to San Francisco deserted the Central Pacific, and to add insult to injury, the California Pacific train-ferry combination made the trip between the two cities in four hours as compared to six hours for the Central Pacific.

In addition, two new locomotives received from Mason in June 1871, were equipped with air brakes, and soon two complete passenger trains on the California Pacific were also equipped, the first to operate on the Pacific Coast. The Central Pacific had installed air brakes on locomotive No. 96, the pay car and Superintendent Towne's business car as an experiment two months earlier, but had not yet begun to adopt the air brake for passenger trains. At this time the California Pacific won the appeal in the courts, the damage payment being set aside as unfair and unreasonable. One can imagine the slow burn of resentment in the minds of Huntington and his directors, but until July 19th there was no visible evidence of it. On that day the Central Pacific announced it had obtained the right to run trains over the Sacramento & Yolo Bridge, and the following day laid their own rails parallel to those of the California Pacific, with switch frogs at both ends of the bridge. They also announced the incorporation of the Northern Railway, to build from Oakland to Tehama, 210 miles, with a branch from Davis to Sacramento which would parallel the California Pacific.

This move produced rumors that the Central Pacific was about to buy the California Pacific, with immediate denials from the latter's officials, but on August 10, 1871, the directors of both railroads met in an office in San Francisco, and there it was disclosed that the Central Pacific had for months been buying California Pacific stock until they had undisputed control. The new directorate of the California Pacific was that of the Central Pacific, and the San Francisco group were "out." The Sacramento & Placerville was also bought at this time for $166,400. The immediate consequences of this merger were the construction of a new approach on the Sacramento side of the bridge across the river, and tracks connecting the Central Pacific station and main line with the California Pacific. Part of the latter's new station was torn down to make room for these tracks, and on November 5, 1871, all overland passenger trains of the Central Pacific went across the bridge to South Vallejo, the old route via Stockton being used by

freights and a daily passenger train for local traffic. Some of the California Pacific's locomotives were taken over by the Central Pacific, though most of them retained their road name and numbers until 1891. This new arrangement lasted exactly one month, for in December 1871, a great rainstorm flooded the Sacramento River and its tributaries and washed out miles of the California Pacific's trestle west of Sacramento. Train service on the Central Pacific returned to its old route, and when the California Pacific's trestle was rebuilt a year later, the Stockton-Niles line remained in use, as many passengers objected to the long steamer ride from South Vallejo to San Francisco.

The California Pacific served a very useful purpose in later years, for a 17 mile branch was built from Suisun, 40 miles west of Sacramento, to Benicia on the north shore of Carquinez Straits. Here the giant train ferry *Solano* was placed in service in December 1879, carrying passenger trains complete with locomotive across the straits to Port Costa. There the train was reassembled and continued its journey to Oakland Pier over a new line the Central Pacific had built from Oakland to Tracy via Martinez. This cut the running time from Sacramento to San Francisco to four hours including both ferry boat rides. In 1914 a new steel-hulled train ferry, the *Contra Costa* was placed in service. These great ferries remained in use until the Carquinez Bridge east of Martinez was placed in service on November 30, 1930.

The Central Pacific locomotive list included 179 engines at the end of 1870. In 1871, several were

The train ferry *Solano* crossing Carquinez Straits with a local train from Sacramento. — GOLDEN WEST COLLECTION

Two views of the car ferry *Solano* at the dock in Port Costa, with a train being assembled for its journey to Oakland, and the four tracks of the ferry which could store the *Overland Limited* even after its Pullmans reached 80 feet in length. — BOTH HUNTINGTON LIBRARY, SAN MARINO, CALIFORNIA

The second Central Pacific Sacramento station, built in 1879 several blocks east of the first station. — RICHARD B. JACKSON COLLECTION

transferred to the newly organized Southern Pacific Railroad, which was to build south from Stockton through California, Arizona and New Mexico, with an eventual destination of New Orleans. It was also planned to build a line from San Jose to Los Angeles, but this dream did not come true for 30 years. The first engine transferred was the *C. P. Huntington* No. 3, which left Sacramento for San Jose on February 7, 1871, renumbered Southern Pacific No. 1. This engine worked on construction trains between San Jose and Hollister, spent years in local service at Oakland, reaching the lowly status of a weed burner in the late 1890's at Sacramento. It was then removed from the roster and ordered scrapped. By a miracle, it escaped this fate, was finally appreciated for what it was, and endures to this day. It ran time and again in various railroad celebrations, made trips to Chicago and Los Angeles, was even paraded up Hollywood Boulevard in 1927. It now sits in the Sacramento County Fair Grounds, not far from where it was landed from the steamer *Pet*.

The *Governor Stanford* was slated to go to Leland Stanford, Jr. University when the latter was opened in 1894. The engine was cleaned up and restored to its former splendor, but the evidence is quite conclusive that it did not reach Palo Alto until 1899. There it remained indoors, subject to the occasional vandalism of students for 64 years. In 1963, when building alterations required removal of the locomotive, arrangements were made with the Pacific Coast Chapter of the Railway & Locomotive Historical Society to turn the engine over to them on a semi-permanent loan, to be placed with the rest of the Chapter's collection of locomotives and rolling stock in a transportation museum

The *C. P. Huntington* on Hollywood Boulevard, advertising the silent film "Iron Horse". The extras are genuine Indians; not pale face actors. — GOLDEN WEST COLLECTION (BELOW) The *C. P. Huntington* stands alongside the latest cab-first articulated for a publicity shot in 1937. — DAVID L. JOSLYN

Shops under General Superintendent of Motive Power E. F. Perkins, who had replaced J. H. Graves in 1868. Stevens soon proved himself so capable that Perkins, who could not accustom himself to the summer heat of the Sacramento Valley and longed to return to his home in New England, resigned in July 1870. Stevens was given Perkins' job but his title was General Master Mechanic.

One of the first things Stevens had suggested to Perkins was to eliminate the Folsom shops of the Sacramento Valley Railroad, repair all the latter's engines at Sacramento, and to send the machinery from Folsom to West Oakland to augment the meager repair facilities there. The Folsom shops were closed December 26, 1869, in spite of a storm of protest from Folsom residents, and on January 6, 1870, a strange train arrived in Sacramento from Folsom. Hauled by the locomotive *Pioneer* No. 4, there were the locomotives *Nevada* No. 2, the *L. L. Robinson* No. 3 and Central Pacific's *Tuolumne* No. 42, a 4-4-0 which with its three mates had been operating most of the Sacramento Valley trains. The *L. L. Robinson* was described by an eye-witness as a mere skeleton of a locomotive, it having been so badly damaged two years earlier by a

The *Governor Stanford* on rails once again after 64 years as a show piece in the Library of Stanford University. — FRED STINDT (BELOW) The *Governor Stanford* in September 1873, after conversion to a fire engine for Sacramento yard service. — GERALD M. BEST COLLECTION

which is still in the formative stage. In June 1963, the engine was trucked to Richmond, California, where it was stored for nearly four years in the old shop building of the Santa Fe Railway. It has since been moved to a safer place to protect it not only from neglect by a disinterested railroad, but the deliberate stealing of parts of the engine as souvenirs. It is hoped that by the time of the Centennial of the Golden Spike, this engine will be on exhibit in Sacramento, where it first raised a head of steam.

The motive power headquarters of the Central Pacific remained at Sacramento as long as the road existed as a separate company. Late in 1869, Huntington brought Andrew Jackson Stevens up from Alameda where he had been Master Mechanic of the San Francisco & Alameda Railroad. Stevens was made Master Mechanic of the Sacramento

At the left, Sacramento & Placerville No. 2 at Folsom in 1879. The engine truck wheels probably came from the locomotive *Sacramento*. — GERALD M. BEST COLLECTION (BELOW) Engine No. 173 as designed by Andrew Jackson Stevens in November 1872. Its classic lines were to endure for a century. — RICHARD B. JACKSON COLLECTION

boiler explosion that it had never been repaired. Stevens was not a man to throw away a good engine chassis, and in March 1871, he turned out the *L. L. Robinson* as good as new, a strange combination of Steven's new designs and the old styling of the New Jersey Locomotive Works. The engine eventually became Sacramento & Placerville No. 2 and lasted until 1889 when it was sold to the Folsom Water Power Company.

Under Stevens, a comprehensive program of rebuilding the older locomotives was begun. In the last half of 1872, ten new Rogers 4-4-0s were purchased, these being the first engines not assigned names. It had been decided to eliminate the names on the locomotives when Stevens took charge, though this was not done all at once. As a locomotive came into the shop, the name was painted out, and all disappeared by 1874. On May 18, 1872, one of the engines wrecked at Alameda Junction two years earlier was brought into the shop. This was Norris-Lancaster No. 173, ex-*Sonoma*, previously Western Pacific "H", a 4-4-0 with 66-inch drivers

and 16½x24-inch cylinders. The boiler and parts of the chassis could be reused, and Stevens had been ordered to rebuild it, so he selected this particular engine as an experiment to see what would be required to build a new locomotive. Though it was carried in the records thereafter as built by the Central Pacific Company, the detailed list of what was done and what parts were reused is in the report signed by gang foreman J. J. McCormack on November 18, 1872. The engine had 54-inch drivers as rebuilt, later increased to 57 inches by the use of thicker tires, 17x24-inch cylinders; McCormack did his work well, for the engine lasted until 1909, working most of the time on Oakland suburban trains.

In the late 1940's, when Walt Disney had decided to build a live steam model locomotive, he saw a picture of No. 173 and admired its beautiful lines. David L. Joslyn, then draftsman in the Sacramento Shops, furnished prints from the original tracings which he had found in storage in a warehouse full of discarded files of the company. The drawings were scaled down to a model scale of two inches to the foot, so Walt could build the *Lily Belle,* which ran on Disney's backyard railroad for many years and is now on exhibit at Disneyland. In 1954, when Disneyland was conceived, engine No. 1 at Disneyland was built to Central Pacific No. 173's drawings redone to ⅝ full size, the engine to run on a 3-foot gauge track. Like its prototype, it is a beautiful locomotive, has run over a quarter of a million miles since Disneyland was opened in 1955, and is still in regular service.

So pleased was the Central Pacific management with No. 173 that in 1873 Stevens was ordered to build twelve new locomotives like it. The first of the new 4-4-0s was turned out June 30, 1873, as Central Pacific 2nd No. 55. Of the remaining new engines, all were like No. 55 in exterior appearance, although some had 60-inch drivers and 18x24-inch cylinders. Two were sold to the Virginia & Truckee in 1873, and one was built for the Los Angeles & San Pedro Railroad; the latter soon became a part of the Southern Pacific. V. & T. No. 18 is still in existence at Los Angeles, the property of Paramount Studios and has been used since 1939 in motion pictures. It is the sole survivor of all the 4-4-0 engines built by Andrew Jackson Stevens. The other locomotive in the Alameda Junction disaster, the *Atherton* No. 177, was brought into the shop in 1872 and remained there a year before it was turned out under the same road number. It could not have been as badly damaged as No. 173 as its cylinders and driving wheels were reused Equipped with a water pump and hose reel, it became a fire engine for service in the snowshed district.

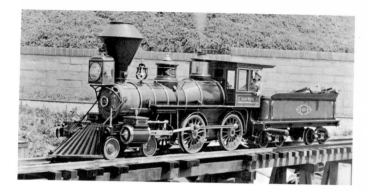

Disney's 2-inch scale live steamer of C.P. No. 173 named *Lily Belle,* ran around his Beverly Hills home for many years. — RICHARD JACKSON

Walt Disney had a ⅝ scale model of Central Pacific No. 173 built for his Disneyland railroad. — GERALD M. BEST

Central Pacific 2nd No. 55 was erected in the Sacramento shops in June 1873. Note the fine builders identification between the driving wheels. — GERALD M. BEST COLLECTION

Locomotive No. 166 was one of Steven's later designs, with his highly sophisticated valve gear and a boiler reminiscent of British practice. — GERALD M. BEST COLLECTION

Central Pacific No. 177 on the Sacramento roundhouse turntable was the first of 13 ten-wheel engines built by Stevens between 1886 - 1888. — GERALD M. BEST COLLECTION

Steven's first new engine, 2nd No. 55 was not equipped with air brakes when placed in service, but shortly thereafter a general order was issued to equip all locomotives and passenger rolling stock with air brakes as soon as possible. Within two years all main line passenger trains had Westinghouse air brakes, and in at least one instance they were used for an unexpected reason. One day in 1876 as the westbound express from Ogden was slowly approaching the station platform at Sacramento, it stopped very suddenly. The engineer was seen to jump down to the ground, run along the track to the vicinity of the first baggage car, then return to the cab and bring his train into the station. When asked why he had applied the emergency brakes, he said, "I sneezed and blew my teeth out the window. If I had'nt stopped and run back, I would never have found them!"

All Central Pacific engines built prior to 1870 were wood burners. There were no coal mines along the line, wood was cheap and plentiful during construction days, and it was not until the Western Pacific was completed that coal mines in Contra Costa county were able to supply coal in sufficient quantity to make it worth while to convert some of the engines to burn coal. The first engines to be so converted were those which operated between Sacramento and Oakland, as they were close to the coal supply. The coal was not of good quality, resulting in late trains because of failure of engines to make steam. Stevens recommended that all engines operating east of Wadsworth be converted to burn coal, and that the high grade coal from Utah be used. In time, this coal became the main source of supply for all locomotives of the Central Pacific until oil replaced coal in 1905. Stevens was a thorough man, for he even made measured tests of the amount of wood consumed by a locomotive running from Sacramento to Truckee and return by attaching a car loaded with wood behind the engine's tender, permitting the fireman to use the same type and quality of wood throughout the test. He then recommended that those engines which operated in districts where wood was much cheaper than coal should continue to burn wood, but all of Steven's new engines of 1873 burned coal.

Thirty new ten-wheel freight and ten new 4-4-0 passenger engines were purchased in 1875 and 1876 from Schenectady and Danforth, these being the last locomotives bought by the Central Pacific from Eastern builders before the 1891 renumbering. The highest road number in the 1878 locomotive list was No. 228, and to top this, a strange and unique locomotive numbered No. 229 was added

After success of No. 173, Stevens built many engines like the No. 188. — GERALD M. BEST COLLECTION

in 1879. This engine consisted of a 2-2-0 locomotive with 42-inch drivers and 7x14-inch cylinders, which formed the front support for a passenger type car body with a four-wheel truck in the rear. It was built by the Vulcan Iron Works in San Francisco in 1865 for the Napa Valley Railroad and appeared on the California Pacific in 1869 where it was named the *Flea*. When not in use as the pay car or for inspection tours, it handled short work trains. In 1879 the *Flea* became Central Pacific No. 229. What the Central Pacific used this steam car for is not known, but it was soon sold, and eventually ended its days on the Sierra Nevada Wood & Lumber Company line between Truckee and Hobart Mills. In 1921, David L. Joslyn photographed what was left of the steam car in back of the Sacramento Shops, where it stood in ruins near the river levee.

The Centennial year 1876 marked the addition of 18 new Silver Palace Sleeping Cars built by Barney & Smith. These were more luxurious and heavier than the earlier Silver Palace cars, and were the last company-owned sleepers to be purchased. When Emperor Dom Pedro Segundo of Brazil was enroute by steamer from Panama to San Francisco,

The last engine acquired from factories other than its own shops. — GERALD M. BEST COLLECTION

The former California Pacific *Flea*, which later became Central Pacific No. 229, on the Sierra Nevada Wood & Lumber Co.'s road as No. 4. — LOUIS STEIN COLLECTION

Locomotive parts of the steam car *Calistog* leaving the Vulcan Iron Works, San Francisco in 1865. — ROY GRAVES COLLECTION

The remains of the *Flea* rusting in the swamp behind the Sacramento Shops of the Southern Pacific in 1921. — DAVID L. JOSLYN

Central Pacific 2nd No. 229 was Stevens first attempt at building a heavy freight engine. It was very successful, but he was not allowed to build more than one of this type. — GERALD M. BEST COLLECTION

One of seven engines built for Oakland suburban service, No. 236 was the only one photographed as it left Sacramento shops in 1882. — RICHARD B. JACKSON COLLECTION

on his way to the Centennial Exposition in Philadelphia, his agents found the Central Pacific's Directors' Car inadequate to the Emperor's needs, and two of Pullman's most luxurious private hotel cars were rushed from Chicago to accommodate the Emperor. The old Directors' car, which had been at Promontory with Governor Stanford in 1869, was obviously outmoded, and a new car named the *California*, representing the height of luxury for railroad executives at that time, was ordered from Harlan & Hollingsworth.

There is every reason to believe that the old Directors' Car was either sold or given to Senator William Sharon of Nevada after the *California* arrived. Various newspaper dispatches from Virginia City and San Francisco mention Sharon as riding with Huntington, Crocker and other Central Pacific executives in the latters' Directors' car prior to the arrival of the Emperor of Brazil, and of Sharon going east in his private car to Washington. Gilbert H. Kneiss and other historians all list Virginia & Truckee coach No. 17 as being formerly Senator Sharon's private car, builder unknown, acquired by the V. & T. in 1876 and at some unknown later date converted to a coach. Frequent newspaper comments from Virginia City in 1876 and later years mention the V. & T. Officers' Car, yet no V. & T. history mentions the existence of this car except as Sharon's private car. As coach No. 17 it was sold to 20th Century-Fox Studios in 1938 and is stored on

their ranch near Thousand Oaks, California, much the worse for 30 years in the open. Some of the journal box lids still have CPRR cast in raised letters, and the roof, especially the clerestory and other features show a remarkable similarity to Governor Stanford's original private car.

Emperor Dom Pedro Segundo met with a slight delay on his journey East over the Central Pacific on May 2, 1876, when his train was held west of Promontory for three hours because of the derailment of a freight train. The latter was coming upgrade westbound, about a mile east of Promontory siding when a bull was seen by the engineer, standing in the middle of the track, pawing the ties and daring the engine to a bucking duel. Refusing to budge when the engineer whistled repeatedly, the bull won the contest, derailing the engine and several cars at the cost of his life. In death the bull had his revenge, for the Emperor's special was delayed for three hours while the engine and cars were placed back on the track. The westbound passenger train which had been following the freight up the hill was forced to back to a siding two miles east of Promontory to permit the Emperor's train to pass, and suffered a six-hour delay. Perhaps the Emperor dined that night on filet of bull steaks.

In 1881 and 1882, seven 2-6-2 side-tank suburban engines were built at Sacramento for use on Oakland and Alameda trains and in April 1882, Stevens turned out the largest locomotive built west of the

Stevens great experiment, the *El Gobernador*, a 4-10-0 with a boiler too small for the demands of the cylinders, and a tender with only enough water capacity for 20 miles of running. The photograph was taken at Sumner (now Bakersfield), where the engine spent most of its days working the steep grades of Tehachapi pass in helper service. — HUNTINGTON LIBRARY, SAN MARINO, CALIFORNIA

Rockies at that time. The *Flea* No. 229 having been sold by then, the new engine No. 229 was a 4-8-0, or mastodon type, with 19x30-inch cylinders, 54-inch drivers and 123,000 pounds total weight, nearly 25 tons heavier than any other locomotive on the railroad. It performed so well that 25 engines of similar design, with 20x30-inch cylinders were ordered from Eastern builders for use on the Southern Pacific.

In 1883, Stevens designed and built the locomotive *El Gobernador* No. 237, the only engine to receive a name after 1871. It was about ten tons heavier than No. 229, was a 4-10-0 with 21x36-inch cylinders, 51-inch drivers, and though its first picture taken on the turntable at Sacramento shows a few sticks of wood in the tender, it was built to burn coal. The wood was undoubtedly used to get up steam at the roundhouse as was the custom at the time. Stevens equipped the engine with rotary valves, but tests on the big hill were very discouraging and the engine went back in the shop for major

changes. The driving wheel diameter was increased to 57 inches, the valves were changed to a modified Stephenson type, using a design worked out by Chief Draftsman George Stoddard. The engine's final weight was 146,000 pounds, with an overall length of 65 feet 4 inches including tender. The latter had only a 3,600 gallon water capacity, too little for so large an engine. Further tests on the hill proved that the engine could be used as a helper on freight trains, but the Sacramento Division superintendent did not want it because of its long driving-wheel base. In 1884 it was leased to the Southern Pacific and sent to work out of Sumner, now East Bakersfield, helping freights to Tehachapi Summit. There it remained for eight years, spending a good deal of its time in the shops, finally returning to Sacramento in 1892 to be stored for two years, then scrapped. The *El Gobernador's* trouble was insufficient steam generating capacity in the boiler, for the size of the cylinders. It was way ahead of its time — a magnificent experiment, but unfortunately a failure.

On April 1, 1885, the Central Pacific Railroad was leased for 99 years to the Southern Pacific Company, and thereafter locomotives of many of the companies controlled by the Southern Pacific began to work on the transcontinental main line. The team of Stevens and Stoddard was ordered to design and built a number of eight and ten-wheel locomotives, the first group having the unique diamond stack first developed by Stevens for No. 173, and with sandbox and steam dome design the same as used on earlier Stevens engines. By 1886 Stevens had developed a straight top boiler, and perhaps with a thought of emulating the plain British style of the times, he placed the sandbox below the boiler, on top of the frames, with a tiny steam dome half-way between the bell and the cab — truly different in appearance than anything turned out by the Eastern builders. All had outside valve gear and balanced valves developed by Stevens. Angus Sinclair called it a modified Hackworth gear and described it as the combined motion of a single eccentric and cross-head lever to impart movements to a sort of wrist plate which actuated two valve stems, one for each valve. This opened the valves sharply for admission until the steam port was wide open; it remained in that position for an instant and then closed quickly. It was an ideal valve motion, performing the functions of quick opening of port, quick cutoff, protracted release and small compression, all remarkably rapid. Sinclair said that had a company powerful enough to influence railroad officials taken up this design in 1883 it would have become the standard valve motion of nearly all American railroads. Employees called it the Stevens Monkey Motion and it was applied to all locomotives built at Sacramento between 1885 and 1889.

All told, Stevens and Stoddard built 62 locomotives at Sacramento between 1882 and 1889, of which 22 were for the Central Pacific and the rest for the Southern Pacific or the newly completed Oregon & California. Thirteen 2-8-0 consolidations were built in 1887 and 1888, six each for the above mentioned roads and one for the Central Pacific. This engine, No. 250, the highest road number ever used by the Central Pacific, was the last engine built for it. Stevens died in 1888, and for many years locomotive building at Sacramento Shops ceased. For those who are interested in the details of Steven's valve gear and locomotive design, the splendid paper by David L. Joslyn in Railway & Locomotive Historical Society Bulletin No. 65 is recommended.

It had been the writer's original intent to list only the locomotives owned by the Central Pacific to 1871, but those acquired after that date are in the minority, and in the interest of completeness all those added between 1871 and 1888 are included in the roster. The 1891 renumbering was done because locomotives of the various Southern Pacific controlled roads were frequently running on the same division, and train dispatchers became confused by having two or three engines bearing the same road number included in one train order. After several narrow escapes from serious accidents, all locomotives of the Southern Pacific lines west of El Paso, Texas, were renumbered beginning with No. 1001. Though the owner road's name still appeared either on the cab panels or on the tender, even these disappeared in a new renumbering in 1901, when the owner road's initials were stencilled on the back of the cab, under the roof. Southern Pacific engines operating east of El Paso were assigned numbers from No. 1 to 1000.

The last of the original Central Pacific locomotives to run in road service was Southern Pacific No. 2205, originally Central Pacific No. 249, one of the Stevens engines and which was scrapped in June 1926. Several of the suburban 2-6-2 tank engines were either converted to shop switchers or sold off the line. One of the latter, built as Central Pacific No. 233, is now on display in front of the Oakland Auditorium. Last but not least, Stockton Terminal & Eastern No. 1 (Norris-Lancaster 1864 and built for the Western Pacific), was sold in 1909 to the Stockton-based shortline where it worked until 1953. Its owner, Dr. John Hiss of Los Angeles, proud to have the oldest operating engine in the State, regretfully retired it when the boiler gave out, replacing it with another steam engine even though the road owned a diesel. He gave old No. 1 to Traveltown in Los Angeles, where it remains today, the colorful centerpiece in a large display of locomotives.

California is very fortunate to have no less than four of the original Central Pacific locomotives preserved for museum purposes. There is also the splendid example of Andrew Jackson Steven's craftsmanship in Los Angeles, former Virginia & Truckee No. 18, built by Stevens in 1873 and owned by Paramount Studios. When the engine has finished its days in motion pictures, wouldn't to be wonderful for Paramount to donate the engine to the State of California, to sit alongside the other pioneer locomotives which all had their beginnings in Sacramento?

When photographer Andrew J. Russell was commissioned to photograph the construction of the Union Pacific, he hired S. J. Sedgwick as his assistant. Sedgwick owned a small camera designed for 3½x4-inch lantern slides, and frequently used it to photograph scenes Russell did not have time for. Most of Sedgwick's pictures have been erroneously credited to Russell, and this scene is a Sedgwick original of a construction train on the seven mile Zig-Zag temporary track, which bypassed the summit tunnel near Wasatch until it was holed through. On the trestle is Sedgwick's transportation, Pony engine No. 5. In later years, Sedgwick bought out Russell's business and became famous in his own right as the producer of Sedgwick's Illustrated Lantern Slide Lectures called *Across the Continent.* — AMERICAN GEOGRAPHICAL SOCIETY

THE UNION PACIFIC

THE EARLY history of the Union Pacific Railroad is a complicated pattern of government red tape through commissions, committees and ambitious capitalists. As related in the Central Pacific history, the Enabling Act signed by President Lincoln July 1, 1862, created the Union Pacific; unlike the Central Pacific which had been incorporated in California, the Union Pacific was formed by government fiat, with a commission composed of 158 members to organize the company. They met in Chicago on September 3, 1862, and efforts were made to comply with the terms of the Enabling Act by selling stock in the company to the amount of $2,000,000. When this sum had been raised, the stockholders would then meet and elect officers.

Among those at the Chicago meeting was Thomas C. Durant, a man with considerable railroad building experience, and it was he who prodded the commissioners and the government into various amendments in the original law so that the stock would be attractive to investors. When first placed on the market, Union Pacific stock was considered a very bad risk by the investing public, and few shares were sold in 1862. It was not until October 29, 1863, that the necessary shares had been sub-

scribed and ten per cent of their price paid in, permitting the meeting of stockholders to elect officers. At this meeting, General John A. Dix, former President of the Chicago, Rock Island & Pacific Railroad and in 1863 the Secretary of the Treasury in President Lincoln's cabinet was elected President of the Union Pacific, with Thomas C. Durant the Vice President.

At the time the eastern terminal of the Union Pacific was set at Omaha in Nebraska Territory, there was not one single railroad west of the Missouri River along the line of the Union Pacific survey. The plains swarmed with hostile Indians and the surveying parties which were sent out to locate the line had to be protected by the government troops who were stationed in forts at strategic points along the wagon road west of Omaha. The nearest western terminal of a railroad which had connections with railroads east of the Mississippi River was the Hannibal & St. Joseph Railroad, which terminated at St. Joseph, Missouri, and reached that town in 1859. It was 135 miles from Omaha by steamer on the Missouri River. Three railroads controlled by different groups were embarked on a race across the State of Iowa at the start of the Civil War. These were the Cedar Rapids

& Missouri River, the Burlington & Missouri River and the Chicago, Rock Island & Pacific.

The Cedar Rapids & Missouri River was the western extension of a railroad which comprised the Galena & Chicago Union Railroad from Chicago to Clinton, Iowa, and the Chicago, Iowa & Nebraska Railroad from Clinton to Cedar Rapids, 81 miles and completed in 1859. The Cedar Rapids & Missouri River got off to a good start in 1861, building 41 miles of track to Otto Creek in that year, to Marshall in 1862, and to Boone, Iowa, 121 miles west of Cedar Rapids, at the end of 1864. There construction work ceased, leaving a 150 mile gap from Boone to Omaha. The Galena & Chicago Union leased the Chicago, Iowa & Nebraska on July 3, 1862, the Chicago & North Western Railroad leased the Galena & Chicago Union on June 3, 1864, and the Cedar Rapids & Missouri River came under Chicago & North Western control through sublease on December 1, 1865. Funds were made available soon after, and construction work towards Omaha was resumed.

The other two railroads embarked on the race for Omaha had railheads at Ottumwa, Iowa, for the Burlington & Missouri River, and the Rock Island was a short distance west of Des Moines, Iowa. On paper it looked like a close race to see which railroad would reach Council Bluffs, across the Missouri from Omaha, and beat the others to priority in furnishing supplies to the Union Pacific. The North Western had the best financing and they won the race by over two years. The last rail was laid by the North Western at the Council Bluffs terminal on January 22, 1867, and the first passenger train through from Chicago arrived six days

later. The Rock Island came in second, its first through Chicago train arriving in Council Bluffs on June 7, 1869, and the Burlington & Missouri River's first train arrived on January 18, 1870. This chronology is given to show the handicaps under which the Union Pacific construction forces worked during the early years of contruction.

Ground was broken with appropriate ceremonies at Omaha on December 2, 1863, and like the Central Pacific eleven months earlier, the Union Pacific had no rails, locomotives nor construction equipment on hand at that time. Under the supervision of Chief Engineer Peter Dey, actual grading began in March 1864, but it was only a token gesture. Later that year bids were opened for the construction of the first hundred miles of railroad, and through the influence of Thomas Durant, his friend Herbert M. Hoxie was the only bidder, at $50,000 a mile. Peter Dey thought this price was outrageously high, and when Durant sent Colonel Silas Seymour to Omaha as his engineering representative, and Seymour proceeded to countermand some of Dey's orders, the latter resigned early in 1865. Such a storm of protest had been caused by Hoxie's contract that he turned it over to the Credit Mobilier, a new company formed by Durant to finance the railroad, and Hoxie was made the Superintendent of Transportation.

A year passed before any further work was done towards building the Union Pacific, during which Congressman Oakes Ames of Boston was asked by President Lincoln to step in and help straighten out the tangled affairs of the road. Ames and his brother Oliver were eventually to lose most of their personal fortunes trying to keep the construction

The first locomotive on the Union Pacific had received a new boiler and was greatly changed from its original condition when photographed. — UNION PACIFIC MUSEUM

The west bank of the Missouri River at Omaha was a scene of great activity during the years from 1865 to 1872. Here the steamer *Colorado* which brought the first locomotive to Omaha in July 1865 is docked at the Omaha landing. — UNION PACIFIC MUSEUM

work going, but their ethics and their sense of responsibility were of the highest.

In the spring of 1864, five locomotives were ordered from builders on the east coast. Two were built in August of that year at the Manchester Locomotive Works, Manchester, New Hampshire, at $14,500 each plus $1,000 freight charges to St. Joseph. The other three were completed at the Danforth, Cooke works in Paterson, New Jersey, in September 1864. They cost $16,450 each including freight to St. Joseph. At that point it was planned to ship them up the Missouri River by steamer as soon as the spring thaws raised the river level to navigable depths. The season was usually from late March to the end of autumn; during the cold weather the river would freeze, the water level would drop and the boats could not operate.

When the locomotives arrived in Hannibal, which must surely have been no later than November 1864, nothing had been done towards construction of the railroad at Omaha, so the engines undoubtedly sat in their crates on the dock at St. Joseph for many months. Two of the five engines never reached the Union Pacific. While they were in storage at St. Joseph, the company sold them to

contractors in December 1864 for sums representing a considerable profit. Hoxie figured that more could be ordered and delivered before the engines were needed at Omaha, and this is borne out by the fact that two engines were ordered from Richard Norris in Philadelphia early in 1865.

The three Danforth, Cooke & Company locomotives were all 4-4-0s with 60-inch drivers and 14x22-inch cylinders, weighing slightly over 27 tons without tender. They were named the *Major General Sherman*, the *Major General McPherson* and the *Lieut. General Grant*. The latter was sold in December 1864 to M. K. Jesup & Company for $21,000. Jesup was a contractor who supplied railroad material, and it is believed that this engine went to the Union Pacific, Eastern District, later the Kansas Pacific, for by the end of 1864 that railroad was operating from Kansas City westward to Lawrence. Kansas Pacific No. 3, the *Pottowattamie* had the same dimensions as the *Lieut. General Grant*, and was built at the same works in 1864.

The two Manchester engines were 4-4-0s, with 60-inch drivers and 16x22-inch cylinders, with an engine weight of about 30 tons. Unfortunately the Manchester factory records did not give engine

weights, so the figure of 30 tons is based on the weight of similar engines built by Manchester at that time for other roads. Manchester had been shut down from 1857 to 1864 and the two engines for the Union Pacific were among the first built there after the factory reopened. They bore no road numbers or names, and the historians can only guess which one was sold to the Kilbourne Lighting Company in December 1864 for $20,000. The identity of this company and its reason for buying a locomotive at that time could not be determined by the writer. For the sake of the record, the one retained by the Union Pacific is shown in the roster as the second of the two Manchesters. It was named *Manchester* No. 3 by the company and bore that name for the short time it was on the road. The government list of locomotives of the Union Pacific in 1866 shows no Manchester locomotive, and there is some evidence that No. 3 became Colorado Central No. 1.

The *Major General Sherman* No. 1 came up the Missouri River on the steamboat *Colorado,* which arrived at Omaha on July 2, 1865. The crated parts were hauled on wagons up the river bank to the site where the roundhouse was under construction. There the engine was set up, and on July 21, 1865, the *Omaha Weekly Republican* reported that — "Quite a lively time was had at the levee this afternoon with the running of the locomotive upon the Union Pacific Railroad. The Iron horse had several hundred admirers and all hailed the *General Sherman.*" The engine had arrived none too soon, for the first rail had been laid at Omaha on July 10, and by the time the engine was tested, two miles of track had been completed. The wrought iron rails used by the Union Pacific for the first 441 miles from Omaha to the west weighed 50 pounds to the yard, with 56 pound rail for the balance of the distance to Ogden. The rails were fastened together by wrought iron chairs which proved unreliable and were always working loose. The 50 pound rail proved too light for the heavy traffic generated when the railroad was completed, and within a few years it was replaced with heavier rail, the joints bolted together with fish-plates. The use of steel for rail manufacture did not become standard until after the transcontinental railroad was finished. The other two engines at St. Joseph came up the river in August, and by the end of September the railroad had three locomotives in service.

On October 6, 1865, the track reached Papillon, 12 miles from Omaha, and on the 20th an excursion train of one platform car and the locomotive *Major General Sherman* made a round trip to Papillon from Omaha, with Thomas Durant as the host and a goodly number of Omaha citizens as guests. One passenger remarked the next day that the train went along at a good clip, probably at least 14 miles an hour. With the closing of the Missouri River in the late fall, it was necessary to bring the parts for two locomotives and many freight car trucks overland from the railhead of the Cedar Rapids & Missouri River, wagons hauled by oxen being the principal means of transport at that time. The locomotives were the *Major General Sheridan* No. 4 and the *Vice Admiral Farragut* No. 5 from Norris Brothers in Lancaster. They had 60-inch drivers, 16x24-inch cylinders and weighed about 30 tons, though in later years after rebuilding they weighed 73,700 pounds for the engine alone. Like the first three locomotives, the new arrivals were of the eight-wheel American type.

As early as 1863, Thomas Durant had tried to persuade Brigadier General Grenville M. Dodge, whose home town was Council Bluffs, Iowa, to leave the Union Army and become Chief Engineer of the Union Pacific. General Dodge had already displayed remarkable capability as a civil engineer in rebuilding railroads torn up by the Confederates, but Dodge felt that the Army needed him, and he refused all offers by Durant, who persisted year after year to entice him to leave the service. When the Civil War ended in the spring of 1865, General Dodge was sent with troops to clear Nebraska and Wyoming of hostile Indians who were making great inroads on the U. P. surveying parties, the trading stations and the wagon trains. In the course of these journeys through the Indian country, General Dodge discovered the pass through the Black Hills range of the Rockies which became the one used by the Union Pacific.

Durant was successful in his efforts to obtain the best possible talent for laying out the line and building the railroad, when in February 1866, Brigadier General John Casement and his brother Daniel agreed to lay the track on the level sections of the Union Pacific for $750 a mile for the labor only, the company to supply the rails, crossties and other track material and to contract for the grading as a separate job. General Casement and his family arrived in Omaha the first week in May, and that same month General Dodge resigned his commission in the Army to become chief engineer of the Union Pacific. With the Casement brothers and

General Dodge in charge, the progress of the Union Pacific became accelerated immediately, spurred on no doubt by the removal of the restriction on the Central Pacific in June of that year to stop work when they reached a point 150 miles east of the California-Nevada line.

The Missouri River became navigable at the end of March, and in April three locomotives, and two passenger coaches left by steamer from St. Joseph for Omaha. The first trip of the *Colorado* marked the delivery of locomotive No. 6 from Hinkley & Williams, formerly the Boston Locomotive Works in Boston, Massachusetts. No. 6 went to the Colorado Central in 1871 where it bore the name *Black Hawk*, the name of a Colorado mining town, and some historians claim this was the name of the engine while on the Union Pacific. As the Hinkley & Williams list for the period from 1857 to 1880 has been lost, there is no way of checking this from the factory records. The engine was smaller than the two Norris engines, with 60-inch drivers, 14x22-inch cylinders and about 26 tons total weight.

The steamer *Colorado* soon returned with two more locomotives, both turned out by the Schenectady Locomotive Works in April 1866. They had 60-inch drivers, 16x22-inch cylinders and weighed 62,250 pounds, and except for the size of the cylinders, were the same design as the locomotive *Jupiter* used by the Central Pacific at the time of the meeting of the rails at Promontory, Utah, three years later. They left the factory without names, but were named *Omaha* and *Idaho* when they arrived in Omaha on May 17, 1866. The *Omaha* was set up and tested on May 25, while the *Idaho* was

Pony engine No. 2 built by Grant in 1868, with its two mates, was used in yard service and later as a shop switcher — GOLDEN WEST COLLECTION

tested on May 31, both engines being put to work immediately. The steamer *Colorado* returned again to Omaha on June 7 with the *Osceola* No. 9, a Rogers-built 4-4-0 purchased in 1862 by the U. S. Military Railroad as the *Osceola*, retaining that name on the Union Pacific. The steamer *Metamora* came up river on June 15 with the *Denver* No. 10 and the *Colorado* No. 11, from the Danforth Locomotive & Machine Works, successors to Danforth, Cooke & Company of Paterson. On August 23rd the *Colorado* brought two locomotives; the *Bellevue* No. 12, a mogul or 2-6-0 type built by Danforth and classed as a freight locomotive, weighing 36 tons, and the *Utah*, an 0-4-0 saddle tank switcher from Danforth and called a "Pony" engine. These were the last engines to bear names. Switching in the Omaha yards and around the shops, the *Utah* attracted a great deal of attention with its huge cab, twice normal size, and the water tank perched on top of the boiler.

According to the *Omaha Republican*, by mid-September 1866 there were a total of 17 locomotives on the line, four more were at St. Joseph awaiting transporation up the river, and one was on the steamer *Metamora* and due any day. These shipments completed the locomotive arrivals for 1866, although after the river froze over in early December, a large amount of material came by wagons across Iowa from the steadily advancing railhead of the Cedar Rapids & Missouri River, now leased to the Chicago & North Western which had a continuous line from Chicago, the result of merger. The last rail was laid in the Council Bluffs station yards on January 25, 1867, and thereafter rails, locomotives, rolling stock and supplies for the Union Pacific came in a never ending stream to Council Bluffs, to be ferried across the river as soon as the ice melted. Until that event, and the passing of the heavy ice down the river, the Chicago & North Western and the Union Pacific each built a

The transfer ferry *H. C. Nutt* has brought a load of empty cars to the Iowa side of the Missouri, with the city of Omaha as a background. These ferries were discontinued when the bridge was completed in 1872. At the right, the steamers *Colorado* and *Denver* with a party of tourists from the East, bound for a ride on the partly completed Union Pacific Railroad. — BOTH UNION PACIFIC MUSEUM

A CHARACTER—SCENE IN THE EMIGRANT WAITING-ROOM OF THE UNION PACIFIC RAILROAD DEPOT AT OMAHA.

Omaha Station-The Way West

New lives in the West! Families quickened to a pioneer dream, packed their belongings and piled on the train for Omaha. From its depot, the rails of the Union Pacific commenced their westward march across the plains, the Rockies, and the Salt Lake Valley. The station and its platform fascinated artists from *Harpers Weekly* who never tired of depicting its ever-changing crowd of frontiersmen, trappers, Eastern capitalists, and miners bound for the Comstock Lode. In the above scene, emigrants heading for the Black Hills region were urged to do their last minute shopping before leaving civilization for the wilds. They boarded the steamcars with their gear, arrived at the nearest point on the Union Pacific to their destination, then took the stage into the untamed West. At the right, the station platform at Omaha with Indians, buffalo hunters and emigrants bound for the new life of the West.

Hunting Buffalo By Train

The building of the Union Pacific across the prairie land of the west opened vistas of adventure. Buffalo hunting by train was considered a prime sport in frontier times. A correspondent from *Leslie's* wrote, "In the dark of the evening the great mass of animals could scarcely be distinguished from the prairie itself save for the flash of gunfire. A little in advance of the engine they closed with the track and ran into the fire of 200 guns. It was a race for life." Before long the shipment to the East of buffalo hides became big business for the Union Pacific. During a period of three years the railroad shipped 1,379,000 hides and 32,000,000 pounds of bones to market. The rich buffalo meat, the prime source of Indian nourishment was left to rot at trackside. This mass annihilation through the heart of the buffalo land, only hastened the near destruction of the species.

branch line from their respective terminals, down the bluffs to the levees at the edge of the Missouri River. By the end of April 1867, the car ferries *Hero* and *Heroine*, each equipped with two tracks, were bringing the supplies for the Union Pacific across the river. Passenger trains of both roads also connected with these ferries, and two of the Union Pacific's stern wheel steamers were added to the car ferries in bringing supplies across the river.

Returning to 1866, all through the spring and summer of that year the Casement brothers had continued advancing the railhead west. They had built a large boarding train to provide dormitory and eating facilities for the tracklayers, who were a motley crew of Civil War veterans from both sides, Irish immigrants, drifters — anyone who was willing to work for the prevailing wage. Most of the men preferred to camp in tents rather than sleep in the crowded dormitory cars. The boarding train carried rifles and ammunition to equip over a thousand of the workers in case of Indian raids. The predatory tribes, who were more interested in stealing rations and guns than killing the workmen, were kept away by an Army guard. Milepost 100, nine miles west of Columbus, Nebraska, was reached on June 14, 1866, with nine stations and sidings between there and Omaha.

During 1866, ten new stalls were added to the five already completed at the Omaha roundhouse, and locomotive repair facilities and a large shop for building cars were completed that year. Durant brought Isaac H. Congdon out from Hamilton, Ontario, where he had been Master Mechanic of the Great Western Railway shops, to supervise the work of setting up locomotives and keeping them in repair. Congdon had served his apprenticeship with the Hartford & New Haven Railroad, later going to the Cleveland, Columbus & Cincinnati before moving to the Great Western. Through the hectic years until the Union Pacific was completed, Congdon set up the new locomotives as they ar-

A construction train follows the tracklayers across the prairie. The excavation parallel to the track provided earth for the roadbed and a drainage ditch at the same time. — UNION PACIFIC MUSEUM

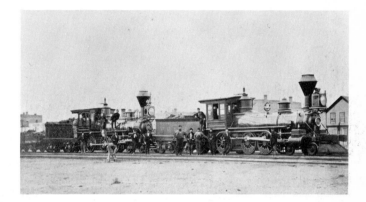

A Union Pacific double-header at Laramie with No. 52, the second engine made notable by the fact that it was a Moore & Richardson ten-wheeler brought on the road by the Casement brothers and later sold to the Union Pacific. — UNION PACIFIC MUSEUM

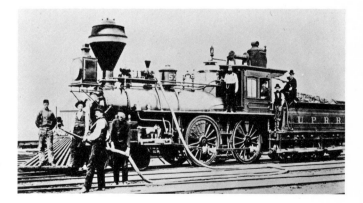

Locomotive No. 53 by Norris & Son was another of the Casement engines, equipped with water pump and hose for fire fighting. The smokestack is one of Congdon's earliest designs. — UNION PACIFIC MUSEUM

One of Russell's best photographs shows engine No. 23, Schenectady 1867 at Wyoming Station, 15 miles west of Laramie. The engineer with his stovepipe hat, the antlers on the headlight, and the man with a rifle standing by the tender, plus the classic batten board sided station, all bespeak the times. — AMERICAN GEOGRAPHICAL SOCIETY

rived and trained a large force of shopmen in all branches of locomotive repair work. Over 500 men were working there when Congdon was promoted to Master Mechanic-Locomotives in 1870, his title being changed to Superintendent, Locomotive Department, in 1871. Congdon's locomotive repair shop escaped the great fire of October 4, 1869, which burned all car repair facilities and the cars which were inside the buildings.

All told, 35 locomotives were on order at the end of 1866, and all were delivered in 1867. They were of the 4-4-0 type, most of them having 60-inch drivers and 16x24-inch cylinders. They included five by Rogers and 14 by Grant, both factories in Paterson, New Jersey, six from Schenectady of the same design as previous engines from that works, five Hinkley & Williams from Boston and five from the Taunton Locomotive Works, Taunton, Massachussetts. The latter firm was to build many more locomotives for the Union Pacific in later years. To speed up construction, the Casement brothers bought six secondhand locomotives in the summer of 1866 and they were brought up the river on the steamers leased by the Union Pacific. Four were ten-wheelers built by Moore & Richardson of Cincinnati, Ohio, and two were 4-4-0s by Richard Norris and Rogers. The original owners of these engines are not known; according to historians who specialize in the locomotives of the U. S. Military Railroad, all were from that road and were probably built in the early days of the Civil War. In January 1868, the Casements sold all six engines to the Union Pacific, which assigned them numbers from No. 51 to 56.

General Sherman arrived in Omaha on August 17, 1866, and rode by special train to the end of track, 190 miles west of Omaha and only five miles from Fort Kearney, a large military outpost. The 100th meridian of Greenwich, 247 miles west of Omaha, was reached on October 5, 1866. By invitation of Thomas Durant, a party of 100 guests left New York City on October 15 by special train and most of them found their way to Hannibal, Missouri, from whence they made the trip to Omaha in two days. A few chose to go overland from Chicago to the end of the Cedar Rapids & Missouri River, arriving in Omaha by stage coach about the same time as the party coming up the river. All the guests had arrived by October 22, and boarded the special train waiting for them in Omaha. This was a strange conglomeration of rolling stock, for it included the Lincoln car, a magnificent car built to carry President Lincoln around the country, but which he never rode in until it carried his body home to Springfield in 1865. Durant had bought the car after Lincoln's funeral, equipped it for service as his business car on the Union Pacific, and had brought it to Omaha. The second deluxe car was the company's new directors' car, built for the Union Pacific in the car shops of the Pittsburgh, Fort Wayne & Chicago in 1866. The most impor-

Grand Island, 154 miles from Omaha, was the first engine changing point. Here No. 76 emerges from the ten-stall roundhouse on a cold winter's day in 1868. — AMERICAN GEOGRAPHICAL SOCIETY

tant guests rode in this latter car, Durant and his family rode in the Lincoln car, and the rest of the passengers were distributed among four first class passenger coaches. At the head end of the train were three baggage cars, one containing a large and well stocked bar, another for preparing food for the passengers, and the third for supplies.

Headed by Vice President Durant, who now ran the company because President Dix was going to France as the new U. S. Ambassador, the officials of the Union Pacific greeted the distinguished party, which included U. S. Senators, Representatives, foreign nobility, even George M. Pullman, who no doubt made the trip with an eye to future business for his sleeping cars after the railroad was completed. The nine-car train left at noon on October 23, hauled by two locomotives as far as Fremont, where the helper engine was removed and the locomotive *Idaho* brought the train to the end of track. The party stayed over night in Columbus, where a special tent camp had been erected, and the following day proceeded past the 100th Meridian to end of track, 279 miles west of Omaha. Returning, the train stopped at a special arch erected over the track at the 100th Meridian, posing for pictures which preserved the event for posterity.

Advancing at over a mile of track laid per day, and sometimes as much as three miles, construction was brought to a complete halt by heavy snows on the plains on December 11, 1866, with the end of track at Milepost 305. The winter quarters for the

Durant's special train headed by the *Idaho* No. 8 stops at the 100th Meridian sign on the return journey to Omaha. Thomas Durant is leaning against the left-hand post, with his hunting rifle across his shoulders. — LIBRARY OF CONGRESS

The only good photograph of the Lincoln car shows it without windows or interior furnishings, clerestory sagging in the center and was probably pictured just before it was to be scrapped. — HUNTINGTON LIBRARY, SAN MARINO, CALIFORNIA

A general view of the Omaha station and shops before Union Pacific was completed. The roundhouse is in the center, with the shop building at the left. The first station at the extreme right is nearly covered from view by the huge piles of wood to be used as engine fuel. — UNION PACIFIC MUSEUM

crews were set up at North Platte, soon to become a principal railroad junction and locomotive service point. All this had been accomplished with the Union Pacific's fleet of 16 locomotives and the Casement brothers' private roster of six engines. Over 200 platform cars for the carrying of rails and crossties were in service by the end of 1866 and a dozen passenger cars, the bodies of which had all been built in the Omaha shops, provided passenger service from Omaha to as far as the contractors would permit the trains to go. During this time, operations were in the hands of the Casements, the road not having been accepted as yet by the government. Unlike the Central Pacific, which grossed $865,000 in 1866 and made a determined effort to exploit the road's commercial possibilities for every mile of track laid, the Casements considered passengers a nuisance and subjected them to uncomfortable rides in a motley assortment of homemade cars on which even the truss rods underneath the frames could not keep from sagging in the middle. Complaints about these cars reached such proportions that in 1867 Durant hired C. L. Gamble as Master of Car Repairs and car building at Omaha was placed on a professional basis. After the rail link with the East was completed, the Union Pacific bought many cars from Eastern builders, as did the Central Pacific.

All locomotives burned wood as fuel, and this was not in plentiful supply. The available wood for crossties was mostly the local cottonwood, which would rot into uselessness within a few years. To prolong the life of cottonwood ties, a process called burnetizing, named for inventor Burnet, impregnated the space between the wood fibres with a zinc solution, and was used in Omaha until ties of better quality could be obtained. Good oak or other hardwood ties from the East, freighted up the Missouri by steamer, brought fantastic prices, as high as $3.50 each (a high grade creosoted tie in 1969 costs $5.50). Photos of the track made by Andrew

J. Russell during the construction days show that most of the crossties in Nebraska were not sawed, but planed or adzed to form opposite flat surfaces, with the curved part of the other two sides still covered with the bark of the tree from which the tie came. The ends of the ties were rough and pointed, showing the marks of the axe which had separated the tie from the rest of the tree. This presents a great contrast to the crossties used by the Central Pacific, which were made of first quality wood, sawed on all four sides and all cut to the same length. Crosstie prices came down quickly after the Chicago & North Western was completed and ferry service established across the Missouri River.

Samuel Reed, boss of Casement's tracklaying gang, inspects the finished roadbed west of Omaha. The hand-hewn crossties which were the Union Pacific's trademark all had to be replaced within a few years. — LIBRARY OF CONGRESS

101

Cecil B. DeMille's re-creation of the Plum Creek massacre, in the motion picture "Union Pacific" cost Paramount Studios a lot more money than the railroad lost in the original wreck. (BELOW) A scene from the picture, as Indians shoot-up a construction train. — BOTH PARAMOUNT PICTURES

Soldiers are joined by tracklayers in this realistic reproduction of an Indian raid, from the DeMille epic. — PARAMOUNT PICTURES

The news from Omaha on January 25, 1867, must have been welcome to the beleaguered forces of the Casements at North Platte, for on that day the rails of the Chicago & North Western were in Council Bluffs, and as previously related, a few weeks later cars loaded with rails brought direct from eastern mills were rolling across the Nebraska prairie to Casement's supply dump in North Platte. Construction began anew in March 1867, and reached Julesburg, Colorado, 86 miles west of North Platte early in June. Here General Dodge met with General Rawlins and most of the field engineers of the Union Pacific, for trouble with the Indians had increased to a point where the surveyors operated under extreme difficulties. The engineering group reached the slopes of the Rockies 139 miles west of Julesburg soon after the North Platte conference, and here a site for a division point and a town to be named Cheyenne was selected. General Dodge and his party continued west while General Rawlins returned home, and during the summer the line was laid out in spite of frequent Indian raids.

The worst of the Indian depredations became known as the Plum Creek Massacre. On the night of August 12, 1867, at a point six miles west of Plum Creek near the present town of Lexington, a band of Indians removed the wooden beams and supports of a small culvert across a dry stream bed, and placed several crossties and a large boulder on the track. A westbound freight hauled by engine No. 22 was derailed by the obstruction, the engine turning on its side while a rail went clear through the boiler; the tender and the first three cars, which were loaded with brick and coal, piled on top of the engine, killing the fireman and mortally injuring the engineer. In the caboose were the conductor, a brakeman and two passengers, and one of the latter, Charles A. Radcliffe, became the principal in the drama which followed. The sudden, jolting stop did not injure the men in the caboose, and they soon discovered the Indians up near the locomotive. Radcliffe managed to work his way forward without being discovered, tried vainly to extricate the engineer, then returned to the caboose, under which the other three men were hiding. Radcliffe then courageously ran back along the line and stopped a following freight train. The other three men followed and the freight backed six miles to Plum Creek station. A telegram to Grand Island resulted in an order to back the train to Elm Creek, taking all the families living at Plum Creek to safety.

In the morning, the freight proceeded west again

The Cheyenne station restaurant, a warm haven for passengers who came in out of the wintry air, was famous for its juicy and tender steaks, a reputation it lost 50 years later. (BELOW) Inside the "Eating House" the goblets are filled with cloth napkins as they stand on the inverted dinner plates, ready for the next train load of hungry passengers. — AMERICAN GEOGRAPHICAL SOCIETY

they discovered the obstructions on the track. One lineman was found killed and scalped, another had escaped east though wounded and scalped, two others showed up later after the troops arrived, and the remaining two linemen were missing and never found. At no time did any of the train crew or the linemen engage in gunfire with the Indians, as the former were not armed.

Thereafter a great deal more caution was exercised in operating trains at night in Nebraska; and the area around the bluffs west of Plum Creek, which had for years been a favorite spot for Indian raids on the wagon trains, was patrolled by troops. The Plum Creek affair, in greatly exaggerated form with the train crew shooting it out with the Indians, provided the dramatic highlight in Cecil B. De-Mille's epic motion picture, "Union Pacific," produced in 1939.

All through the summer of 1867 Casement's forces continued laying track at a rate of from one to nearly two miles per day, until they reached Cheyenne, Wyoming Territory, on November 13, 1867. In the 516 miles from Omaha the line had climbed from an altitude of 966 feet above sea level to 6,041 feet at Cheyenne, an average of less than ten feet per mile though it was level in some sections and as much as 44 feet per mile in others. Work continued west of Cheyenne through Evans Pass, which had been selected by General Dodge, but after the route for ten miles east of the summit was vetoed by Silas Seymour and the snow closed in, the railhead stopped in Granite Canyon, 23 miles west of Cheyenne. Approximately 234 miles had been built during the year, and Oakes Ames, responsible for building 667 miles west of the 100th Meridian, was somehow managing to buy enough supplies to form a stockpile that winter at Cheyenne.

and stopped at a safe distance, the Indians being observed through field glasses. They were all very drunk from the liquor found in one of the cars, were dancing around the burning train, looting it of all manner of merchandise, while twelve Indian lookouts were seen on top of the bluffs overlooking the scene. Towards evening a company of soldiers arrived by train from Lone Tree, 112 miles west, and quickly drove the Indians away. It was then discovered that a telegraph repair crew of six men who had started out an hour ahead of the freight to repair a break in the telegraph wire, caused by the Indians without doubt, had been ambushed just as

A train of empty cars crosses the Missouri from Omaha to the east bank of the river before the permanent bridge was completed. The track did not actually rest on the ice, being laid on stringers supported by piling driven into the river bottom.
— UNION PACIFIC MUSEUM

At the end of 1867, the company had 53 locomotives, 14 passenger cars, 4 baggage cars and 1,010 freight cars of all types. The first two Pullman cars to cross the Missouri were the *Denver* and the *Central City*, which arrived in Omaha on October 16, 1867, and were permanently assigned to the Union Pacific. The equipment had to service a line already 539 miles long, as compared to the Central Pacific's 138 miles completed that same month. The latter had more locomotives and rolling stock than the Union Pacific, all concentrated in a much shorter distance, these serving potential traffic centers of greater importance at the moment than those along the Union Pacific.

In 1867, while the location parties were surveying west of the summit at Sherman, great deposits of coal were discovered 75 miles west of Laramie, Wyoming. Thus the fuel problem for the railroad would be solved as soon as the rails reached the location of the coal mines, and all locomotives ordered after May 1868 were equipped with grates to burn coal. The conversion from wood to coal caused the company to try out no less than 20 different designs of smokestacks during the following 25 years, in an effort to rid the locomotives of the cinder problem.

The Casements were determined to keep the supply of rails coming across the Missouri River and west to the supply dumps at Cheyenne during the winter. The Missouri was frozen solid in the middle of December 1867 and the ferries were tied up, the river steamers having long since ceased operations for the year. A temporary trestle was built across the river, this being a combination of piling and wooden stringers which were laid on top of the ice, their ends supported by piling. On this combination the crossties and rails were laid, and on January 6, 1868, the first train crossed the Missouri River from Iowa to Nebraska. Soon the

Omaha yards were filled with cars loaded with rail from the east, hemlock crossties from Chicago at 80 cents each, and the Chicago & North Western passenger trains terminated their runs in the Omaha station. This bonanza lasted until March 6, exactly two months, at which time the ice showed signs of breaking up, and it was decided to stop traffic across the bridge. One last train of empty platform cars crossed the bridge to Council Bluffs, and barely an hour later, great floes of ice came down the river and carried away the entire bridge, there being no time to salvage it. The Union Pacific was luckier the following winter, for the ice was solid enough to stand the weight of the track on December 12, 1868, and trains began crossing the rebuilt trestle the same day. Trains of supplies, new locomotives and rolling stock, and the daily passenger trains crossed on the trestle, until on March 3, 1869, the rails were removed and most of the material salvaged before the ice went down the river. That same month, the caissons for the new permanent bridge across the Missouri were sunk into the muddy river bottom, but it was not until 1872 that the bridge was completed and the ferries completely eliminated.

The Union Pacific purchased 83 locomotives in 1868; of this number, eight are believed to have been diverted to some other railroad. Ten locomotives were built by Rogers in 1868 on one order from the Union Pacific, though only the two engines built in February were delivered. The other eight were turned out in May and June of 1868, but no Union Pacific list shows these engines, which bore the numbers from No. 133 to 140 when they left the factory.

Of the 75 engines actually received in 1868, 47 were 4-4-0s, 25 were 4-6-0s and there were three 2-8-0 consolidation types from Baldwin; 47-ton giants which were the first of many to be ordered by the railroad a decade later. The 1868 locomotives came from the principal builders of the east; Baldwin, Rhode Island, Rogers, Hinkley & Williams, Grant, Schenectady, Taunton and Danforth. Included among the 4-4-0s were ten coal burners with extended smokeboxes and Hudson's patent straight stack, used in combination with adjustable cinder screens in the smokebox, controlled by the fireman by means of a lever extending from the cab. Five of the engines, Nos. 116 to 120, were from the Rogers Locomotive Works, and five, Nos. 121 to 125, were from the Schenectady Locomotive Works. They were the first to have an injector, besides the two crosshead pumps mounted one on each side, and had small drivers of 54-inch diameter, making them admirable for freight service and for handling construction trains. All ten of them

Engine No. 74, one of the five high-wheeled Rogers passenger engines which were delivered in 1868, has one of Congdon's enormous stacks, and the new, patented Bissell engine truck. — UNION PACIFIC MUSEUM (BELOW) Omaha roundhouse in winter, as photographed by S. J. Sedgwick, shows diamond stacked Rogers No. 75 in a pose which would delight a locomotive photographer's heart. On the front of the headlight bracket are two bronze eagles, each holding a red silk tassel in its beak. — AMERICAN GEOGRAPHICAL SOCIETY

One of five Rogers-built freight engines used on the Casement's construction trains as the railhead approached Promontory. This photograph of No. 116 by C. R. Savage is a classic three-quarter engine view of the time. — UNION PACIFIC MUSEUM (BELOW) Schenectady-built No. 26 and Rogers No. 71 are lined up in a canyon west of Bryan, in the upper reaches of the Echo River. — GERALD M. BEST COLLECTION

Saddle tank Pony engine No. 3 built by Grant helped build the yards at Promontory after the railroad was completed. Photographer Russell exposed one of his large, wet-plate negatives on this subject.
— AMERICAN GEOGRAPHICAL SOCIETY

were sent to the west end of the line as soon as received, and many of them appear in various photographs made by Andrew J. Russell in the last weeks of construction before the meeting of the rails at Promontory on May 10, 1869. Also included in the 1868 orders were three more 0-4-0 saddle tank switchers listed as "Pony" engines, similar to the *Utah* No. 1 which had arrived in 1866. All told there were 134 locomotives in service at the end of 1868, not counting the eight Rogers engines which were not delivered and the *Manchester* No. 3 which had been sold.

The Laramie station and eating house were combined in one building, which housed the division offices on the second floor. In this picture, Russell was able to capture the raw beginnings of what was for many years a great locomotive terminal. A train loaded with crossties on the right, passes the unfinished platform and walk leading to the depot.
— AMERICAN GEOGRAPHICAL SOCIETY

The railhead reached Sherman Summit in the last week of April 1868, and was pushed westward to Laramie, arriving there on June 18. Continuing at a rate of over two miles per day, the rails reached Benton, near the army post at Fort Steele, 694 miles from Omaha in July, and to Point of Rocks, Wyoming, on September 11, 1868. As of September 1, regular train service between Omaha and Benton was furnished, with one passenger and three mixed trains daily each way. On this date the Central Pacific passenger trains were running to Brown's Station, 235 miles east of Sacramento, though Crocker's graders were working many miles east of there. Truly it was a race that summer between the two groups, each striving to lay more and more miles of track per day, not only from a competitive standpoint but to qualify for more government bonds,

Laramie roundhouse survived until the end of steam though it was used as a storehouse and hiding place for rotary snowplows in its last years. Behind the woodpile are engines No. 48 and No. 87. On the right, a closeup of engine No. 87 enlarged from the view above. — AMERICAN GEOGRAPHICAL SOCIETY

At the left, the Bushnell party at Rock Creek Station, 50 miles west of Laramie, in the summer of 1868. Behind the engine is a subsistence car, containing all the provisions for the party as well as the kitchen. (RIGHT) This Sedgwick view of the interior of Bushnell's private car shows the host seated at the head of the table. Mirrors, polished brass lamps and ornate roof braces belie the plain exterior of this early day hotel on wheels. — BOTH AMERICAN GEOGRAPHICAL SOCIETY

The Bushnell Party

One of the directors of the Union Pacific, and the most active supporter of Thomas Durant in the formation of the Credit Mobilier and the financing of the Union Pacific was Cornelius S. Bushnell of New Haven, Connecticut. He was a banker there and a director of the Shore Line Railroad. He was directly responsible for bringing the Ames brothers into the company, and in 1868 he brought his family and several of his friends to Omaha for an inspection trip over the completed portions of the railroad, little enough reward for what he had done for Thomas Durant. The two cars of the Bushnell special train made history a year later when they were the first two cars in Durant's special train to Promontory for the golden spike ceremony.

As soon as the first 300 miles of the Union Pacific was completed and accepted by the government, Samuel B. Reed was promoted from the tracklaying gang to General Superintendent. Soon posters began to appear in railroad stations east of the Missouri, advertising the great saving in time for travelers going to Denver or points west. A year later, Treasurer John Cisco was thriftily combining his publicity for the company's gold bonds with news the railroad was open for business almost to the western border of Wyoming Territory. — GOLDEN WEST COLLECTION

land grants of 12,800 acres per finished mile, and permission to sell their own secondary bonds. Green River, later a division point, was reached at the end of September. A roundhouse and shop site was selected at Bryan, 13 miles west of Green River, that same month. On October 27, 1868, General Casement entertained Thomas Durant and several friends, on Durant's orders, by beating the Central Pacific's track laying record of six and a half miles in one day, laying seven and a half miles west of Bryan between daybreak and sunset. Charles Crocker sent congratulations and replied that his forces would beat that record in their own time, before witnesses. According to an entry in the diary of Daniel L. Harris, a special government director of the Union Pacific appointed by President Grant on March 8, 1869, this display of track laying prowess cost the company at least $20,000 more than the expense required to lay track at two miles per day. "How so?" writes director Harris in his diary. "Because for three days previous all the track and bridge force men were ordered to remain idle at the Company's expense until the tie contractors should have distributed all the materials. This involved his own force of 250 men and 90 teams and the rail contractor's force of 800 or 900 men and 80 teams, some of which they were in the habit of charging $25.00 a day for." Harris did not comment

Those who believe "Piggyback" loading of road vehicles on railroad cars a modern invention need only look at Russell's photograph of a train load of wagons halted near the end of track in western Wyoming in the fall of 1868. (BELOW) General John S. Casement stands beside his boarding and supply train in Wyoming. Photographer Russell's darkroom wagon is at the right. — BOTH AMERICAN GEOGRAPHICAL SOCIETY

At the left, Schenectady-built engines No. 65 and
No. 63 stand at the end of track west of Green
River. The supply wagon train is bound for the
camps of the grading crews beyond the railhead.
— AMERICAN GEOGRAPHICAL SOCIETY

The often-published Russell picture of Casement's supply and boarding train with
engine No. 66 at the end has usually appeared with the front and rear of the train
cut off. The entire train is shown here, with 17 cars visible. Engine No. 66 distinguished itself on May 7, 1869, when it ran to the end of track at Promontory
and met Central Pacific's *Whirlwind* in an informal preview of the joining of the
rails three days later. — HUNTINGTON LIBRARY, SAN MARINO, CALIFORNIA

West of the crossing of the Green River, the Union Pacific grade was cut out of
solid rock for several miles. Photographer Sedgwick posed engine No. 86 and the
Russell photo car on the rocky ledge above the river, in this frigid, mid-winter
setting. — AMERICAN GEOGRAPHICAL SOCIETY

At the left, Citadel Rock, famous landmark behind Green
River, Wyoming, is one of Russell's greatest photographs.
In the foreground are the granite piers of the permanent
bridge, with the temporary trestle at the right. At the
time of this photograph, the town of Green River did not
exist. — AMERICAN GEOGRAPHICAL SOCIETY

on what Charles Crocker must have spent in extra costs when his forces laid ten miles of track in one day, but it must have been plenty. The first serious construction train accident occurred on August 15, 1868, when engine No. 10 and a train of 20 platform cars loaded with telegraph poles hit an ox which had strayed on the track, derailing the locomotive and piling up the first eight cars in a heap. Riding on the first two cars were 40 men, of whom six were killed and eight injured, the rest escaping with cuts and bruises.

Granger, Wyoming, was reached on October 31. The Oakes Ames contract had expired, and the Credit Mobilier, which had been the clearing house for funds, was financially in bad shape. A tie contractor named James W. Davis was persuaded by Durant and Sidney Dillon to take over the contract to build the road from Granger to a meeting with the Central Pacific, with the help of the Casements. The easy grade west was ended too, for the line now had to climb to the summit of the Wahsatch Mountains at Aspen, and after passing Evanston, Wyoming, 955 miles from Omaha, the surveyed line descended through Echo Canyon, dropping down into the Weber River Canyon and finally into the valley of the Great Salt Lake at Ogden. From the head of Echo Canyon at the point where the railroad entered it, the grade descended from an altitude of 6,879 feet at the summit, to 4,340 feet at Ogden, in a distance of 65 miles. Heavy snows brought the work to a complete halt at Wahsatch,

Engine No. 71 at end of track near Granger, Wyoming, at a station known as Church Buttes. Icicles hang from the tender frame and trucks of this train of bridge abutment granite which is headed for the front. — AMERICAN GEOGRAPHICAL SOCIETY (**BELOW**) A group of men "Workin' on the Railway" from *Harper's Weekly* — Sept. 7, 1867. — HUNTINGTON LIBRARY, SAN MARINO, CALIFORNIA

GROUP OF WORKMEN ON THE UNION PACIFIC RAILROAD.—[SKETCHED BY T. R. DAVIS.]

As the race to Promontory assumed dramatic aspects, photographer Russell was out on the line with his assistant S. J. Sedgwick trying to capture the railroad scene. On this beautiful glass plate, Sedgwick captures Pony engine No. 5 at the east portal of tunnel No. 2 near Wasatch. — AMERICAN GEOGRAPHICAL SOCIETY

Construction train of platform cars fills in part of the approach to one of the trestles of the Zig-Zag, while Pony engine No. 5 stands below the center arch of the trestle. Note the typical Union Pacific track construction with hand-hewn wooden ties. The Zig-Zag was only a temporary bypass until summit tunnel was completed — AMERICAN GEOGRAPHICAL SOCIETY (RIGHT) The east approach to the Zig-Zag at the right, shows the turnout to the tunnel during the construction period. This temporary track was replaced by the track in the photo at the left. U.S. GEOLOGICAL SURVEY At the left, photographer Sedgwick captured on glass this fine view of engine No. 119 as it leaves the east approach to tunnel No. 2. This engine made history a few months earlier by hauling Vice-President Durant's special train to Promontory. — AMERICAN GEOGRAPHICAL SOCIETY

The ballasting of the Union Pacific track was the last step in completing the railroad. In this splendid photograph inscribed on the glass plate "Steam Shovel at Hanging Rock, Echo Canyon," Russell captured an early model of the steam shovel. In this scene a train loaded with ballast is ready to back out of the gravel pit, while the smokestack of an empty gravel train's locomotive may be seen behind the loaded cars. The main line, such as it was at the time, is barely visible on the extreme right. — AMERICAN GEOGRAPHICAL SOCIETY

ten miles west of Evanston, where a roundhouse and locomotive service station were built. Supplies of rail were accumulated there until the graders and bridge builders who braved the snow and cold could cut, fill, and tunnel their way down Echo Canyon. While the largest of the tunnels was being bored, the graders built a temporary switchback line around it, which was used after tracklaying was resumed, until late in May 1869 when the tunnel was completed.

In the last week of January 1869, the railhead was 1,000 miles west of Omaha, at a point a mile west of Weber Quarry. There a tree at the exact spot where Milepost 1,000 was erected received the name "Thousand-Mile Tree," and was an object of curiosity to visitors for as long as it lived. At this time the Mormon grading crews hired by Leland Stanford were building a grade from Ogden to Echo Summit, closely paralleling the Union Pacific grade. Other Mormon workers were building a Central Pacific grade west from Ogden until they met the graders of Charles Crocker at the west end of Great Salt Lake. During this time the Union Pacific staked out and partially graded a line all the way to Humboldt Wells, 218 miles west of Ogden, a useless duplication of grading totaling 258 miles. The Union Pacific officials were not as smart as C. P. Huntington, who filed a map of his com-

On October 26, 1868, the Union Pacific rails reached the trading post of Black's Fork, 14 miles west of Green River, where an enginehouse, a small shop and town were built by the railroad to serve as the winter headquarters. The name was changed to Bryan, and in the above scene, the hastily built enginehouse was full of engines like Nos. 82 and 124 at the left and center. — AMERICAN GEOGRAPH-ICAL SOCIETY

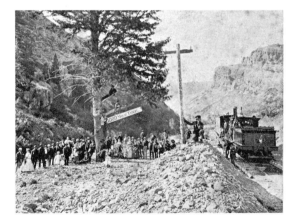

Eighteen miles west of Hanging Rock, near the town of Weber was a tree exactly 1,000 miles from Omaha station. Quickly made famous as the "1,000 Mile Tree," the excursion party in the picture stopped for photographer Savage to make a stereo view that sold by the thousands. — WARD KIMBALL COLLECTION

124

In this camera study by Andrew J. Russell, locomotive No. 120 with a four car train stands just west of the crossing of the Weber River, with tunnel No. 3 in the rugged Utah background. — AMERICAN GEOGRAPHICAL SOCIETY

When Devil's Gate bridge aroused some skepticism among train crews and enginemen who would have to take their trains over it, the Union Pacific engineering department posed a test train to run over it consisting of three locomotives and two cabooses. Photographers Russell and Sedgwick were on hand to capture the event on glass for the ages. Although this scene is often reproduced in volumes featuring the Union Pacific they have always been the Russell exposure. To be distinctive the publisher uncovered the Sedgwick version in the files of the American Geographical Society and it is shown below.

pleted survey and grade in Washington, claimed the bonds due him for finishing the roadbed to Echo Canyon Summit, and got them.

The Union Pacific reached Ogden on March 3, 1869, when locomotive No. 117 brought in a construction train on that date. Both companies were pushing their crews at staggering costs, for supplies had to be brought by rail over a thousand miles from Omaha, and the Central Pacific was extending its lifeline four or five miles daily. A letter published in the *Salt Lake City Telegraph* in April 1869 gives a graphic description of the Casement Brothers construction train in the days after the rails were being laid from Ogden west towards Nevada. The train, hauled by engines Nos. 117 and 119, consisted of 22 cars as follows;

No. 1 Blacksmith car carrying switchstands, frogs, bolts, etc.
No. 2. Feed store and saddlers' shop.
No. 3. Carpenter shop and wash house.
No. 4. Mule whackers' sleeping car.
No. 5. Bunk car for 144 men.
No. 6. Sitting room and dining compartment.
No. 7. Dining car seating 200 men.
No. 8. Kitchen car with counting room and telegraph office.
No. 9. Store car.
No. 10 to 16. Bunk cars similar to car No. 5.
No. 17. Captain Clayton's kitchen and dining car for self and wife.
No. 18. Parlor and bedroom car for Captain Clayton.
No. 19. Sleeping car for other officials.
No. 20. Supply car.
Nos. 21-22. Water cars.

Captain Clayton was the General Superintendent of the track laying forces. The permanently assigned engineer of engine No. 117 was George McCamish, with Samuel Bradford assigned to engine No. 119. The track force using this train operated in the following manner; 20 men in groups of two would bed a tie every 14 feet — they were known as the joint tie men. Next came the fillers who filled in the spaces with crossties. There were ten iron men, four to each rail with one man always standing by as a replacement. Following the iron men were four gaugers, who aligned the rails. The head spikers followed and drove six spikes in each rail. The back spikers and screwers were next, finishing the spiking of each rail, mounting the fish plates and bolting them to the rails. The spikers were preceded by spike peddlers who walked on each side of the track, distributing the spikes two to a crosstie on each side.

Next came the chain gang, or backfillers, who shoveled earth between the ties and tamped it down. The track liners followed, with crowbars to align the track, or to jack it up if too low. Behind the track liners were the back iron men, who loaded rails on the small truck cars from piles previously dumped by the side of the track. Water carriers were everywhere, and the tail piece man picked up all the loose bolts, spikes, tools, etc., and distributed them where they belonged. The trucks loaded with rails were hauled by a horse named "Champion Tom," who had been with this train all the way from Omaha. Many horses were used in hauling wagons loaded with crossties and such items as spikes, fish plates, and other track material. Some idea as to the number of men required to staff a complete tracklaying train such as the one described here can be visualized from a statement made by Central Pacific's track boss Strobridge. "On the day my crew laid ten miles of track, we used 848 men and 92 horses." The men used in the grading operations ran into the many thousands more, the bridge gang alone requiring 900 men.

Shortly after the Casement brothers tracklaying train left Ogden, a compromise was reached between Huntington and Durant in Washington on April 9, and the following day Congress issued a decree setting the meeting point at Promontory, Utah, 53 miles west of Ogden. As previously related, the Central Pacific with 14 miles to go to reach Promontory, laid ten miles of track in one day, a record the Union Pacific was powerless to beat or duplicate since their railhead was only nine miles from Promontory that day.

Central Pacific tracklayers came marching up to Promontory on May 1, and laid their track to the exact meeting point of the surveyed lines. Two deep excavations in the hills several miles east of Promontory, called Carmichael's and Clark's cuts, named after the foremen of the grading gangs who did the work, were completed on May 6, and the long, spindly trestle connecting the two cuts was already finished. On May 7 the Union Pacific tracklayers worked west to within a couple of rail lengths of the meeting point, with a long siding branching off a short distance east of the latter, for storage of engines and cars. One of the Casement brothers came up to inspect the work in a train consisting of engine No. 66 and a caboose coach. Standing on the Central Pacific track a hundred feet away was Central Pacific *Whirlwind* No. 62, and the engineers of both locomotives whistled at each other several times in salute to the meeting. A reporter for the San Francisco newspaper *Alta Cali-*

A panorama of the upper Great Salt Lake Valley made from the roof of a freight car at the station of Corinne. This view shows the railroad making a 90 degree turn to the right, to head south to Ogden. In the distance is Brigham City, and faintly visible partly up the mountain side is the ancient shoreline of Great Salt Lake some millions of years ago. — AMERICAN GEOGRAPHICAL SOCIETY

In its haste to reach Promontory to meet the Central Pacific at the appointed time, a hastily built trestle was erected four miles east of Promontory, with the intention of filling it in later. The Central Pacific grade passed to the north of this point and was on a solid rock fill across the gully in the foreground. Engine No. 116 stands on this trestle in November 1869, after the first snowfall. A few weeks later the trestle was abandoned and the Central Pacific grade was used. Today the earth fills at the trestle approaches mark the site of one of Union Pacific's largest structures. — AMERICAN GEOGRAPHICAL SOCIETY (LEFT) Newspapers and station bulletin boards carried the advertisement poster announcing the completion of the Union Pacific and its connection with the Central Pacific to California. — UNION PACIFIC MUSEUM

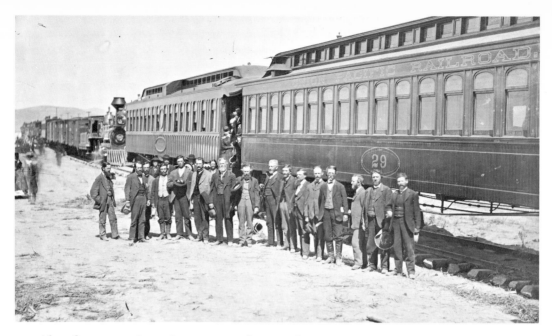

After the ceremonies at Promontory, photographer Russell posed all the Union Pacific officials and guests alongside of Durant's business car No. 29, behind which is the first Pullman car to come west of Corinne. Thomas Durant stands with silk hat in hand, in line with the far end of the business car. On Durant's right is director Sidney Dillon, later president of the company, while on Durant's left is director John Duff, then Major General Grenville M. Dodge — AMERICAN GEOGRAPHICAL SOCIETY

fornia who was present at this time stated that the Union Pacific tracklaying crew were the hardest lot he had ever seen. He said, "Imagine the Presidio's 19th U. S. Infantry struck by lightning and you have them!"

The ceremony at Promontory was described in the Central Pacific portion of this story, but the reason for the delay of the Union Pacific official train and the postponement of the ceremony to May 10 was not entirely due to bad weather. When Durant's special train had reached Piedmont, 83 miles west of Green River, it was detained by a mob of unpaid tie cutters, who refused to let the train pass until they had been paid. Behind the special was another train loaded with excursionists from the East, bent on making the first transcontinental trip. After the two trains were held at Piedmont from the evening of May 6 to the morning of May 8, Oakes Ames, who had succeeded his brother Oliver as President of the Union Pacific, was sent a telegram urging him to forward enough money by wire to pay off the mob of lumberjacks. Though at the end of his own personal resources, Ames managed to get the money, and on May 8 the men were paid and the trains passed through. There was heavy storm damage at this time in Echo Canyon, and the special train carrying Thomas Durant, directors Sidney Dillon and John Duff, General Dodge and others too numerous to list was so late

that it did not reach Promontory until 10 a.m. on the morning of May 10.

The engine which brought the Durant special west from Ogden was No. 119, one of the Rogers coal burners previously described, which had been turned out of the factory on November 19, 1868. It must have arrived in Omaha some time in December, and together with the other four of the class was sent to the west end of the line. After Sidney Dillon became President of the Union Pacific, he was asked why engine No. 119 had been selected to haul the official train. He was not sure, but thought it had been placed on the train at Ogden because it was serviced and ready, and therefore "first out." Being well suited to handle the special train up the grade to Promontory, it was picked by sheer happenstance, for it could have been any other of the ten small-drivered coal burners working out of Ogden at the time. The train No. 119 pulled consisted of a "subsistence" car, a business car, the Union Pacific "Directors' Car" No. 29, and a Pullman sleeping car, the first to run west of Corinne. No eyewitness of that day recorded the name of the Pullman, nor has its name been found in railroad company or Pullman records. No. 119's crew probably spent considerable time cleaning the boiler jacket, polishing the brass cap on top of the stack and making the engine presentable for the meeting with the Central Pacific special.

After the ceremony at Promontory, No. 119 spent its working years on the main line, was renumbered No. 343 in 1885 and its driving wheel diameter increased to 57 inches by means of thicker tires. When class designations were adopted in 1885, it became Class BK-4, the code for all engines with 57-inch drivers and 16x24-inch cylinders. In April 1903 it was vacated from the equipment rolls and scrapped. Its four mates had either been scrapped earlier or sold to F. M. Hicks in Chicago. In 1903, E. H. Harriman was busy consolidating all his railroads into one system and obviously gave no thought to No. 119's fate; the Union Pacific motive power officials probably cared even less.

Only twelve additional locomotives were purchased by the Union Pacific in 1869 and these were all delivered by May 10. The line was 1,085 miles long when completed, and it was served by fewer locomotives than the Central Pacific, which was much shorter. As of June 1869, there were 145 locomotives in service as compared with 179 either delivered or enroute to the Central Pacific. The difference can only be attributed to the fact that the Union Pacific's treasury had been emptied, and the locomotive fleet was kept low because of this condition. Though five more engines were purchased in 1870, an equivalent number were sold to subsidiaries such as the Colorado Central — Julesburg Branch, and to the Utah Central.

Union Pacific No. 119 on a construction train near Ogden in the last weeks of tracklaying. Behind the engine are some of the Casement brothers' boarding cars, to which No. 119 and its sister engine, No. 117 were assigned. — UNION PACIFIC MUSEUM

Two weeks after the transcontinental railroad was completed, a party of excursionists from California accompanied Charles Crocker on his journey east to Omaha. On their return to the west, the party made an inspection stop in the upper end of Weber Canyon. Russell photographed the group on its westbound journey as it paused at Devil's Gate bridge. The rear car is a Union Pacific flat car equipped with benches, the following is the first Silver Palace Sleeping Car to come west and lettered "I", Governor Stanford's business car which was at Promontory, the subsistence car, and behind the engine a caboose-coach. — AMERICAN GEOGRAPHICAL SOCIETY

Like the Central Pacific, division points were selected as the railroad progressed westward, and the largest shops were located at Omaha and North Platte. After the bridge across the Missouri River was completed in 1872, the transfer station for all passengers boarding or leaving Union Pacific trains was located about a half-mile east of the bridge, and two miles west of the town of Council Bluffs. The largest roundhouse was at Omaha, which was the headquarters for the Platte Division, 291 miles from Omaha to North Platte. In the late 1870s this division was renamed the Eastern Division. A small roundhouse of six stalls was erected at Fremont to handle the helper engines which brought the trains west up the grade out of Omaha, and at Grand Island, 154 miles from Omaha, was a large roundhouse with shops for running repairs. All locomotives were changed at this point, it being considered in the 19th century that a locomotive should not run more than 150 to 200 miles without going into the roundhouse for service. The Central Pacific was to disprove this theory a few years later.

North Platte was headquarters for the Lodge Pole Division, which extended 282 miles to Laramie, Wyoming, the name being changed to Mountain Division in 1875. At North Platte was a 20-stall roundhouse, a blacksmith and machine shop, all of granite blocks brought from the western part of the railroad. For many years the North Platte shops were second only to the Omaha shops in importance. Julesburg, Colorado, 76 miles west of North Platte, was at first only a way station, but eventually became the eastern terminus of the Colorado Central — Julesburg Branch, a tie line between Julesburg and the town of LaSalle, Colo-

This closeup of Union Pacific No. 117 was made by photographer A. A. Hart of Sacramento on May 8, 1869, when Governor Stanford and his party were taken by special train as far as Taylor's Mills east of Uintah. The location is probably a wye at Taylor's Mills where the train was turned for the return trip. — HUNTINGTON LIBRARY, SAN MARINO, CALIFORNIA (BELOW) The Union Pacific bridge across the Missouri between Omaha and Council Bluffs, though construction began in November 1868, was not opened for traffic until March 1872. It was quickly replaced with a larger bridge, which in turn was succeeded by the present structure. — UNION PACIFIC MUSEUM

Engine No. 76 built by Rogers, on the turntable at Omaha in the winter of 1868. The
roundhouse doors were closed tight to retain heat. — AMERICAN GEOGRAPHICAL SOCIETY

rado, on the Denver Pacific's Cheyenne-Denver
line. Locomotives were changed at Sidney, Nebraska, 123 miles west of North Platte, where a
ten-stall roundhouse and small shops were erected
long before the railroad was completed. From Sidney to Cheyenne was a 102 mile run, and at Cheyenne all passenger trains stopped for meals as well
as a change of engines. There the Denver Pacific
Railroad, built between 1868 and 1870, had its
northern terminus. This railroad came under the
control of the Kansas Pacific Railroad in 1872 and
provided the latter with a through railroad of 743
miles from Kansas City to Cheyenne, via Denver.
Years later the Union Pacific was to absorb this
railroad as a part of its ambitious expansion plans.
Cheyenne first had a 20-stall roundhouse and small
shops, but as the years passed, it became a very important locomotive service point. The roundhouse
was enlarged, shops were built for general locomotive repair, and a large storage yard for freight
trains was added. Helper engines were needed on
all trains from Cheyenne to Sherman summit, so as
the traffic developed the Cheyenne roundhouse
tracks swarmed with locomotives.

The balance of the Lodge Pole Division, Cheyenne to Laramie, was only 57 miles long, during
which the line ascended from an altitude of 6,041
feet at Cheyenne to 8,242 feet at Sherman, then
descended to 7,123 feet at Laramie. This was the

shortest run for engines and engine crews on the
whole railroad and the change of crews at Cheyenne and Laramie persisted into modern times.
Much relocation work on this line was done in
later years, first after the double-tracking and again
quite recently, in an effort to cut down on the grade
to the summit in each direction. Laramie was the
headquarters for the Laramie Division, with a 20-
stall roundhouse made of granite, machine shops
and a rolling mill for re-rolling old rails, the latter
set up in 1874. The stone roundhouse, though not
used in the last days of steam, remained there until
dieselization of the railroad eliminated all steam
facilities at Laramie.

The Laramie Division was 285 miles long, ending at Bryan, Wyoming. At Medicine Bow, 74
miles west of Laramie, was a five-stall roundhouse
and service facilities for the engines handling the
coal trains from the mines at Carbon, four miles
west. This coal was used principally by the railroad, most of it going east towards Omaha, for
more and better quality coal was available west of
Rawlins. Locomotives were changed at Rawlins,
136 miles west of Laramie, with a 20-stall roundhouse and small shop located there. At Rock
Springs, west of Rawlins, were large coal mines
which supplied the railroad with locomotive fuel,
also catering to the demand for home heating coal,
it being of a much better grade than eastern Wyom-

A closeup of three of the engines as shown in the illustration below. No. 156 in the center stall was later to distinguish itself by handling the Jarrett & Palmer special train from Grand Island to North Platte, Nebraska. The wooden slats nailed to the pilots were the forerunner of the steel pilot plows of later years. — AMERICAN GEOGRAPHICAL SOCIETY

On a warm day in the fall of 1869, Sedgwick posed all the engines at the stone roundhouse at Rawlins. From left to right, the locomotives are Nos. 92, 106, 156, 93, 107 and 127. The plate has begun to crack from improper storage over the years. — AMERICAN GEOGRAPHICAL SOCIETY

One of the most unusual pictures to come to light recently is the original Sedgwick photograph of locomotive No. 120 at Wasatch in 1869. Details of the Bissell engine truck, and other chassis features are clearly shown. — AMERICAN GEOGRAPHICAL SOCIETY

ing coal. In due time the coal mines in northeastern Utah were to produce the finest coal in the West. In 1900 the distance between Laramie and Rock Creek was reduced by 17 miles, by eliminating the devious route used by Colonel Silas Seymour in an effort to avoid fills and cuts through the rocks and thereby save construction time. This aroused the wrath of General Dodge, who had made the original survey, but Seymour's locations was allowed to stand, until at the start of a program of improvements initiated by E. H. Harriman, Dodge was vindicated by the adoption of his survey for the new line.

Green River, Wyoming, 845 miles west of Omaha, was originally and is today primarily a railroad town, but at the time of the building of the road it was the scene of conflict between real estate promoters and the railroad company. Weeks before the railhead reached Green River, a town had been laid out a short distance south of the present city, and by September 1868 it had a population of 2,000. The railroad company did not propose to be dictated to as to the site of a division point, and continued tracklaying 13 miles west of Green River to Bryan. There the Union Pacific built a roundhouse, repair shops and yards, laying out a town to which the inhabitants of Green River soon came, leaving the old town a deserted ruin. This arrange-

ment lasted until after the railroad was completed and a traffic pattern had developed, at which time it became obvious that Bryan was not the place for a division point. Everything was moved east to Green River, the town being located to the north of the tracks instead of south as in 1868. A 15-stall roundhouse with repair facilities was set up, becoming the eastern terminal for trains operating on the Oregon Short Line after 1882.

The Utah Division, changed to Western Division in 1875, was 187 miles long, from Green River to Ogden, with an additional 53 miles to Promontory until that section was sold to the Central Pacific. As originally set up, the engine changing point and meal station was at Wahsatch, 121 miles west of Green River and near the head of Echo Canyon. Here a roundhouse and shops were in use until the early 1870s, when all the facilities were moved eleven miles east to Evanston. This became the engine changing point as well as the place where helper engines on eastbound trains out of Ogden could be serviced and sent back to their home base. There was originally a 20-stall roundhouse at Evanston, later reduced to half that size. From Wahsatch the Union Pacific descended through Echo Creek Canyon to the valley of the Weber River, on a grade which in many places reached the maximum permissible 2.2 percent. Ogden, 1,032 miles from

Ogden station of the Union Pacific with two fine examples of the Congdon stack on the locomotives heading two passenger trains. The date is probably in the early 1880s. — GERALD M. BEST COLLECTION

Omaha, became the western terminus of the Union Pacific about March 1, 1870, although it retained title to six miles north and west of Ogden on the Promontory line until 1874 when it sold the section to the Central Pacific.

At Ogden a large roundhouse and shops were built during the fall of 1869, the temporary shops and roundhouse at Uintah being dismantled in October of that year. Within a week of the completion of the transcontinental railroad, the Utah Central began construction south from Ogden. Sponsored by a new company headed by Brigham Young, the 37 mile railroad from Ogden to Salt Lake City was built in record time. Grading was completed over most of the route by September 1869, the bridge across the Weber River at Ogden being the biggest obstacle, which was not overcome until October 18, when Union Pacific engine No. 117, which brought the first U. P. train into Ogden, crossed the bridge with a train of five cars loaded with rail. The Union Pacific sold their No. 15 to the Utah Central at this time, for use on construction trains, and new locomotives from the Schenectady Works arrived a month after the line was completed. The last spike was driven in Salt Lake City on January 10, 1870, and regular train service was begun the following day.

The sale of the Union Pacific's track from a point near Ogden to Promontory has already been discussed in the Central Pacific story. Though the Union Pacific built the station, restaurant and freight house on their own property east of the junction of the two railroads, they spent a minimum amount on yards and locomotive facilities because of the certainty that Promontory would soon be abandoned as the western terminus of the Union Pacific. Locomotives were turned around on

Engine No. 121 was the Ogden station switcher in the 1870 period and it still carried the link and pin coupler. — RICHARD B. JACKSON COLLECTION

137

William Henry Jackson photographed the golden spike site in July 1869, after the yards of both railroads had been completed. The telegraph pole with the flag is still in place directly opposite the junction of the railroads, and the last Central Pacific tie can be seen beyond the westernmost hand-hewn U.P. tie. The siding switch led to the freight house and the C.P. switch and the gallows of the turntable can be seen in the distance. — GERALD M. BEST COLLECTION

Utah Central No. 1, formerly Union Pacific No. 15, shortly after it went to work during construction of the railroad from Ogden to Salt Lake City. Daughters of the Utah Pioneers Museum in Salt Lake City has the original print.

a "Y," and a water tank and small coal dump provided necessary supplies. No maintenance had been done on the track from Ogden to Promontory and as a result there were several bad derailments in the nine mile section between Promontory and Blue Creek during the summer and fall of 1869. On July 27, a mixed train fell through a trestle between Blue Creek and Corinne, killing the engine crew and one passenger, besides injuring other passengers and employees.

Once the Central Pacific received title to the line from Promontory to Ogden, they dispatched a trainload of Chinese stonemasons and bridge workers, together with many carloads of dump carts and excavation equipment, to work on the line east of Promontory and to construct a roundhouse, shops, and a station at Ogden. Portions of the Union Pacific grade just east of Promontory were abandoned in favor of the better location of the Central Pacific line, eliminating several high trestles which had a possible life expectancy of only two or three years. During the period December 1869 to March

1870, Union Pacific employees staffed the stations at Promontory and other intermediate locations.

Having had their fill of the depredations of gamblers and toughs who inhabited the tent city at Promontory and the flagrant robbing of a westbound immigrant family, the railroads (no doubt at the request of the Central Pacific officials in charge of the takeover) gave tent city residents notice to leave town. The evacuation was immediate, and the Union Pacific agent and all railroad employees prepared a special train consisting of a locomotive and a coach to hasten their passage. The hooligans were given 15 minutes to board the train with their personal possessions or be run out of town on a rail. The passengers aboard the special were taken to Corinne and dumped. This action ended the last of the tent cities which followed the Union Pacific railhead since leaving Omaha.

Even after the Central Pacific completed the relocation of the first nine miles of line east of Promontory, a serious derailment occurred on April 2, 1870, when a mixed train with several immigrant

Replacing the original wooden station at Omaha was this huge brick building erected in 1872 and known to the locals as the "Cow Shed." Its capacity was limited and in 1898 was replaced with open tracks with covered platforms. — UNION PACIFIC MUSEUM

Until the Missouri River bridge was completed in March 1872, passenger ferries connected the Union Pacific with the three railroad terminals on the east bank. The sign at the right advertises the Chicago, Rock Island & Pacific, the sign directly over the center of the steamer *P. F. Geisse* belongs to the Kansas City, St. Joseph & Council Bluffs, and the Chicago & North Western trains stand behind the small, white buildings between the two steamers. — UNION PACIFIC MUSEUM

The westbound *Atlantic & Pacific Express* on one of its first runs, stands in the station at Corinne, Utah. Behind the last baggage car is the Lincoln car, then Directors' car No. 29; between the small building and the tent is the Pullman *Wahsatch*, behind the tent is the Pullman *Denver*, first to cross the Missouri River, and at the end of the train is Silver Palace Sleeping Car *D.* — AMERICAN GEO-GRAPHICAL SOCIETY

This bulletin issued by the Pullman Company heralding the *Atlantic & Pacific Express* gives the date of the first train as November 11, 1869. This was actually the third round trip, for the first train arrived in San Francisco on October 22, 1869. — GOLDEN WEST COLLEC-TION

cars on the rear was derailed four miles east of Promontory and rolled down the bank, injuring a number of passengers and crew.

A considerable part of the story of through sleeping car and dining car service between Omaha and Oakland Pier was presented in the Central Pacific section. Unlike the latter, the Union Pacific reached an agreement with George Pullman and operated his cars from Omaha to Ogden. Though all passenger trains stopped at meal stations for many years, and the Union Pacific owned no dining cars, Pull man diners operated during the first two or three years after the railroad was completed, first on the Atlantic & Pacific Express and later at least one day a week each way. Until well after 1885, Union Pacific passengers ate their meals at the company meal stations, where the food ranged from splendid to very mediocre. For use on second sections of regular passenger or excursion trains, the Union Pacific purchased 23 new sleeping cars of the same general design as the Central Pacific's Silver Palace Sleeping Cars, but these were relegated to immigrant or tourist car service by 1885 and the Pullmans ruled the consist of the expresses.

Like the Central Pacific, the Union Pacific was lucky to avoid serious passenger train accidents during the construction period. The very slow schedules of all trains was probably responsible for the lack of disastrous, high speed collisions or derailments, though there were plenty of the latter. This does not include accidents resulting from Indian raids, these being confined to construction trains. On October 30, 1869, just two weeks before the Central Pacific had its first calamity, there was a rear-end collision halfway between Wahsatch and Evanston, Wyoming, which made the headlines. The westbound daily express to which Pullman sleepers were attached was standing on the main track waiting for a stalled freight train to move, when it was hit by a westbound immigrant train running as an extra. Four passengers on the *Wahsatch*, the rear Pullman car were killed, one being a man from Petaluma, California, who was standing on the rear platform and though told to jump, he failed to do so and lost his life. Three Mormon immigrants in the first coach of the following train were killed when the car was telescoped by the baggage car. The express was able to continue after several hours delay, minus one sleeping car.

On January 29, 1870, the regular passenger train which had left Omaha on the 27th met with disaster while rounding a curve five miles west of Aspen, Wyoming. The train consisted of a baggage car, two coaches, the Pullman dining car *Elk Horn Club* and the Pullman sleepers *America* and the ill-fated *Wahsatch*, just back from an overhaul at the Pullman shops in Chicago. The outside rails on the curve gave way due to excessive speed of the train, and a coach and all three Pullmans rolled down the bank, landing upside-down at the bottom. By a miracle, only two men were killed; they were riding on a coach platform in defiance of the rules, jumped when the coach began to roll over and were crushed beneath it. Nearly a hundred passengers were injured or cut by glass, but there were no deaths in either the Pullmans or the coach except the two platform riders. A relief train was made up at Evanston and sent east to the scene

141

of the wreck, bringing the passengers into Ogden twelve hours late. The Pullmans were all rerailed and returned to Chicago for repairs, but two months later, when the *America* had been back on the western run less than a week, it was derailed by a herd of cattle in western Wyoming.

August 14, 1870, marked the last serious attempt by bands of hostile Indians to disrupt traffic on the Union Pacific, when the rails were torn up late in the evening a few miles west of Bennett, Nebraska, in the expectation that express train No. 3, due there about 9:30 p.m., would be wrecked. Fortunately, their depredations were seen by an alert track patrolman, who borrowed a horse from a nearby ranch and rode into Bennett, the first station east of Antelope. He arrived in time to hold the train there and warn the military, who quickly drove off the marauders. The damage to the track was so great that it required 24 hours for the track repair gang to restore the line to service.

Though Pullman sleepers from Omaha to Oakland Pier were discontinued at the Central Pacific's request in July 1870, and thereafter transcontinental passengers changed trains three times on a trip from New York to San Francisco — Chicago, Omaha and Ogden. During the first year of operation, the Union Pacific not only built a number of refrigerator cars called "Fruit Cars," but handled the cars of various eastern packing companies over their lines, carrying eggs, oysters, fresh lake fish from Chicago and bringing back table grapes and California fruit on the return trips. In the spring of 1870 the yardmaster at Omaha was astonished to see a box car from the Erie Railway, a six-foot gauge railroad, but equipped with temporary standard gauge trucks, come across the Mis-

souri on the ferry, way-billed to San Francisco with a consist of shoes. It returned a couple of weeks later with a load of wool, and this car was but one of many "foreign" freight cars which began to come through from various eastern cities with consignments destined for towns along the transcontinental railroad.

The first silk train movement of record left San Francisco on November 22, 1870, with a total of eleven cars and caboose, bound for New York City. It was followed the next day by the first of two trains totalling 40 cars loaded with tea from China, all landed at San Francisco from one ship a few days earlier. Silk and tea trains were given the right-of-way over all other freight trains, and in later years were to be run at schedules which were faster than most passenger trains. This was because the insurance on silk in particular was very

Though photographed on the Central Pacific at Blue Canyon, the 20-car double-headed tea and silk train pictured above was enroute to the eastern seaboard from San Francisco, via Union Pacific. — RICHARD JACKSON COLLECTION (BELOW) The Union Pacific pioneered in the operation of trains of refrigerated "Fruit Cars," the first such train arriving in Sacramento from Omaha in August 1869. This train consists of 19 Union Pacific fruit cars, with the herald of "California Fast Freight Line" on the side of each car. — GERALD M. BEST COLLECTION

This superb photograph finds Pony engine No. 5 out on the line with the Union Pacific photograph car. After Andrew J. Russell and his assistant S. J. Sedgwick had returned to New York in 1869, another member of Russell's group, J. B. Silvis, made a number of trips over the Union Pacific. The car was equipped with a portrait studio as well as a darkroom, thus transferring the itinerant photographer with his horse and wagon, to more comfortable quarters in a railroad car. — UNION PACIFIC MUSEUM

high, and no time was lost in transporting the expensive commodity to its destination.

Since the first train holdup on the Central Pacific has been described, it is apropos at this point to include the first known holdup on the Union Pacific. Though the robbery of a train at Ogalalla, Nebraska, in 1877 is credited with being the first, it was preceded by another which is an outstanding example of daring and ingenuity. On the evening of August 27, 1875, the eastbound express had left Bitter Creek, Wyoming, 60 miles east of Green River, when two men climbed to the roof of the express car then lowered themselves down the side by ropes fastened to the ventilators, opened an unbarred window and crawled inside. While the express messenger slept, the robbers filched the keyring from his pocket and proceeded to unlock the padlock on the strongbox. The snap of the unlocked padlock awakened the messenger and when he tried to resist, the bandits fired several wild shots, none hitting their mark. In the confusion, the messenger pulled the bellrope as the train neared Agate station and realizing the train was coming to a halt, the robbers opened the door and fled into the darkness with several packages. The stolen articles later proved to be of little or no cash value. The robbers were never caught, but thereafter the windows of express cars were securely locked.

Returning to the Union Pacific motive power, six Schenectady, three Hinkley & Williams, and three Taunton 4-4-0s were delivered in 1869, and except for four more Taunton 4-4-0s purchased in 1870, this ended locomotive buying on the Union Pacific for four years. Though the highest locomotive number was No. 165, a number had been sold or scrapped by January 1870, leaving 150 road engines and five "Pony" engines in service. One of the latter was an odd-ball Schenectady 4-4-0 engine without tender, having side tanks for water and a coal bunker in the back of the cab. It was first used to haul officials on inspection trips over the line, and hauled the official photographer, A. J. Russell, and his photo car from Omaha to Promontory in 1869. This engine remained on the roster for a few years and then disappeared from the records.

As early as 1864, motive power Superintendent Congdon had patented a design for an extended smokebox with two exhaust nozzles, one in front of the other, with an adjustable netting above them. The smokestack itself was straight, and it is believed that Union Pacific No. 119 and the other four Rogers engines of that class were so equipped. This stack was replaced with a Jarrett type diamond stack in 1870, a modification called the Fountain stack taking its place in 1873. In 1878 Congdon patented another stack which had been in use since 1875 and this stack became known as the Congdon stack. Its appearance was much the same as a bonnet stack except that the circular section above the screen was very high, giving the impression of enormous height and bulk. Congdon's experiments were brought about by the discovery of coal beds in Nebraska which were close to the surface, therefore easily mined, and the product, called lignite, was extremely fine and dusty. To

Union Pacific No. 130 by Taunton with Congdon's final smokestack design.
— GERALD M. BEST COLLECTION

145

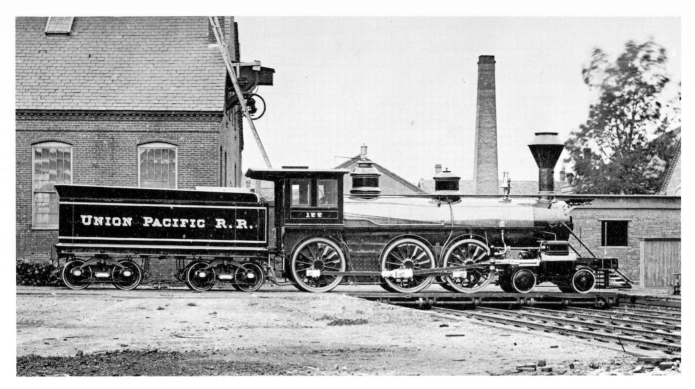

Engine No. 177 at the Taunton Locomotive Works in 1877, and equipped with a Taunton diamond stack. — GERALD M. BEST COLLECTION

Union Pacific No. 985, formerly No. 238, was built by Taunton in 1881, and still retained its factory-built stack after 1885, when it was renumbered. — GERALD M. BEST COLLECTION

quote an expert fuel consultant of that day, the lignite, which burned very much like wood, was easily sucked through the flues when the engine was working hard. The locomotive's progress through the night closely resembled the flight of a sky rocket, which rendered the prospects of extensive prairies fires exceedingly promising. The lignite was so cheap that the company would not haul the good Utah or western Wyoming coal east of Cheyenne, resulting in the adoption of the Congdon stack for all the locomotives of the system.

Unlike Central Pacific's Andrew Jackson Stevens, Congdon was content to keep the locomotives in good repair, adapted them for air brakes as the money became available, and kept the locomotive dead line to the irreducible minimum. It was not until after Congdon's time that the Union Pacific embarked on modernization of locomotives which is not pertinent to this story.

In 1874 the first eight of a large number of ten-wheel freight engines built at the Taunton Locomotive Works arrived on the road, followed in 1875 by five handsome Taunton 4-4-0s with 66-inch drivers and 18x24-inch cylinders. All of these locomotives were equipped with Congdon stacks at the factory. The freight engines had 54-inch drivers and 18x24-inch cylinders and weighed 38 tons. These were followed in 1878 by 30 more Taunton 4-6-0s, the first ten having 60-inch drivers and intended for passenger service, and the following 20 were like the first Taunton 4-6-0s, with 54-inch drivers. In 1880, 14 similar engines came from Danforth, which also delivered four 2-6-0 freight

engines of 50-inch drivers and 18x22-inch cylinders, the latter a standard type on the Erie Railway. The Union Pacific did not favor the mogul type, and unlike the Southern Pacific during the Harriman era, bought very few 2-6-0s in its history.

The new Taunton eight-wheelers were given a chance to show their worth in 1876 when the Union Pacific participated in hauling the Jarrett & Palmer special from New York to San Francisco. Three famous Shakespearian actors, Lawrence Barrett, Patrick Thorne and C. B. Bishop were to appear in the play "Henry V" at McCullough's California Theater in San Francisco on June 5, 1876. Their agent, Henry C. Jarrett, and manager Palmer of Booth's Theater in New York City knew that the regular transcontinental journey required seven days, and so they conferred with representatives of four railroads and worked up a schedule of 84 hours for the trip. Some reporters said that it was all arranged as a publicity stunt for the actors and their managers; others that the players did not finish the run of the play in New York until too late to reach San Francisco on the regular overland train. Publicity was no doubt the prime factor, for the sleeper berths which were not to be occupied by the actors and their managers were eagerly snapped up at $500 each, this cost including a return on any regular train and a week's lodging at the new Palace Hotel in San Francisco. Elaborate tickets mounted in a booklet with solid silver covers, all contained in a white satin casket with lilac satin lining, cost the promoters $40 each and these must have taken considerable time to prepare.

Regardless of the motive, the passengers left the New York ferry terminal of the Pennsylvania Railriad at 12:40 a.m. Eastern time on June 1, and the train pulled out of the Jersey City terminal at 12:50 a.m. The locomotive was P. R. R. No. 573, Altoona-built in 1872, with 60-inch drivers and 17x24-inch

The 14 Danforth ten-wheelers delivered in 1880 could be identified from the Tauntons by having the sandbox forward of the front pair of drivers. Crosshead pumps were still being installed on new engines as late as 1881. — GERALD M. BEST COLLECTION

cylinders. The consist was the Pullman Hotel car *Marlborough,* a coach and a baggage car, the latter two being exchanged for a combination baggage and passenger car at Chicago. The run of 439 miles to Pittsburgh was made non-stop, as the locomotive took water from track pans and carried enough coal for the distance. A Pennsylvania Railroad controlled subsidiary, the Pittsburgh, Fort Wayne & Chicago hauled the train to Chicago, where it arrived on the evening of June 1, having averaged 43 miles an hour from Jersey City. Here the Chicago & North Western received the train and made the run to Council Bluffs at an average speed of 42 miles an hour, with four locomotive changes and five water stops enroute.

An unexplained 43 minutes were lost between the time the train arrived at the Council Bluffs interchange station and the time it departed from the Union Pacific's Omaha station, only one and a half miles distant. The train left Omaha at 10:43 a.m. central time on June 2, with high-wheeled engine No. 146, built by Schenectady taking it to Grand Island. Eight locomotives were used by the Union Pacific during the run to Ogden, five of them being new Tauntons with 66-inch drivers. The time for the 1,032 mile trip was 25 hours, 14 minutes, the highest speed attained being 72 miles an hour on one of the long tangents between Grand Island and North Platte, with an average of 41 miles an hour for the Union Pacific's share of the trip. This unheard of speed on track not intended for use at more than 45 miles per hour produced such a rough

147

ride in Wyoming that it was impossible for the cooks to prepare hot meals on the range in the hotel car.

Union Pacific's engine No. 153 brought the special to the Ogden interchange on the morning of June 3, a few hours over two days from Jersey City. During this time the newspapers all over the country were filled with headlines about the record-breaking trip, and practically the entire population of the small towns enroute turned out to see the train pass through. At Ogden, the Central Pacific engine No. 149, ex *Black Fox*, one of the *Jupiter's* class from Schenectady, was waiting to take the train to Oakland. No. 149 had been equipped with a special tender mounted on six-wheel trucks, with a water capacity of 3,700 gallons and nearly double the normal coal carrying space. The Central Pacific usually changed engines at every division point just as the roads west of Pittsburgh had done, but Superintendent Towne decided to gamble everything on a daring plan and ran No. 149 all the way through from Ogden to Oakland Pier. At the throttle was engineer Henry S. Small, regular engineer on the pay train and familiar with every mile of the railroad. To spell him when it was necessary to take time out for meals, there were Benjamin Smith, Road Foreman of Engines, and James Wright, the regular engineer of No. 149. Hard-working firemen W. C. Dean, J. W. Brown and Martin Duxstad shoveled 37,350 pounds of coal into No. 149's firebox between Ogden and Oakland Pier.

The Jarrett & Palmer special pulled into the Ogden station at 9:43 a.m. and the engine change was made in one minute, the train departing west at 9:44 a.m. Not far from Promontory it was necessary to halt the train for 18 minutes to cool and lubri-

Rogers-built No. 77 hauled the Jarrett & Palmer special from North Platte to Cheyenne. — WALTER LUCAS COLLECTION (BELOW) Union Pacific No. 151 at the Taunton factory, was also on the Jarrett & Palmer special from Rawlins to Green River. — GERALD M. BEST COLLECTION

Union Pacific No. 654, formerly No. 156, hauled the Jarrett & Palmer special train from Grand Island to North Platte. Except for the eagle on the bell and the antlers on the headlight, there seems to be no change in appearance from the illustration on page 135. — GERALD M. BEST COLLECTION

At the right, Jarrett & Palmer's train at the end of its run on Oakland Wharf. The special was widely publicized in the nation's press and many were on hand to watch the train pull in. Note the sailing vessels to the left of the special train. — HUNTINGTON LIBRARY, SAN MARINO, CALIFORNIA (BELOW) Central Pacific No. 149, after returning to Sacramento. The men who ran the train from Ogden to Oakland pose beside their engine. — GERALD M. BEST COLLECTION

cate a hot journal, and it was soon found that the brakes on the two cars were so worn that air brake control of the train was difficult, so hand braking was used when necessary. At Truckee an empty coach was added next to the engine for extra braking power. A helper engine assisted No. 149 to Summit, where another empty coach was added to enable the train to make fast time down the hill. Going through Stockton, engineer Small blew the whistle so hard that its cylindrical top blew off and fell in the coal piled in the tender. Another helper had to be used from Ellis, west of Stockton, to Altamount Summit, from whence No. 149 made it to Oakland Pier, covering the last two miles in two minutes. The passengers transferred to a ferry and reached San Francisco at 9:45 a.m., June 4, or 83 hours, 55 minutes from New York. A photograph of the 13 passengers made in San Francisco a day later states the run was made in 83 hours, 53 minutes, 45 seconds, but to quote the late Lucius Beebe—"The time difference was no matter; there was glory enough in it for all." Engineer Small received a diamond studded gold medal from Messrs. Jarrett and Palmer and a fine gold watch and chain from the passengers. Over half a century was to pass before the Union Pacific's regular passenger trains between Omaha and Ogden beat the Jarrett & Palmer special's run on a regular daily basis.

By 1883, when this Taunton consolidation No. 268 was built, Congdon stacks were standard equipment on all new locomotives. — FRED JUKES COLLECTION

Baldwin-built No. 224 at Green River shortly after it went into service in 1881. — FRED JUKES COLLECTION (BELOW) National de Tehuantepec No. 521, formerly Union Pacific No. 223, at El Paso, Texas, in 1933. Engine was not scrapped until 1956. — GERALD M. BEST COLLECTION

On January 24, 1880, the Union Pacific Company underwent a major corporate change. It was merged with the bankrupt Kansas Pacific and its subsidiary, the Denver Pacific, to form the Union Pacific Railway Company. Sidney Dillon, a Director of the company since 1868 and President of the Union Pacific Company since 1874, remained to head the new company. This was when Congdon received his new and more impressive title of General Superintendent of Motive Power and Rolling Stock. Besides the two railroads mentioned above, the Union Pacific controlled a number of smaller lines, both standard and narrow gauge, which retained their identity until 1885.

Beginning in 1881, the Union Pacific began buying what had become a standard freight locomotive for heavy service on most of the eastern railroads, the 2-8-0 or consolidation type. The three which the company had purchased in 1868 had proved very satisfactory and 37 new 2-8-0s were added to make a total of 40 of this class by 1883. They were all alike, with 50-inch drivers, 20x24-inch cylinders and weighing 51 tons, except that the last twelve from Taunton weighed 53 tons. Besides the latter, there were 15 from Baldwin and ten from Cooke, the latter firm being the successor to Danforth. Until the arrival of these 37 consolidations, the bulk of the heavy freight trains were hauled by the 4-6-0s, many of which were becoming worn out and would soon need rebuilding. One of the Baldwin consolidations, U. P. No. 223 was sold in 1905 to the National de Tehuantepec in Mexico and remained in service until 1956 after a life of 75 years. For a long time it was a familiar sight at El Paso, Texas, on the daily passenger train from Juarez.

150

The Oregon Short Line was organized by the Union Pacific Railway in April 1881, to build a connection from the Union Pacific at Granger, Wyoming, 156 miles east of Ogden, to a connection with the Oregon Railway & Navigation Company at Huntington, Oregon, a distance of 540 miles. It was built in the record time of three years, and it gave Superintendent Congdon a splendid opportunity to get rid of a lot of the oldest locomotives on the road, a total of 29 being sold to the O. S. L. in 1882. They all came back into the fold in 1885 when the O. S. L. was absorbed by the Union Pacific, but Congdon left the company soon afterwards and it was not his worry. A number of other early-day Union Pacific engines had been sold to various shortlines branching off the main line in Nebraska, to the Colorado Central and to Brigham Young's various Utah railroads. One of those sold in this manner was No. 1, formerly the *Major General Sherman*, which was purchased by the Omaha & Republican Valley in 1880. This line was taken over by the Union Pacific in 1885 and all of its engines except No. 1 were renumbered. The latter was given back its original lettering, was posed for a photograph at Omaha and was laid aside as a museum piece. Due to extensive rebuilding, it bore little resemblance to a Danforth, Cooke & Company engine of 1864. It remained in storage for some years at Omaha, and then vanished from view.

On July 1, 1885, all locomotives of railroads controlled by the Union Pacific Railway were renumbered into one group. Locomotives of some of these roads included the Colorado Central's three-foot gauge lines, the Kansas Central, Utah Northern, and Denver, South Park & Pacific, and their loco-

motives were grouped in the narrow gauge section of the new roster, from No. 1 to 299. Standard gauge locomotives were renumbered from No. 300 up, the highest numbers used being No. 1394 to 1399. No attempt is made here to chronicle the rosters of the other roads involved in this renumbering, as this is primarily the story of the locomotives of the Union Pacific main line, the eastern half of the transcontinental railroad. Motive power boss Congdon retired in December 1885, and his place was taken by Clem Hackney, who left his position as Assistant Superintendent of Motive Power of the Atchinson, Topeka & Santa Fe Railway. Under Hackney the great program of rebuilding the old engines or replacing them with new and larger machines began. The 4-4-0 type, favored by Hackney, was purchased in astonishing numbers between 1886 and 1889, no less than 191 going into service during those four years. Hackney was replaced by J. H. McConnell in 1890. Like Congdon, McConnell is best remembered for the unique smokestack he designed and with which many Union Pacific locomotives were equipped.

With the 1885 renumbering, this story ends. The disappearance of No. 1 at Omaha, the scrapping of No. 119 and the disposal of all the other engines built prior to May 10, 1869, reflected the disinterest in historic locomotives on the part of the Harriman System. When No. 119 was scrapped in 1903, Superintendent of Motive Power William R. McKeen, Jr. was more interested in standardizing all locomotives of the Harriman lines so that parts could be interchangeable, and this included the old Central Pacific, which by then was a part of the vast Harriman empire. The only reason that two historic Central Pacific locomotives eluded the scrapper

Schenectady No. 611 built in 1889, has a McConnell stack, probably installed in 1891. This locomotive is a splendid example of the 191 standardized 4-4-0s which the Union Pacific bought between 1885 and 1889. — R. H. KINDIG COLLECTION

151

was that one had been donated in 1899 to Stanford University and was not company property and in the case of the *C. P. Huntington,* it was hidden away in the Sacramento shops for years by affectionate employees who kept eagle-eyed officials from seeing it.

The last two pioneer main line engines of the Union Pacific of which there is any record were scrapped in May 1916 at Pocatello, Idaho, these being old Union Pacific Nos. 16 and 58, Grant-built 1867 4-4-0s which in their last days were Oregon Short Line Nos. 208 and 214. The Union Pacific did retain a 4-4-0 for exhibition purposes, this being No. 943, which had been built in Omaha in 1893

from parts of older locomotives, though it received a new boiler and many modern additions. As Union Pacific No. 9 it was exhibited at the Century of Progress Exposition in Chicago in 1933-1934, was returned to Omaha and scrapped in 1935. No. 947, the last surviving 4-4-0, built at the Omaha Shops in 1891, was retired in 1936 and donated to the University of Idaho where it remained on the campus together with an old Sumpter Valley mogul which had once been on the Utah Northern. The latter sported a Congdon stack, the last survivor of this type. In 1942 President William M. Jeffers of the Union Pacific headed a Presidential board organized to obtain scrap metal for wartime use. Jef-

At the left, Union Pacific No. 947, the last surviving 4-4-0, with a stack which is neither fish nor fowl, in its last months before scrapping in 1942. On the right, Sumpter Valley No. 11, former Union Pacific No. 11 and originally Utah & Northern No. 7 (3-foot gauge) on the campus of the University of Idaho. It had the last known example of the Congdon stack when scrapped in 1942. — BOTH ARTHUR PETERSEN

The monument at Promontory, erected by Southern Pacific in the 1910 era, has been moved to a new location at the Golden Spike National Historic Site, to make way for the new Visitor Center building which will be ready on May 10, 1969. — UNION PACIFIC MUSEUM

fers became the "Indian-giver" by requesting that the University of Idaho turn back both engines to the Union Pacific for scrapping. This was done and a few days later the two engines were cut up in Pocatello.

The Southern Pacific wisely failed to do anything about the *C. P. Huntington*, leaving it undisturbed on the station lawn at Sacramento. Jeffers probably did not know about the *Governor Stanford* at Palo Alto, and had he asked them to donate the engine for scrap, they would have refused. It is very odd that the United States should have made such a fetish of seeking out the few historic locomotives still in existence, when the countryside was strewn with auto wrecking establishments, many of which were never harvested for scrap iron. England, in spite of the bombings, kept intact their beautiful historic locomotives in the Kensington Museum in London and the railroad museum at

York; even the Austrians and the French managed to save their locomotive relics by hiding them away in obscure roundhouses and sheds during the war.

When the Centennial of the completion of the transcontinental railroad is celebrated on May 10, 1969, it will be in commemoration not only of the herculean feat of civil engineering, of coordination by many men, but the achievement of the steam locomotive in bringing together all the means for accomplishing this end. A century after Promontory, the passenger train is disappearing, the emphasis is on the hauling of freight, and the weight of the diesel locomotives on a present-day Union Pacific freight train exceeds that of a steam locomotive and its entire train in 1869. The Tauntons, the Schenectadys, the Grants and the Rhode Islands, just to mention a few, together with their builders are all gone, but their deeds in formulating railroad history are not forgotten. ▬

Fig. 86.
A^{14}
Front View.
Furnace Door. Scale ½".-1'

Longitudinal Section of Boiler. Scale ½".-1'

Fig. 82
Plan of Crown Bar
Scale ¼".-1'

Fig. 83
Side view of Crown Bar

Fig. 84.
Cross Section thr.
Crown Bar. rivet

Cross Section thr. Crown Bar.

Fig. 81
h
g
f

Fig. 78
Fig. 77

Fig. 56.
Cross Section.

Fig. 79. Plan

Fig. 73. Plan.

Fig. 74. Section thr. a.b.

Smoke Stack Saddle.

Cab Bracke

Cylinder Oil Cup.
on Boiler.

Fig. 65.
Section. Fig. 64. Side View.

Fig. 62.
Front View.

A^{11} Fig. 63.
Cross Section.

Fig. 76. Fig. 75.
Section. Front View.

Fig. 70
Cylinder Oil Cup

Scale 3".-1'

Fig. 71
Fig. 69.
Fig. 72

Gauge Cock
Dripper

Steam Locomotives

CENTRAL PACIFIC - UNION PACIFIC

SCALE MODEL DRAWINGS

ROSTER OF MOTIVE POWER

THE LOCOMOTIVE lists of the Central Pacific and the Union Pacific Railroads follow. Where known, the construction number of each locomotive is given, the year and month built, and the principal dimensions at the time it went into service. These dimensions include the driving wheel diameter including the tire, the cylinder bore and stroke, and the total weight of the engine, not including the tender. It is realized that after the two railroads operated for several years, considerable rebuilding and the addition of air brake equipment changed the dimensions of some of the locomotives. For this reason and because of lack of space, the weight on drivers and such variable items as boiler pressure and tractive effort and changes in weights or dimensions after rebuilding are not included.

All Central Pacific locomotives were renumbered in 1891 and those still in existence in 1901 were again renumbered. A few were later renumbered once again in 1906. The first general renumbering of Union Pacific locomotives was June 1885, followed by another in 1915. Between those dates, a few of the 4-4-0 type engines received different numbers in 1888, and during the rebuilding of many of them between that date and 1895, the numbers were changed. Very few engines in existence prior to 1885 reached the 1915 renumbering, and none of those on the original roster.

In both lists, the names of several locomotive builders may differ from previously published lists. One of the companies which built so many engines for both railroads started as Danforth, Cooke & Company in 1852, was reorganized as the Danforth Locomotive & Machine Works in 1865, and on April 28, 1882, it became the Cooke Locomotive & Machine Works. These corporate names are observed throughout both lists, even though some company records lump together the engines built under all three names as Cooke, or Danforth, or Danforth & Cooke. The other case in point is the firm which began business as Hinkley & Drury in 1841, changed its name to Boston Locomotive Works in 1848, became Hinkley & Williams from 1858 to 1872 and was finally known as the Hinkley Locomotive Company.

There is a strange gap in the Union Pacific roster which includes numbers 147 to 155. These were obviously vacant until 1874 and 1875 at which time they were filled with new Taunton engines. These road numbers were probably set aside for a group of locomotives which were ordered, but for reasons not known today were not delivered. This gap, besides the one previously mentioned between 133 and 140, remained for over five years, leaving the total number of locomotives in use at a considerably lower figure than the highest road number, No. 165, reached in 1870.

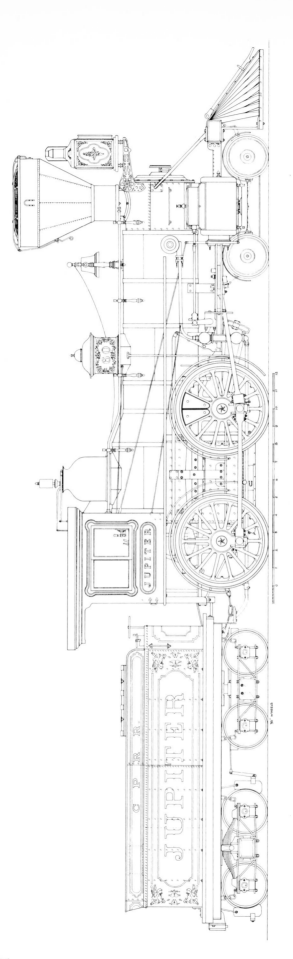

Jupiter No. 60
CENTRAL PACIFIC

The *Jupiter* was the product of the only locomotive builder of any importance in New York State in 1868. It represented 17 years of development of the 4-4-0 type locomotive by the Schenectady Locomotive Works, which concentrated its efforts on this eight-wheel design known as the American type. The *Jupiter* was the first of 28 locomotives of its type ordered from Schenectady during the Central Pacific's construction days and was designed as an all-purpose locomotive for either freight or passenger service

Since no original drawings of the *Jupiter* have survived, and drawings of the engine and tender suitable for use in scale model building of the locomotive were needed for a contest held by the National Model Railroad Association, draftsman William Plunkett has produced the remarkably accurate drawings shown on these pages, using photographs for most of his source material.

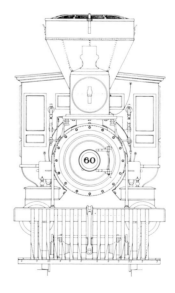
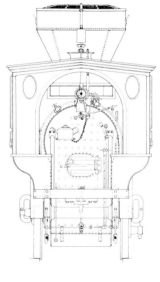

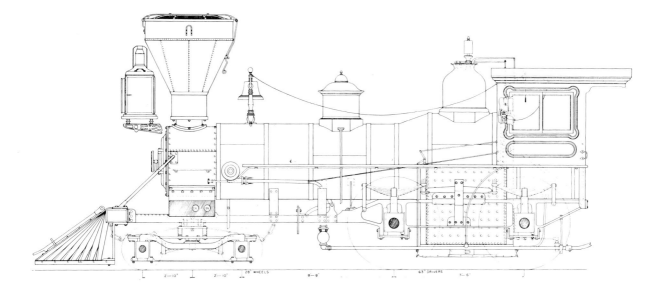

PRINCIPAL DIMENSIONS

Builder	Schenectady Locomotive Works
Type	4-4-0 American
Diameter of Cylinders and Stroke	16 x 24-inch
Air Brakes	None
Driving Wheels	60-inch including 1½-inch tires, 57-inch wheel centers
Boiler	Shell — 50-inch outside diameter
	Firebox — 66¾ x 36 x 66-inch
	Flues — 179 of 2-inch diameter and 11 feet long
Wheelbase	Rigid — 7 feet 6 inches
	Total — 21 feet 6½ inches
Weight On Drivers	39,000 pounds
Total Engine Weight	65,400 pounds
Water Tank Capacity	2,000 gallons, approx.
Fuel	Wood

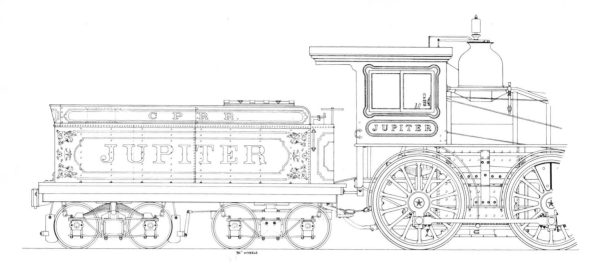

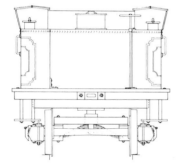
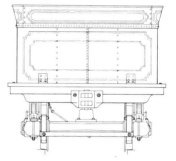

CENTRAL PACIFIC—No. 60 *Jupiter*
Locomotive Color Data

BOILER JACKET—Russian Iron color, which was a light grey-blue. *CAB*—Authorities disagree. Some believe it was dark reddish stained walnut; others say it was wine red, the same color as the tender. Gold striping around the moulding and edges of the cab. *FIREBOX, SMOKEBOX AND HEADLIGHT BRACKETS* — Greyish black. *STACK*—Semi-gloss stovepipe enamel black. *CYLINDER HEAD COVERS, JACKET, STEAMCHEST SIDES AND TOP*—Polished brass. *HEADLIGHT CASE*—Wine red. *FRONT NUMBER PLATE*—Polished brass edge with wine red center, numerals *60* in gold leaf. *SAND BOX, STEAM DOME BASE AND RUNNING BOARDS*—Wine red. *STEAM DOME COVER*—Polished brass. *BOILER JACKET BANDS, HANDRAILS AND POSTS, BELL, CHECK VALVES AND CROSSHEAD PUMPS, HAND BRACKETS AND WHISTLE*—Polished brass. *BELL FRAME PEDESTALS*—Polished brass. *BELL YOKE AND BASE*—Black. *DRIVING AND ENGINE TRUCK WHEELS, PILOT*—Crimson with no striping on the tires. *RODS, EQUALIZERS, BOILER BRACES, MOVING PARTS*—Polished steel. *TENDER TANK AND FRAME* —Wine red. *TENDER TRUCKS*—Black with white outline around the edges of the journals. *STRIPING, LETTERING AND FILIGREE WORK ON TANK*—Gold leaf with dark shading.

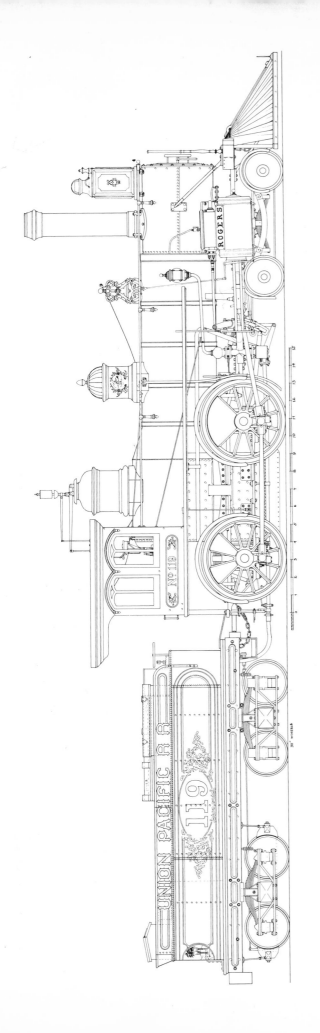

No. 119
UNION PACIFIC

Union Pacific No. 119 was built by the Rogers Locomotive Works at Paterson, New Jersey, builders of 31 years experience, during which time the company turned out over 1,500 locomotives of many types. The Union Pacific bought 24 Rogers locomotives of the American type before the railroad was completed, and No. 119 was one of five identical engines with small drivers, designed for freight service or for hauling passenger trains on heavy grades. Though different from the *Jupiter* in external appearance, it bore a remarkable similarity in such dimensions as the boiler, wheelbase, cylinders, etc. As no drawings of the original engine were preserved by the Union Pacific, it was again necessary for draftsman William Plunkett to do the same painstaking research required for the *Jupiter's* drawings, in turning out those of Union Pacific No. 119, which are reproduced in 3/16-inch scale. Drawings are copyrighted by the National Model Railroad Association and reproduced through the courtesy of the N.M.R.A. and William Plunkett.

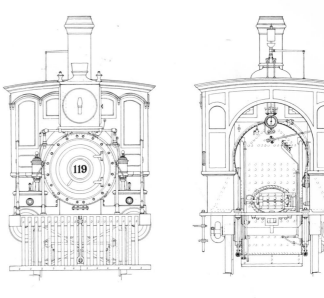

SCALE: 3/16 inch to the foot

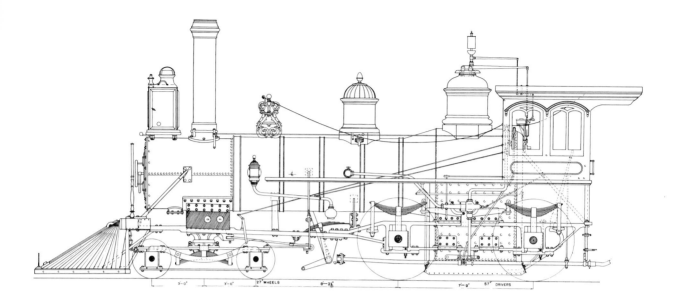

PRINCIPAL DIMENSIONS

Builder	Rogers Locomotive and Machine Works
Type	4-4-0 American
Class	BK-4
Diameter of Cylinders and Stroke	16 x 24-inch
Air Brakes	None
Driving Wheels	54-inch including 2½-inch tires, 49-inch centers
Boiler	Shell — 50-inch outside diameter
	Firebox — 66¾ x 36 x 66-inch
	Flues — 179, 2-inch diameter and 11 feet long
Wheelbase	Rigid — 7 feet 9 inches
	Total — 21 feet 9 inches
	Engine & Tender combined 41 feet 10 inches
Weight On Drivers	41,800 pounds
Total Engine Weight	68,400 pounds
Water Tank Capacity	1,942 gallons, approx.
Fuel	Coal
Fuel Tender Capacity	6 tons

SCALE: 3/16 inch to the foot

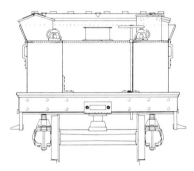

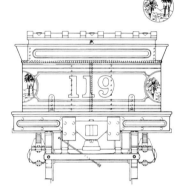

UNION PACIFIC—No. 119
Locomotive Color Data

BOILER JACKET—Russian Iron color. *CAB*—Dark reddish walnut. *FIREBOX, SMOKEBOX*—Greyish black. *SMOKESTACK*—Stovepipe enamel black. *CAP ON THE STACK*—Polished brass or copper, probably painted black at the time of the Golden Spike ceremony. *CYLINDERS AND STEAMCHESTS*—Polished brass at the factory, but cylinder jackets and steamchest sides either tarnished brass or painted at the time of the ceremony. *FRONT NUMBER PLATE*—Polished brass edge with wine red center, numerals "119" in gold leaf. *HEADLIGHT CASE AND BELL FRAME*—Crimson. *HEADLIGHT PLATFORM*—Trimmed in half-round polished brass. *SAND-BOX AND STEAM DOME BASE*—Wine red. *STEAM DOME, BELL, WHISTLE, CROSSHEAD PUMPS, CHECK VALVES, FLAG HOLDERS ON THE PILOT BEAM, HANDRAILS, POSTS, BOILER JACKET BANDS*—Polished brass. *DRIVING AND ENGINE TRUCK WHEELS*—Crimson with white tires, fender edging and axle centers. *ALL MOVING PARTS SUCH AS RODS, ETC.*—Polished steel. *STRIPING, LETTERING AND NUMBERS*—Gold leaf with light red shading. *TENDER TANK AND FRAME*—Wine red. *TENDER TRUCKS*—Black. *MURALS ON THE REAR CORNERS OF THE TANK*—Palmetto and date palms with orange groves, road and mountain background. *MURAL ON THE SAND BOX*—Illustrates a man sowing grain in a field.

Central Pacific's *Bison* No. 57 was one of the earliest ten-wheel type built by the Schenectady Locomotive Works. Designed as a freight engine, it served the road for 42 years. — GOLDEN WEST COLLECTION

CENTRAL PACIFIC RAILROAD

LIST OF LOCOMOTIVES, 1863—1891

No.	Names	Type	Builder and Construction No.		Year Built	Date in Service	Dimensions Dr.—Cyls.—Wt.	1891 No.	Remarks
1	Gov. Stanford	4-4-0	R. Norris & Son	1040	1862	11-9-63	57-16x22-56000	1174	Note 1
2	Pacific	4-4-0	Wm. Mason	141	9-1863	3-25-64	60-16x24-61000	1189	Note 2
3	C. P. Huntington	4-2-4	Danforth-Cooke		1863	4-15-64	54-11x15-39000	1001	Note 3
4	T. D. Judah	4-2-2	Danforth-Cooke		1863	4-9-64	54-11x15-30000		Sold 1889 Wellington Coll. Co.
5	Atlantic	4-4-0	Wm. Mason	145	11-1863	6-21-64	60-15x22-58000	1006	Scrapped 3-1894
6	Conness	4-6-0	Wm. Mason	153	2-1864	3-16-65	48-17x24-70500	1509	To #2000 in 1901
7	A. A. Sargent	4-4-0	Booth & Co.	3	11-1865	12-16-65	60-16x24-56500	1190	To 2nd #1214 and 1487
8	Nevada	2-6-0	Danforth L&M		7-1865	3-23-66	48-18x22-70000	1522	Scrapped 1-1900
9	Utah	2-6-0	Danforth L&M		7-1865	3-24-66	48-18x22-70000	1264	Note 4
10	Humboldt	2-6-0	Danforth L&M		7-1865	4-15-66	48-18x22-70000		Rebuilt 4-4-0 on 2-2-71. Scrapped 1889.
11	Arctic	4-4-0	Wm. Mason	212	9-1865	6-15-66	60-15x22-58000	1120	Scrapped 6-1892.
12	Truckee	4-6-0	Wm. Mason	217	11-1865	7-1-66	48-17x24-70500	1510	To 0-6-0 #1054 on 2-1896.
13	Hercules	2-6-0	Danforth L&M		12-1865	7-17-66	48-18x22-70000	1266	Rebuilt 4-4-0 on 10-1871, to #1514.
14	Oneonta	2-6-0	Danforth L&M		12-1865	11-24-66	48-18x22-70000	1267	Rebuilt 4-4-0 on 6-24-71, scrapped 8-99.
15	Washoe	2-6-0	Danforth L&M		12-1865	11-15-66	48-18x22-70000		Note 5
16	Owyhee	4-6-0	Wm. Mason	224	2-1866	10-25-66	48-17x24-70500	1511	Scrapped 1-1893.
17	Idaho	4-6-0	Wm. Mason	223	2-1866	10-25-66	48-17x24-70500		Note 6.
18	Piute	4-6-0	Danforth L&M		12-1865	11-5-66	48-18x22-70000		Scrapped in 1884.
19	Carson	4-6-0	Danforth L&M		12-1865	11-16-66	48-18x22-70000		Scrapped in 1885.
20	Amazon	4-6-0	McKay & Aldus		7-1866	2-26-67	54-17x24-73800	1523	To 0-6-0 No. 1048 in 1-1895.
21	Tamaroo	4-6-0	McKay & Aldus		8-1866	8-15-67	54-17x24-73800	1524	To 0-6-0 No. 1055 in 3-1896.
22	Auburn	4-6-0	McKay & Aldus		8-1866	8-20-67	54-17x24-73800	1525	Scrapped 11-1892.
23	Mono	4-6-0	McKay & Aldus		8-1866	8-25-67	54-17x24-72300	1526	To 0-6-0 No. 1051 in 1-1896.
24	Montana	4-6-0	McKay & Aldus		8-1866	10-25-67	54-17x24-74000	1527	To 0-6-0 No. 1065 in 11-1897.
25	Yuba	4-6-0	McKay & Aldus		8-1866	10-17-67	54-17x24-73800		Note 7
26	Samson	0-6-0T	Danforth L&M		2-1867	1-30-68	45-17x22-73800	1012	Later 48-70,000, scrapped 1-1900.
27	Goliah	0-6-0T	Danforth L&M		2-1867	2-10-68	45-17x22-73800	1013	Later 48 inch driv. Same No. 1901.
28	Gold Run	4-4-0	McKay & Aldus		2-1867	10-25-67	60-16x24-62100	1191	Scrapped 12-20-1898.
29	Antelope	4-4-0	McKay & Aldus		2-1867	8-14-68	60-16x24-62100	1192	Scrapped 4-1900.
30	Tahoe	4-4-0	R. Norris & Son		5-1867	2-7-68	60-16x22-60100		Scrapped 9-1887.
31	Klamath	4-4-0	R. Norris & Son		5-1867	2-24-68	60-16x22-60100		Note 8.
32	Ajax	0-6-0T	New Jersey L&M	493	5-1867	2-3-68	48-16x24	1257	Note 9.
33	Achilles	0-6-0T	New Jersey L&M		5-1867	2-20-68	48-16x24	1258	Note 10.
34	El Dorado	4-4-0	R. Norris & Son		6-1867	7-17-68	54-17x24-66250	1268	Note 11.
35	Boise	4-4-0	R. Norris & Son		6-1867	7-29-68	54-17x24-66250	1269	Note 12.
36	Shoshone	4-4-0	R. Norris & Son		6-1867	*	60-16x22-60100		Note 13.
37	Mohave	4-4-0	R. Norris & Son		6-1867	*	60-16x22-60100	1175	2nd No. 1208.
38	Ogdensburg	4-6-0	McKay & Aldus		7-1867	8-5-68	54-18x24-73800	1528	To 0-6-0 No. 1071 in 11-1899.
39	Malone	4-6-0	McKay & Aldus		7-1867	5-9-68	54-18x24-73800	1529	Note 14.
40	Solano	4-4-0	R. Norris & Son		7-1860	9-67	54-14x24-58000	1007	Note 15.
41	Stanislaus	4-4-0	R. Norris & Son		6-1867	1-30-68	54-14x24-58000	1003	Note 16.
42	Tuolumne	4-4-0	R. Norris & Son		7-1860	9-67	60-14x24-58000	1004	Note 17.
43	Tulare	4-4-0	R. Norris & Son		7-1860	9-67	60-14x24-58000	1005	Note 18.
44	Colossus	4-6-0	McKay & Aldus		8-1867	*	54-18x24-72300	1530	To 0-6-0 No. 1060 in 6-1897.
45	Majestic	4-6-0	McKay & Aldus		8-1867	*	54-18x24-72300	1531	To 0-6-0 No. 1052 in 2-1896.
46	Unicorn	4-6-0	McKay & Aldus		9-1867	*	48-17x22	1259	Note 19.
47	Griffin	4-6-0	McKay & Aldus		9-1867	*	48-17x22	1260	Note 20.
48	Toiyabe	4-6-0T	Grant	553	12-1867	9-23-68	48-17x22-69000	1366	Note 21.
49	Toquima	4-6-0T	Grant	554	12-1867	8-27-68	48-17x22-69000	1261	Note 22.
50	Champion	4-4-0	McKay & Aldus		10-1867	6-26-68	60-16x24-62100	1176	Became 2nd No. 1209.
51	Climax	4-4-0	McKay & Aldus		10-1867	*	60-16x24-62100	1177	Scrapped 12-20-1898.
52	Tip Top	4-4-0	McKay & Aldus		10-1867	7-9-68	60-16x24-62100	1271	Scrapped 1-15-1900.
53	Summit	4-4-0	McKay & Aldus		10-1867	8-11-68	60-16x24-62100	1194	Scrapped 1-1900.
54	Red Deer	4-4-0	McKay & Aldus		10-1867	2-28-69	60-16x24-62100	1178	Scrapped 8-28-1899.
55	Black Deer	4-4-0	McKay & Aldus		10-1867	3-28-69	60-16x24-62100		Note 23.
56	Grizzly	4-6-0	Schenectady	493	5-1868	12-12-68	48-18x24-71250	1532	Scrapped 1-4-1894.
57	Bison	4-6-0	Schenectady	576	6-1868	12-31-68	48-18x24-71250	1533	Became No. 2020
58	Placer	4-6-0	Schenectady	495	7-1868	2-21-69	48-18x24-71250	1534	Became No. 2021.
59	Pluto	4-6-0	Schenectady	494	7-1868	*	48-18x24-71250	1535	Became No. 2022.
60	Jupiter	4-4-0	Schenectady	505	9-1868	3-20-69	60-16x24-65500	1195	Note 24.

* — No data on "in service" date.

No.	Names	Type	Builder and Construction No.		Year Built	Date in Service	Dimensions Dr.—Cyls.—Wt.	1891 No.	Remarks
61	Storm	4-4-0	Schenectady	510	9-1868	4-5-69	60-16x24-65500	1273	Became No. 1517
62	Whirlwind	4-4-0	Schenectady	511	9-1868	4-4-69	60-16x24-65500	1196	Scrapped 4-1900.
63	Leviathan	4-4-0	Schenectady	512	9-1868	4-5-69	60-16x24-65500	1197	Became 2nd No. 1216 - 1489.
64	Emigrant	4-4-0	McKay & Aldus		2-1868	*	60-16x24-62100	1198	Became 2nd No. 1217.
65	Mikado	4-4-0	McKay & Aldus		2-1868	10-13-68	60-16x24-62100	1199	Scrapped 1-1900.
66	Tycoon	4-4-0	McKay & Aldus		3-1868	10-13-68	60-16x24-62100	1200	Became 2nd No. 1218 - 1490.
67	Hector	4-4-0	McKay & Aldus		3-1868	*	60-16x24-62100	1201	Scrapped 7-1895.
68	Peoquop	4-6-0	McKay & Aldus		4-1868	11-24-68	54-18x24-73800	1536	Became No. 2001.
69	Vulcan	4-6-0	McKay & Aldus		4-1868	*	54-18x24-73800	1537	Note 25.
70	Saturn	4-6-0	McKay & Aldus		5-1868	8-10-69	54-18x24-73800	1538	Became No. 2003.
71	Vesuvius	4-6-0	McKay & Aldus		5-1868	6-30-69	54-18x24-73800	1539	Scrapped 5-1893.
72	Niagara	4-6-0	Danforth L&M		3-1868	7-15-69	56-18x24-72300	1540	Scrapped 1898-1900 ?
73	Terrible	4-6-0	Danforth L&M		3-1868	9-27-68	56-18x24-72300	1541	Scrapped 1898 - 1900 ?
74	Dragon	4-6-0	Danforth L&M		4-1868	7-15-69	56-18x24-72300	1542	Scrapped 7-1895.
75	Growler	4-6-0	Danforth L&M		4-1868	11-5-68	56-18x24-72300	1543	Became No. 2009 - 1012 (0-6-0T).
76	Carrier	4-4-0	Rhode Island	50	4-1868	11-23-68	60-16x24-72300	1274	Scrapped 8-28-1899.
77	Confucius	4-4-0	Rhode Island	51	4-1868	11-29-68	60-16x24-72300	1202	Scrapped 1-1898.
78	Mars	4-4-0	Rhode Island	52	4-1868	11-22-68	60-16x24-72300	1203	Became 2nd No. 1224 - 1495.
79	Apollo	4-4-0	Rhode Island	53	4-1868	11-23-68	60-16x24-62100	1204	Became 2nd No. 1225 — 2nd No. 1366.
80	Phil Sheridan	4-4-0	Danforth L&M		2-1868	9-27-68	60-16x24-66400	1205	Became 2nd No. 1226 - 1496.
81	U. S. Grant	4-4-0	Danforth L&M		2-1868	9-27-68	60-16x24-66400	1206	Same No. in 1901.
82	Buffalo	4-6-0	Rogers	1513	4-1868	11-5-68	54-18x24-77450	1544	Scrapped 3-3-1894.
83	Mountaineer	4-6-0	Rogers	1514	4-1868	11-5-68	54-18x24-77450	1545	Scrapped 2-1893
84	Gazelle	4-4-0	Schenectady	480	3-1868	10-5-68	60-16x24-65450	1207	Scrapped 8-28-1899.
85	White Bear	4-6-0	Rogers	1515	5-1868	11-5-68	54-18x24-77450	1546	Scrapped 3-3-1894.
86	Gorilla	4-6-0	Rogers	1516	5-1868	12-14-68	54-18x24-77450	1547	Scrapped 10-6-1899.
87	Tempest	4-6-0	Rogers	1517	5-1868	12-29-68	54-18x24-77450	1548	Scrapped 8-28-1899.
88	Hurricane	4-6-0	Rhode Island	56	6-1868	2-27-69	54-18x24-72300	1549	To 0-6-0 No. 1067 on 9-1899.
89	Giant	4-6-0	Rhode Isalnd	57	6-1868	*	54-18x24-72300	1550	To 0-6-0 No. 1058 2-1897.
90	Gladiator	4-6-0	Rhode Island	58	6-1868	3-10-69	54-18x24-72300	1551	To 0-6-0 No. 1049 1-1895.
91	Tiger	4-6-0	Rhode Island	59	7-1868	3-14-69	54-18x24-72300	1552	To 0-6-0 No. 1059 on 2-1897.
92	Verdi	4-6-0	Rhode Island	60	7-1868	3-12-69	54-18x24-72300	1553	To 0-6-0 No. 1050 on 1-1895.
93	Oronoco	4-4-0	R. Norris & Son		7-1860	2-20-69	60-14x24-52000		Note 26.
94	Eclipse	4-4-0	McKay & Aldus		7-1868	1-27-69	60-16x24-62100	1208	Scrapped 3-2-1901.
95	Driver	4-4-0	McKay & Aldus		7-1868	*	60-15x24-60000	1164	Scrapped 2-18-1893.
96	Clipper	4-4-0	McKay & Aldus		7-1868	*	60-15x24-60000	1165	Note 27.
97	Racer	4-4-0	McKay & Aldus		7-1868	1-22-69	60-15x24-60000		Note 28.
98	Rattler	4-4-0	McKay & Aldus		7-1868	2-11-69	60-15x24-60000	1209	Became 2nd No. 1219 - 1491.
99	Ranger	4-4-0	McKay & Aldus		7-1868	2-4-69	60-15x24-60000		Note 29.
100	Rover	4-4-0	McKay & Aldus		7-1868	2-8-69	60-15x24-60000		To S.P. No. 16 (1872).
101	Hunter	4-4-0	McKay & Aldus		7-1868	2-28-69	60-15x24-60000	1166	Scrapped 6-1895.
102	Runner	4-4-0	Rogers	1592	8-1868	2-20-69	56-15x22-60250	1122	Scrapped 7-1892.
103	Rusher	4-4-0	Rogers	1593	8-1868	2-14-69	56-15x22-60250	1123	Sold 7-1892.
104	Rambler	4-4-0	Rogers	1594	8-1868	3-21-69	56-15x22-60250		Note 30.
105	Roller	4-4-0	Rogers	1598	8-1868	3-16-69	56-15x22-60250		Note 31.
106	Pacer	4-4-0	Rogers	1600	9-1868	3-30-69	56-15x22-60250	1124	Sold 1891-1896 ?
107	Courser	4-4-0	Rogers	1601	9-1868	4-1-69	56-15x22-60250	1125	Sold 1891-1896 ?
108	Stager	4-4-0	Rogers	1604	9-1868	12-24-68	56-15x22-60250	1126	Sold 1891-1896 ?
109	Flier	4-4-0	Rogers	1605	9-1868	1-5-69	56-15x22-60250		Note 32.
110	Fire Fly	4-4-0	Rogers	1606	9-1868	1-20-69	56-15x22-60250		Note 33.
111	Chamois	4-4-0	Rogers	1607	10-1868	1-25-69	56-15x22-60250	1127	Scrapped 4-1893.
112	Hawk	4-4-0	Danforth L&M		7-1868	2-22-69	56-15x22-60250	1128	Scrapped 9-1891.
113	Falcon	4-4-0	Danforth L&M		7-1868	2-13-69	56-15x22-60250	1129	Scrapped 1895.
114	Heron	4-4-0	Danforth L&M		7-1868	3-20-69	56-15x22-60250	1130	Sold 6-1892.
115	Eagle	4-4-0	Danforth L&M		7-1868	3-19-69	56-15x22-60250		Wrecked & rebuilt to 2nd No. 176.
116	White Eagle	4-4-0	Danforth L&M		7-1868	3-1-69	56-15x22-60250	1131	Scrapped 9-1891.
117	Red Eagle	4-4-0	Danforth L&M		7-1868	4-4-69	56-15x22-60250		Note 34.
118	Grey Eagle	4-4-0	Danforth L&M		8-1868	1-25-69	56-15x22-60250	1133	Scrapped 8-1899.
119	Golden Eagle	4-4-0	Danforth L&M		8-1868	1-26-69	56-15x22-60250	1134	Scrapped 9-1891.
120	Bald Eagle	4-4-0	Danforth L&M		8-1868	2-5-69	56-15x22-60250	1135	Scrapped 9-1892.

— No data on "in service" date.

Principal actor in the dramatic head-on collision at Blue Canyon, November 4, 1870, was the former *Buffalo* No. 82. The locomotive looks none the worse for its experience in this 1878 photograph at Truckee. — GERALD M. BEST COLLECTION

Engines were still burning wood as late as 1888 when this photograph was taken at the Rocklin engine terminal. Engines are No. 86 (ex *Gorilla*), No. 56 (ex *Grizzly*), and Southern Pacific No. 329, newly arrived from the Rhode Island Works. — GUY L. DUNSCOMB COLLECTION

Two of Steven's handsome 4-4-0's turned out by the Sacramento Shops in 1886 are shown at the top and left. (BELOW) Central Pacific No. 130 *Favorite*, the last of the Mc Kay & Aldus engines at Merced on the Southern Pacific in 1870.
— GERALD M. BEST COLLECTION

No.	Names	Type	Builder and Construction No.		Year Built	Date in Service	Dimensions Dr.—Cyls.—Wt.	1891 No.	Remarks
121	American Eagle	4-4-0	Danforth L&M		8-1868	4-18-69	56-15x22-60250		Note 35.
122	Willamette	4-4-0	Globe Loco. Wks.		1865	4-27-69	60-16x24-63500		Retired 1886. Note 36.
123	Geo. L. Woods	4-4-0	Globe Loco. Wks.		1865	8-28-68	60-16x24-63500		Retired 1886. Note 36.
124	Umpqua	4-4-0	Globe Loco. Wks.		1865	8-21-68	60-16x24-63500	1212	Note 36, same No. in 1901.
125	J. R. Moores	4-4-0	Globe Loco. Wks.		1865	9-1-68	60-16x24-63500		Retired 1886. Note 36.
126	Swiftsure	4-4-0	McKay & Aldus		8-1868	3-14-69	56-15x22-60000	1136	Scrapped 6-1892.
127	Mercury	4-4-0	McKay & Aldus		8-1868	3-21-69	56-15x22-60000	1137	Became 2nd No. 1200 - 1484.
128	Herald	4-4-0	McKay & Aldus		8-1868	3-19-69	56-15x22-60000	1138	Scrapped 9-1891.
129	Fleetfoot	4-4-0	McKay & Aldus		8-1868	3-28-69	56-15x22-60000	1139	Scrapped 7-1895.
130	Favorite	4-4-0	McKay & Aldus		8-1868	4-4-69	56-15x22-60000	1140	Scrapped 4-1894.
131	Greyhound	4-4-0	Rhode Island	76	11-1868	2-23-69	56-15x22-60000		Sold 1-1872.
132	Deerhound	4-4-0	Rhode Island	77	11-1868	2-18-69	56-15x22-60000		Note 37.
133	Foxhound	4-4-0	Rhode Island	78	11-1868	2-28-69	56-15x22-60000	1141	Scrapped 1891.
134	Trapper	4-4-0	Rhode Island	79	11-1868	3-2-69	56-15x22-60000	1142	Scrapped 1891.
135	Peeler	4-4-0	Rhode Island	80	11-1868	4-21-69	56-15x22-60000		Note 38.
136	Swallow	4-4-0	Rhode Island	82	12-1868	*	60-16x24-62100	1213	Same No. in 1891.
137	Lark	4-4-0	Rhode Island	81	12-1868	4-30-69	60-16x24-62100	1214	Scrapped 7-1895.
138	Blue Bird	4-4-0	Schenectady	513	10-1868	12-30-68	56-15x22-60100	1143	Scrapped 9-1894.
139	Blue Jay	4-4-0	Schenectady	514	10-1868	1-14-69	56-15x22-60100	1144	Scrapped 9-1894.
140	Ostrich	4-4-0	Schenectady	515	10-1868	12-30-68	56-15x22-60100	1145	Scrapped 9-1891
141	Magpie	4-4-0	Schenectady	516	10-1868	4-18-69	56-15x22-60100	1146	Scrapped 9-28-1892.
142	Raven	4-4-0	Schenectady	517	10-1868	4-24-69	56-15x22-60100		Sold to S.P. as No. 19.
143	Swan	4-4-0	Schenectady	518	10-1868	4-23-69	56-15x22-60100	1147	Scrapped 9-1891.
144	Crane	4-4-0	Schenectady	519	10-1868	5-2-69	56-15x22-60100	1148	Scrapped 1891.
145	Dart	4-4-0	Schenectady	520	10-1868	4-30-69	56-15x22-60100	1149	Scrapped 1891.
146	Arrow	4-4-0	Schenectady	521	11-1868	5-4-69	56-15x22-60100	1150	Scrapped 1891.
147	Reindeer	4-4-0	Schenectady	522	11-1868	*	56-15x22-60100	1151	Scrapped 4-1894.
148	Red Fox	4-4-0	Schenectady	530	11-1868	*	60-16x24-65500	1215	Scrapped 8-8-1900.
149	Black Fox	4-4-0	Schenectady	531	12-1868	7-9-69	60-16x24-65500	1216	Scrapped 1895.
150	Grey Fox	4-4-0	Schenectady	532	1-1869	*	60-16x24-65500	1217	Scrapped 8-1899.
151	Yellow Fox	4-4-0	Schenectady	533	1-1869	*	60-16x24-65500	1218	Scrapped 7-1895.
152	White Fox	4-4-0	Schenectady	534	1-1869	*	60-16x24-65500	1219	Scrapped 8-1899.
153	Young America	4-4-0	Rhode Island	83	12-1868	11-21-69	60-16x24-62100	1220	Became No. 1492.
154	Charmer	4-4-0	Rhode Island	84	12-1868	11-21-69	60-16x24-62100	1221	Same No. in 1901.
155	Sunbeam	4-4-0	Rhode Island	87	12-1868	11-26-69	60-16x24-62100	1222	Became No. 1493.
156	Success	4-4-0	Rogers	1654	4-1869	5-24-69	60-16x24-67700	1223	Became No. 1494.
157	Excelsior	4-4-0	Rogers	1659	4-1869	5-24-69	60-16x24-67700	1224	Scrapped 8-1896.
158	Eureka	4-4-0	Schenectady	558	5-1869	6-13-69	60-16x24-65500	1225	Scrapped 1-1901.
159	Diana	4-4-0	Schenectady	559	5-1869	6-19-69	60-16x24-65500	1226	Scrapped 8-1899.
160	Sultana	4-4-0	Schenectady	565	6-1869	8-5-69	60-16x24-65500	1227	Scrapped 1895.
161	Juno	4-4-0	Schenectady	566	6-1869	8-5-69	60-16x24-65450	1228	Same No. in 1901.
162	Flash	4-4-0	Schenectady	571	7-1869	8-6-69	60-16x24-65450	1229	Scrapped 12-1899.
163	Fancy	4-4-0	Schenectady	572	7-1869	8-6-69	60-16x24-65450	1230	Scrapped 1-1900.
164	Esmeralda	4-4-0	Danforth L&M		11-1868	4-30-69	60-16x22-66000	1179	Became 2nd No. 1210 - 1486.
165	Aurora	4-4-0	Danforth L&M		11-1868	5-2-69	60-16x22-66000	1180	Scrapped 6-1893.
166	No name	4-4-0	Schenectady	573	7-1869	8-20-69	60-12x22-40000		Sold 1869.
167	San Leandro	4-4-0	Schenectady	574	7-1869	8-20-69	60-12x22-40000		Sold 10-1873.
168	Sacramento	4-4-0	Wm. Mason	239	9-1866	1-68	60-15x22-60000		Note 39.
169	Stockton	4-4-0	Baldwin	1519	9-1866	1-68	60-14x22-60000		Note 40.
170	Santa Clara	4-4-0	Baldwin	1512	8-1866	12-24-67	60-14x22-60000		Note 41.
171	San Mateo	4-4-0	Baldwin	1513	8-1866	1-68	60-14x22-60000		Note 42.
172	Merced	4-4-0	Norris-Lanc.	37	1865	8-20-68	66-16½x24-66250		Note 43.
173	Sonoma	4-4-0	Norris-Lanc.	13	1864	1-68	66-16½x24-66250		Note 44.
174	San Jose	4-4-0	Wm. Mason	238	9-1866	1-68	60-15x22-60000		Note 45.
175	William Penn	4-2-0	Norris-Lanc.		1865	8-5-68	54-10x18-24000		Note 46.
176	J. G. Kellogg	4-4-0	S.F.&Alameda R.R.		1864		60-11x22-42700		Note 47.
177	F. D. Atherton	4-4-0	Grant		1868		60-12x22-		Note 48.
178	Liberty	4-4-0	S.F.&Oakland R.R.		1863		54-11x22-42000		Note 49.
179	Oakland	4-2-0	Danforth, Cooke		1864		60-11x15-		Note 50.

* — No data on "in service" date.

No.	Type	Builder and Construction No.		Date Built	Dimensions Dr.—Cyls.—Wt.	1891 No.	Later Nos.	Remarks
180	4-4-0	Rogers	2078	10-1872	56-17x24-72100	1287	1524	
181	4-4-0	Rogers	2084	10-1872	56-17x24-72100	1288	2nd 1369	
182	4-4-0	Rogers	2085	10-1872	56-17x24-72100	1289		
183	4-4-0	Rogers		11-1872	56-17x24-72100	1290	2nd 1311	
184	4-4-0	Rogers	2093	11-1872	56-17x24-72100	1291	2nd 1325	
185	4-4-0	Rhode Island	77	11-1868	56-15x22-60000	1155		Note 51
186	4-4-0	C. P. Shops, Sacto.	11	1-1874	56-17x24-74000	1292	1525	
187	4-4-0	C. P. Shops, Sacto.	8	10-1873	60-18x24-74000	1367		Scrapped 8-6-1899.
188	4-4-0	C. P. Shops, Sacto.	7	10-1873	60-18x24-74000	1368		Scrapped 8-28-1899.
189	4-6-0	Schenectady	981	5-1875	54-18x24-79150	1554	2023	
190	4-6-0	Schenectady	982	5-1875	54-18x24-79150	1555		Rebuilt to 0-6-0 No. 1068 on 9-1899.
191	4-6-0	Schenectady	983	5-1875	54-18x24-79510	1556		Scrapped 5-1-1891.
192	4-6-0	Schenectady	984	5-1875	54-18x24-79510	1557	2013	
193	4-6-0	Schenectady	985	6-1875	54-18x24-79510	1558	2024	
194	4-6-0	Schenectady	986	6-1875	54-18x24-79510	1559	2025	
195	4-6-0	Schenectady	987	6-1875	60-18x24-80000	1560	2014	
196	4-6-0	Schenectady	988	7-1875	60-18x24-80000	1561	2026	
197	4-6-0	Schenectady	989	7-1875	60-18x24-80000	1562	2027	
198	4-6-0	Schenectady	990	7-1875	60-18x24-80000	1563	2015	
199	4-6-0	Schenectady	991	7-1875	60-18x24-80000	1564		Rebuilt to 0-6-0 No. 1061 on 4-1898.
200	4-6-0	Schenectady	992	8-1875	60-18x24-80000	1565	2028	
201	4-6-0	Danforth L&M	956	1875	54-18x24-71500	1566		Scrapped 1898-1900 ?
202	4-6-0	Danforth L&M	1006	1875	54-18x24-71500	1567		Scrapped 1898-1900 ?
203	4-6-0	Danforth L&M	1007	1875	54-18x24-71500	1568		Scrapped 3-3-1894.
204	4-6-0	Danforth L&M	1020	3-1876	54-18x24-71500	1569	2004	
205	4-6-0	Danforth L&M	1021	3-1876	54-18x24-71500	1570	2005	
206	4-6-0	Danforth L&M	1022	3-1876	54-18x24-71500	1571		Rebuilt to 0-6-0 No. 1056 on 3-1896.
207	4-6-0	Danforth L&M	1023	3-1876	54-18x24-71500	1572		Rebuilt to 0-6-0 No. 1057 on 3-1896.
208	4-6-0	Danforth L&M	1024	4-1876	54-18x24-71500	1573	2006	
209	4-6-0	Danforth L&M	1025	4-1876	54-18x24-71500	1574	2007	
210	4-6-0	Danforth L&M	1026	4-1876	54-18x24-71500	1575	2010	
211	4-6-0	Danforth L&M	1027	6-1876	54-18x24-71500	1576		Rebuilt to 0-6-0 No. 1066 on 5-1899.
212	4-6-0	Danforth L&M	1028	6-1876	54-18x24-71500	1577	2008	
213	4-6-0	Danforth L&M	1029	6-1876	54-18x24-71500	1578	2011	
214	4-6-0	Danforth L&M	1030	7-1876	54-18x24-71500	1579		Rebuilt to 0-6-0 No. 1053 on 2-1896.
215	4-6-0	Danforth L&M	1031	7-1876	54-18x24-71500	1580	2012	
216	4-6-0	Schenectady	1016	8-1876	54-18x24-79500	1581	2029	
217	4-6-0	Schenectady	1018	8-1876	54-18x24-79500	1582	2030	
218	4-6-0	Schenectady	1020	8-1876	54-18x24-79500	1583	2031	
219	4-4-0	Schenectady	975	6-1876	66-17x24-68700	1293		Scrapped 12-1899.
220	4-4-0	Schenectady	970	6-1876	66-17x24-68700	1294		Scrapped 8-28-1899.
221	4-4-0	Schenectady	973	7-1876	66-17x24-68700	1295	2nd 1314	
222	4-4-0	Schenectady	1002	7-1876	60-17x24-66700	1296		Scrapped 3-21-1900.
223	4-4-0	Schenectady	1017	8-1876	60-17x24-66700	1297	2nd 1317	
224	4-4-0	Schenectady	1019	8-1876	60-17x24-66700	1298		Same No. in 1901.
225	4-4-0	Schenectady	1021	8-1876	60-17x24-66700	1299		Same No. in 1901.
226	4-4-0	Schenectady	1022	9-1876	60-17x24-66700	1300		Same No. in 1901.
227	4-4-0	Schenectady	1023	9-1876	60-17x24-66700	1301		Same No. in 1901.
228	4-4-0	Schenectady	1024	9-1876	60-17x24-66700	1302		Same No. in 1901.
229	2-2-4	Vulcan Iron Wks.	6	1865	42-7x14-64900			Note 52.
230	2-6-2T	C. P. Shops Sacto.	13	12-1881	48-16x24-100000	1501	1900	Later SPMW No. 577.
231	2-6-2T	C. P. Shops Sacto.	14	1-1882.	48-16x24-100000	1502	1901	Later SPMW No. 571.
232	2-6-2T	C. P. Shops Sacto.	15	1-1882	48-16x24-100000	1503	1902	
233	2-6-2T	C. P. Shops Sacto.	16	1-1882	48-16x24-100000	1504	1903	
234	2-6-2T	C. P. Shops Sacto.	17	2-1882	48-16x24-100000	1505	1904	
235	2-6-2T	C. P. Shops Sacto.	18	2-1882	48-16x24-100000	1506	1905	
236	2-6-2T	C. P. Shops Sacto.	19	2-1882	48-16x24-100000	1507	1906	Later SPMW No. 566.
237	4-10-0	C. P. Shops Sacto.	21	1883	57-21x36-146000	2050		Note 53.
238	4-6-0	C. P. Shops Sacto.	30	2-1887	57-18x30-105100	1765	2194	
239	4-6-0	C. P. Shops Sacto.	31	2-1887	57-18x30-105100	1766	2195	
240	4-6-0	C. P. Shops Sacto.	32	3-1887	57-18x30-105100	1767	2196	

In the above view, No. 162 formerly the *Flash*, which was built after the Central Pacific was completed. At the left, Central Pacific No. 210 on loan to the Southern Pacific of Arizona. (BELOW) No. 240, one of Steven's 1887 design, on the Sacramento turntable. — **PACIFIC COAST CHAPTER — R&LHS COLLECTION**

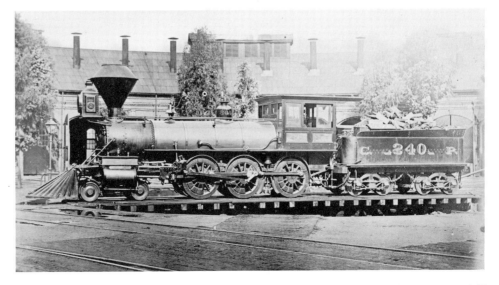

No.	Type	Builder and Construction No.		Date Built	Dimensions Dr.—Cyls.—Wt.	1891 No.	Later Nos.	Remarks
241	4-6-0	C. P. Shops Sacto.	33	3-1887	57-18x30-105100	1768	2197	
242	4-6-0	C. P. Shops Sacto.	34	5-1887	57-18x30-105100	1769	2198	
243	4-6-0	C. P. Shops Sacto.	35	5-1887	57-18x30-105100	1770	2199	
244	4-6-0	C. P. Shops Sacto.	36	5-1887	57-18x30-105100	1771	2200	
245	4-6-0	C. P. Shops Sacto.	37	5-1887	57-18x30-105100	1772	2201	
246	4-6-0	C. P. Shops Sacto.	51	1-1888	57-18x30-105100	1773	2202	
247	4-6-0	C. P. Shops Sacto.	52	1-1888	57-18x30-105100	1774	2203	
248	4-6-0	C. P. Shops Sacto.	53	1-1888	57-18x30-105100	1775	2204	
249	4-6-0	C. P. Shops Sacto.	54	1-1888	57-18x30-105100	1776	2205	
250	2-8-0	C. P. Shops Sacto.	62	6-1888	51-19x30-120300	1900	2500	

REPLACEMENT OR SECOND NUMBERS

No.	Type	Builder and Construction No.		Date Built	Dimensions Dr.—Cyls.—Wt.	1891 No.	Later Nos.	Remarks
3	4-4-0	Rogers	2058	8-1872	56-17x24-72100	1263	1512	
10	4-4-0	C. P. Shops Sacto.	74	10-1889	63-17x24-96100	1265	1513	
18	4-6-0	C. P. Shops Sacto.	22	1884	56-17x30-90000	1521		Scrapped 11-1892.
19	4-6-0	C. P. Shops Sacto.	23	12-1885	56-18x30-112000	1762	2208	
25	4-4-0	Norris Lancaster	14	1864	60-16x22-60100			Note 54.
31	4-4-0	Norris-Lancaster		1864	66-16½x24-67800			Note 55.
36	4-4-0	Rogers	2064	9-1872	56-17x24-72100	1270		Scrapped 8-26-1896.
55	4-4-0	C. P. Shops Sacto.	1	6-1873	56-17x24-74000	1272	1516	
93	4-2-2	Danforth, Cooke		1863	54-11x15-30000			Note 56.
97	4-4-0	Rogers	2067	9-1872	56-17x24-72100	1275	1518	
99	4-4-0	C. P. Shops Sacto.	2	7-1873	56-17x24-76300	1276	1519	
100	4-4-0	Wm. Mason	405	5-1871	66-15x22-60250	1121		Note 57.
104	4-4-0	Schenectady	1557	3-1882	60-17x24-73700	1277	2nd 1320	
110	4-4-0	Schenectady	1558	3-1882	60-17x24-73700	1278	2nd 1349	
115	4-4-0	Wm. Mason	404	5-1871	60-16x24-61000	1210		Note 58.
117	4-4-0	Rhode Island	80	11-1868	56-15x22-60250	1132		Note 59.
121	4-4-0	Wm. Mason	250	3-1867	60-16x24-61000	1211		Note 60.
122	4-4-0	C. P. Shops Sacto.	26	11-1886	68-17x26-88500	1362		Same No. in 1901.
123	4-4-0	C. P. Shops Sacto.	27	11-1886	68-17x26-88500	1363		Same No. in 1901.
125	4-4-0	C. P. Shops Sacto.	28	11-1886	68-17x26-88500	1364		Same No. in 1901.
131	4-4-0	Rogers	2072	10-1872	56-17x24-72100	1279	2nd 1367	
132	4-4-0	Rogers	2075	10-1872	56-17x24-72100	1280		Same No. in 1901.
135	4-4-0	C. P. Shops Sacto.	4	8-1873	56-17x24-74070	1281		Scrapped in 1891.
142	4-4-0	C. P. Shops Sacto.	9	11-1873	56-17x24-74000	1282	1520	
166	4-4-0	Boston Loco. Wks.	555	1-1855	48-14x22-46000			Note 61.
166	4-4-0	C. P. Shops Sacto.	29	11-1886	68-17x26-85800	1365		Same No. in 1901.
167	4-4-0	C. P. Shops Sacto.	12	2-1874	56-17x24-74000	1283	1521	
175	4-6-0	C. P. Shops Sacto.	24	7-1886	56-18x30-100800	1763	2192	
176	4-4-0	Danforth L&M Co.		7-1868	54-15x22-60000	1154		Note 62.
177	4-4-0	C. P. Shops Sacto. Rblt.		8-1873	48-15x22-64400			Note 63.
177	4-6-0	C. P. Shops Sacto.	25	7-1886	56-18x30-100800	1764	2193	
178	0-4-0	Wm. Mason	246	2-1867	48-15x22-48000	1008		Note 64.
179	4-4-0	C. P. Shops Sacto.	10	12-1873	56-17x24-74000	1286	2nd 1368	
229	4-8-0	C. P. Shops Sacto.	20	4-1882	54-19x30-123000	1950	2800-2925	
Betsy	2-2-0	Vulcan Iron Wks. S.F.		9-1864	60-9x18			Note 65.

Note 1 — The *Governor Stanford* No. 1 was officially retired in 1894, was restored and presented to Leland Stanford Jr. University, but was not delivered until 1899.

Note 2 — The *Pacific* No. 2 has been erroneously credited to the San Francisco & San Jose Railroad No. 3. It was in continuous service on the Central Pacific during its entire life. SF&SJ No. 3 was running on that railroad in October 1863, and was probably a Richard Norris engine the same as Nos. 1 and 2 of that road.

Note 3 — The *C. P. Huntington* No. 3 was to have been renumbered No. 1001 on 1-1-1901, but this was not done. Its first appearance on public exhibit as a relic was at the Midwinter Exposition in San Francisco in 1894. It was stored for many years and was finally rebuilt as an operating locomotive for special events. Title to the locomotive now rests with the Governor of California. Became Southern Pacific No. 1 on February 5, 1871.

Note 4 — Certain 0-6-0T, 2-6-0 and 4-6-0 locomotives were rebuilt to 4-4-0 type at Sacramento, mostly in 1871, the last in 1883. Their dimensions as 4-4-0's were as viz:

9	2-6-0	57-17x24-72500	9-1871
10	2-6-0	54-18x22-68800	2-2-1871
13	2-6-0	54-17x24-66800	10-1871
14	2-6-0	54-17x24-72500	6-24-1871
15	2-6-0	54-18x22-66800	8-8-1871
32	0-6-0T	54-17x22-65000	2-2-1871
33	0-6-0T	54-17x22-65000	12-11-1872
46	4-6-0	54-17x22-65000	6-5-1872
47	4-6-0	54-17x22-65000	7-19-1872
48	4-6-0T+tender	54-17x30-85000	1883
49	4-6-0T+tender	54-17x22-65000	9-18-1871

Note 5 — The *Washoe* No. 15 was rebuilt to a 4-4-0 on August 8, 1871. Scrapped prior to 1891.

Note 6 — The *Idaho* No. 17 blew up one mile east of Summit Tunnel, California, January 2, 1879, and was scrapped.

Note 7 — The *Yuba* No. 25 blew up at Clipper Gap on October 8, 1868, and scrapped.

Note 8 — The *Klamath* No. 31 blew up near Elko, Nevada, March 30, 1869, and scrapped.

Note 9 — The *Ajax* No. 32 rebuilt to a 4-4-0 on February 2, 1871. See Note 4.

Note 10 — The *Achilles* No. 33 rebuilt to a 4-4-0 on December 11, 1872. See Note 4.

Note 11 — The *El Dorado* No. 34 had her drivers reduced from 66 inches to 54 inches April 18, 1871.

Note 12 — The *Boise* No. 35 had her drivers reduced from 66 inches to 54 inches on February 15, 1871.

Note 13 — The *Shoshone* No. 36 was sold to the San Francisco & San Jose as their No. 13.

Note 14 — The *Malone* No. 39 became No. 2002. Was wrecked in 1889, and rebuilt at Sacramento Shops. New dimensions were 54-18x24-98500.

Note 15 — The *Solano* No. 40 blew up at Oakland 4-20-1872. Rebuilt 7-20-1872. Converted to a 4-4-2T at Sacramento during August 1876. Rebuilt in 1887 with these dimensions 54-15x22-79600. Carried No. 1007 in 1901.

Note 16 — The *Stanislaus* No. 41 was rebuilt to a 4-4-2T at Sacramento in 1882. Carried No. 1003 in 1901.

Note 17 — The *Tuolumne* No. 42 was rebuilt to a 4-4-2T at Sacramento 2-15-1871. New dimensions were 54-14x24-58000. Scrapped in 1892.

Note 18 — The *Tulare* No. 43 was rebuilt to a 4-4-2T at Sacramento 11-13-1876. New dimensions were 54-14x24-52000. Scrapped in 1896.

Note 19 — The *Unicorn* No. 46 was rebuilt to a 4-4-0 on June 5, 1872. See Note 4.

Note 20 — The *Griffin* No. 47 was rebuilt to a 4-4-0 on July 19, 1872. See Note 4.

Note 21 — The *Toiyabe* No. 48 was built as a tank engine and tender was added at Sacramento, September 7, 1868. Saddle tank removed and rebuilt to a 4-4-0 in 1883. New dimensions were 54-17x30-85000.

Note 22 — The *Toquima* No. 49 was built as a tank engine and tender added at Sacramento, October 1, 1868. Saddle tank removed and rebuilt to a 4-4-0.

Note 23 — The *Black Deer* No. 55 was sold to the San Francisco & San Jose as their No. 15. The SF&SJ was consolidated with the Southern Pacific on October 12, 1870. A number of Central Pacific locomotives were transferred to the SP between 1871 and 1874, although some were later returned.

Note 24 — The *Jupiter* No. 60 was sold to the Gila Valley, Globe & Northern as their No. 1 in 1893.

Note 25 — The *Vulcan* No. 69 was sold to the Gila Valley, Globe & Northern as their No. 2 in 1894.

Note 26 — The *Oronoco* No. 93 was former Sacramento Valley No. 6. Was rebuilt August 29, 1872, and became Southern Pacific No. 17 in September, 1872.

Note 27 — The *Clipper* No. 96 was the first Central Pacific engine equipped with air brakes 3-29-1871. Burned in the Rocklin roundhouse fire November, 1873, was rebuilt 2-1874 with 68-inch drivers taken from wrecked engine No. 173. Sold 8-1892.

Note 28 — The *Racer* No. 97 was sold to San Francisco & San Jose as their No. 12.

Note 29 — The *Ranger* No. 99 became California Pacific 2nd No. 5 (1872). Became Southern Pacific No. 1161.

Note 30 — The *Rambler* No. 104 was sold to the Sacramento & Placerville as their No. 3. Became Northern Railway No. 1021.

Note 31 — The *Roller* No. 105 became Oregonian Railway No. 12 in 1890.

Note 32 — The *Flier* No. 109 became Oregonian Railway No. 13 in 1890.

Note 33 — The *Fire Fly* No. 110 became Sacramento & Placerville No. 1 — 7-24-1879.

Note 34 — *Red Eagle* No. 117 was sold to San Francisco & San Jose as their No. 14.

Note 35 — *American Eagle* No. 121 was sold to the Stockton & Visalia as their No. 1 in November, 1871. Later was Stockton & Copperopolis No. 1.

Note 36 — Engines Nos. 122 to 125 were ordered by the Oregon Central Railroad in 1865 and sold to the Central Pacific July 24, 1868.

Note 37 — *Deerhound* No. 132 was leased to the San Francisco & North Pacific. On return it became Central Pacific No. 185.

Note 38 — *Peeler* No. 135 became S.P. No. 18, on return became Central Pacific 2nd No. 117.

Note 39 — *Sacramento* No. 168 was former Western Pacific "A." Became No. 1152 and was scrapped 3-1894.

Note 40 — *Stockton* No. 169 was former Western Pacific "C." Became No. 1117 and scrapped 3-1894.

Note 41 — *Santa Clara* No. 170 was former Western Pacific "D." Became No. 1118 and was scrapped 9-1891.

Note 42 — *San Mateo* No. 171 was former Western Pacific "E." Sold to Eugene Sable Co. 9-11-1889.

Note 43 — *Merced* No. 172 was former Western Pacific "F." Became No. 1284-1522. Converted to 4-6-0 10-2-1872 and converted back to 4-4-0 by 1878.

Note 44 — *Sonoma* No. 173 was former Western Pacific "H." Became No. 1285-1523. Listed in some classification books as built by Central Pacific. Rebuilt from salvageable parts of engine wrecked at Alameda Junction 11-14-1869. Not a complete new engine.

Note 45 — *San Jose* No. 174 was former Western Pacific "B." Became No. 1153. Scrapped 9-1891.

Note 46 — *William Penn* No. 175 was former Western Pacific "J." Sold to Pacific Iron & Nail Co., Oakland, 12-1885. Converted from a 4-2-0T to a tender engine without saddle tank at Sacramento 10-1868.

Note 47 — *J. G. Kellogg* No. 176 was former San Francisco & Alameda. Rebuilt at Sacramento 5-26-1872. Sold to Stockton & Copperopolis as No. 2. Later lists state engine built by Oakland Railway Co., probably an abbreviation of the San Francisco, Oakland & Alameda Ry.

Note 48 — *F. D. Atherton* No. 177 was former San Francisco & Alameda. Engine wrecked 11-14-1869 with No. 173. Parts used in 2nd No. 177 in 1873.

Note 49 — *Liberty* No. 178 was former San Francisco & Oakland. Rebuilt at Sacramento 3-14-1872. Sold to Stockton & Copperopolis as No. 3.

Note 50 — *Oakland* No. 179 was former San Francisco & Oakland. Doubtful if this engine received a Central Pacific engine number, though listed as No. 179 in the 1871 list. It was shopped 4-3-1873 and placed in yard service at Sacramento as the *Oakland,* and a 2nd No. 179 was built in December 1873. The *Oakland* appears in newspaper accounts of various mishaps in the yards until late 1877.

Note 51 — Engine No. 185 is former Central Pacific No. 132. Leased to the San Francisco & North Pacific and returned to CP. Scrapped 7-1895.

Note 52 — Engine No. 229 was former California Pacific *Flea*. Sold prior to 1882.

Note 53 — Engine No. 237 was named *El Gobernador*. Scrapped 7-15-1894.

Note 54 — Engine 2nd No. 25 was former Western Pacific "I" *Industry*. Was listed in the locomotive list in 1878, but not later.

Note 55 — Engine 2nd No. 31 was former Western Pacific "G" *Mariposa*. Became No. 1193, 2nd No. 1215 — 1488. Later was Stockton Terminal & Eastern No. 1, 1-6-1909 and now resides at Travel Town, Los Angeles, California.

Note 56 — Engine 2nd No. 93 was former Sacramento Valley No. 5. Original Freeport Railroad *G. F. Bragg* acquired in 1874. Sold to Union Coal Co. 8-1888.

Note 57 — Engine 2nd No. 100 was former California Pacific No. 14 acquired in 1874. Scrapped 6-1895.

Note 58 — Engine 2nd No. 115 was former California Pacific No. 13, acquired in 1874. Scrapped 8-1899.

Note 59 — Engine 2nd No. 117 former Southern Pacific No. 18 — Original Central Pacific No. 135. Scrapped 3-1900.

Note 60 — Engine 2nd No. 121 was former California Pacific No. 5 acquired in 1872. Carried same number in 1901.

Note 61 — Engine 2nd No. 166 was originally Sacramento Valley No. 2 *Nevada*. Became Central Pacific No. 166 *Argenta* in 1869. To Northern Railway No. 1020, Southern Pacific No. 1116. Scrapped in 1898.

Note 62 — Engine 2nd No. 176 was former Central Pacific 1st No. 115. Rebuilt in 1876. Scrapped 9-1891.

Note 63 — Engine 2nd No. 177 was built from parts of 1st No. 177. Scrapped prior to 1886.

Note 64 — Engine 2nd No. 178 was former California Pacific No. 2 acquired 3-14-1872. Rebuilt from a 4-4-0. Scrapped 3-3-1894.

Note 65 — Engine *Betsy* was former San Francisco & Alameda *E. B. Mastick*. According to newspaper reports, it was the first engine on the San Francisco & Alameda. It apparently never received a Central Pacific road number, but was used as a roundhouse goat at Oakland. As the *Betsy,* it was shopped in Sacramento 8-25-1872 and returned to Oakland. Retired in 1874, it was sent to Sacramento and scrapped there 9-10-1874.

In June, 1878, three new 4-4-0 passenger engines were built by the Schenectady Locomotive Works for the Central Pacific as follows:

229	Schen.	#1088	6-1878	60-17x24-92000
230	Schen.	#1089	6-1878	60-17x24-92000
231	Schen.	#1090	6-1878	60-17x24-92000

They were set up in Sacramento in July, 1878, were sent on trial trips to Oakland and were immediately transferred to the Southern Pacific of California, where they bore the numbers 45-47 incl.

LOCOMOTIVES OF THE SACRAMENTO VALLEY RAILROAD

No.	Name	Type	Builder and Construction No.		Date Built	Dimensions Dr.—Cyls.—Wt.	Remarks
1	Sacramento	4-4-0	Boston L. Wks.	554	1-1855	60-14x22-49000	Note 1.
2	Nevada	4-4-0	Boston L. Wks.	555	1-1855	60-14x22-49000	Note 2.
3	L. L. Robinson	4-4-0	New Jersey L. Wks.		1855	66-16x20	Note 3.
4	Pioneer	4-4-0	Globe Loco. Wks.		1849	71-15x20	Note 4.
5	Geo. F. Bragg	4-4-0	R. Norris & Son		7-1860	54-14x24	Note 5.
5	G. F. Bragg	4-2-2	Danforth-Cooke		1863	54-11x15-30000	Note 6.
6	Oronoco	4-4-0	R. Norris & Son		7-1860	60-14x24-52000	Note 7.

Note 1 — The *Sacramento* No. 1 was obtained by the Central Pacific during December, 1866. After being used as a hoisting engine, it was returned to Sacramento, shopped and returned to service 5-3-1869 as Sacramento Valley 2nd No. 2. It blew up and was destroyed at Latrobe 9-16-1876.

Note 2 — The *Nevada* No. 2 was transferred to the Central Pacific in 1869 and renumbered Central Pacific 2nd No. 166. It was renamed *Argenta* in 1870. It became Northern Railway No. 1020, then Southern Pacific No. 1116 in 1891.

Note 3 — The *L. L. Robinson* No. 3 was acquired secondhand from C. K. Garrison & Co. in 1855. Engine blew up at Folsom 12-13-1867 and rebuilt at Sacramento during March 1871. Sold to Sacramento & Placerville as No. 2 in 1879. Sold to the Folsom Water Power Co. in 1889.

Note 4 — The *Pioneer* No. 4 was originally called the *Elephant,* changed to *C. K. Garrison* in 1855, and to the *Pioneer* in 1869. New boiler, hook motion replaced by Stephenson valve gear, general rebuilding in Sacramento 12-1-1869. Became 2nd No. 1 in 1870. Scrapped in 1886.

Note 5 — The *Geo. F. Bragg* 1st No. 5 was leased from the California Central and returned in 1864 when the Central Pacific took over the operation of the California Central trains. See California Central No. 4 in roster.

Note 6 — The *G. F. Bragg* 2nd No. 5 is the former Freeport Railroad No. 1 acquired in 1865. Became Central Pacific 2nd No. 93 in 1874. Original name was *Nebraska*.

Note 7 — The *Oronoco* No. 6 is the former California Central No. 1 the *Harry Wilson*. Assigned to the SVRR by the Central Pacific in October, 1867. Rebuilt after a boiler explosion and assigned to the Central Pacific as 1st No. 93, 2-29-1869.

LOCOMOTIVES OF THE CALIFORNIA PACIFIC RAILROAD

No.	Name	Type	Builder and Construction No.		Date Built	Dimensions Dr.—Cyls.—Wt.	Remarks
1	Vallejo	4-4-0	Wm. Mason	245	1-1867	54-16x22-60500	Note 1.
2	Marysville	4-4-0	Wm. Mason	246	1-1867	54-16x22-60500	Wrecked prior to 1869. See CP 2nd No. 178.
3	Solano	4-4-0	Wm. Mason	247	2-1867	54-16x22-60500	To Southern Pacific No. 1183.
4	Yuba	4-4-0	Wm. Mason	248	2-1867	54-16x22-60500	To Southern Pacific No. 1184.
5	Yolo	4-4-0	Wm. Mason	250	3-1867	54-16x22-60500	Wrecked and rebuilt by CP as 2nd No. 121.
6	Napa	4-4-0	Wm. Mason	251	3-1867	56-15x22-61000	To Southern Pacific No. 1162.
7	Wm. Mason	4-4-0	Wm. Mason	289	9-1868	54-16x22-60500	To Southern Pacific No. 1185 – 2nd No. 1207.
8	Sacramento	4-4-0	Wm. Mason	290	9-1868	54-16x22-60500	To Southern Pacific No. 1186.
9	J. W. Ryder	4-4-0	Wm. Mason	318	7-1869	66-16x22-61200	To Southern Pacific No. 1187.
10	D. W. Rice	4-4-0	Wm. Mason	319	7-1869	66-16x22-61200	To Southern Pacific No. 1188.
11	D. C. Haskins	4-4-0	Wm. Mason	361	6-1870	56-16x24-61000	Note 2.
12	Wm. F. Rolofson	4-4-0	Wm. Mason	362	6-1870	60-16x24-61000	To Southern Pacific No. 1242.
13	London	4-4-0	Wm. Mason	404	5-1871	60-16x24-61000	Sold to CP 2nd No. 115 (1872).
14	Frankfort	4-4-0	Wm. Mason	405	5-1871	66-15x22-60250	Sold to CP 2nd No. 100 (1872).
	Flea	2-2-4	Vulcan Iron Wks.	6	1865	42-7x14-64900	Note 3.

SECOND NUMBERS

No.	Name	Type	Builder and Construction No.		Date Built	Dimensions Dr.—Cyls.—Wt.	Remarks
2	Calistoga	4-4-0	Booth & Co.	10	5-1869	60-14x22-52000	To Southern Pacific No. 1115.
5		4-4-0	McKay & Aldus		7-1868	60-15x24-60000	To Southern Pacific No. 1161 Ex CP 1st 99.

Note 1 — *Vallejo* No. 1 rebuilt to an 0-4-0 with new dimensions of 48-14x22-52000. Became Southern Pacific No. 1114-1002.

Note 2 — *D. C. Haskins* No. 11 was leased to the Stockton & Copperopolis No. 1, *Andrew Jackson,* 2-1-1871. Returned to the California Pacific 8-1871 and its old name and road number were restored. Became Southern Pacific No. 1241.

Note 3 — *Flea* was sold to the Central Pacific in 1879 and became No. 229. Apparently sold to the San Joaquin Valley Coal Mining Co. by the Central Pacific in 1882. It was again sold after 1893 to the Sierra Nevada Wood & Lumber Co. Ex Napa Valley Railroad *Napa City* steam car. Scrapped at Sacramento about 1921.

Southern Pacific No. 17 originally California Central No. 1 built by Richard Norris in 1860, is photographed at Cisco after 1872. The engine still had its ornate bell frame and headlight brackets. — SOUTHERN PACIFIC

No.	Name	Type	Builder	Date Built	Dimensions Dr.—Cyls.—Wt.	Remarks
1	*Harry Wilson*	4-4-0	R. Norris & Son	7-1860	60-14x24-52000	See Note.
2	*Lincoln*	4-4-0	R. Norris & Son	7-1860	60-14x24-	See Note.
3	*Garibaldi*	4-4-0	R. Norris & Son	7-1860	60-14x24-	See Note.
4	*Sam Brannan*	4-4-0	R. Norris & Son	7-1860	54-14x24-	See Note.

California Central R.R.

The four locomotives of this road were shipped from New York in July, 1860, and arrived in San Francisco in January, 1861. They were held there under a writ of attachment for unpaid freight charges. Three were soon released and arrived in Sacramento on March 22, 1861. They were set up at the Sacramento Valley R.R. enginehouse, and as received were named the *Northerner, Southerner* and the *Pacific.* Their names were changed to *Harry Wilson, Lincoln* and *Garibaldi,* not necessarily in sequence. The first two were sent to Folsom on May 10, 1861, to work on construction trains, the *Garibaldi* remaining unused until May, 1862. At that time, the fourth engine, named *Atlantic* at the factory, stored in San Francisco since January, 1861, came up the river and was set up in Sacramento. It was leased to the Sacramento Valley R.R. which renamed it the *Geo. F. Bragg.* Some time in July, 1864, the *Geo. F. Bragg* was returned to its owner, who by this date was Sam Brannan. He renamed the locomotive after himself. The Sacramento Valley R.R. then renamed the Freeport R.R. engine *G. F. Bragg,* thereby creating confusion for historians. All four California Central engines together with the rolling stock were purchased from Sam Brannan by the Central Pacific, at a Sheriff's sale in Sacramento in December, 1865. The *Harry Wilson,* in first class running order, brought $5,000, but the other three were in such bad shape that they were sold for $1,000 each. They were sent to Folsom in 1866, the gauge narrowed to standard, and on September 24, 1867, the four locomotives and all the rolling stock were brought into Sacramento, to be pooled with Central Pacific equipment. The *Harry Wilson* immediately became the *Oronoco* No. 6 on the Sacramento Valley. The other three engines were shopped at Sacramento, and with a single new Richard Norris 4-4-0 No. 41, formed a group of four engines which operated most of the trains on the Sacramento Valley and Sacramento & Placerville railroads for some years.

Locomotives of the
Western Pacific Railroad of California

The ten locomotives of this road were delivered at San Francisco between 1865 and 1867. They bore names and were lettered from "A" to "J" instead of using road numbers. The engines *Merced* and *William Penn* were sent to San Jose in 1866 and used during the construction of 20 miles of line between San Jose and Niles. In the winter of 1867-68 after the Central Pacific controlled the Western Pacific, the other eight engines were shipped to Sacramento, set up in the shops there, and in January, 1868, were reported stored in the dead-line at Sacramento, waiting for construction to begin on the eastern end of the Western Pacific. This work was postponed until the summer of 1869 and the stored Western Pacific engines were turned over to the Central Pacific. In July, 1868, the two engines on the orphan San Jose-Niles line were taken to San Francisco, shipped to Sacramento by river boat, and joined the other W. P. engines on the Central Pacific.

In the above view, the former *Denver* No. 10 as Union Pacific No. 553, showing the effects of rebuilding with a new boiler and extended smokebox. (BELOW) Grant-built No. 45 at the factory in 1867. — UNION PACIFIC MUSEUM

UNION PACIFIC RAILROAD

LIST OF LOCOMOTIVES, 1864—1885

No.	Type	Builder and Construction No.		Date Built	Dimensions Dr.—Cyls.—Wt.	Remarks
1	4-4-0	Danforth, Cooke		9-1864	60-14x22-54500	Named *Major General Sherman* — Note 1.
2	4-4-0	Danforth, Cooke		9-1864	60-14x22-54500	Named *Major General McPherson* — Note 2.
3	4-4-0	Manchester	51	8-1864	60-16x22-55000	Named *Manchester*, gone in 1866.
4	4-4-0	Norris-Lancaster		1865	60-16x24-73700	Named *Major General Sheridan* — Note 3.
5	4-4-0	Norris-Lancaster		1865	60-16x24-73700	Named *Vice Admiral Farragut* — Note 4.
6	4-4-0	Hinkley & Williams		1866	60-14x24-52800	Named *Black Hawk*, Ex 1st No. 19 — Note 5.
7	4-4-0	Schenectady	411	4-1866	60-16x24-62250	Named *Omaha*, renumbered to No. 574.
8	4-4-0	Schenectady	418	4-1866	60-16x24-62250	Named *Idaho*, renumbered to No. 575.
9	4-4-0	Rogers	1025	7-1862	60-13½x22-62932	Named *Osceola* — Note 6.
10	4-4-0	Danforth L&M		1866	63-16x24-69740	Named *Denver*, renumbered to No. 553.
11	4-4-0	Danfotth L&M		1866	63-16x24-69740	Named *Colorado* — Note 7.
12	2-6-0	Danforth L&M		1866	54-18x22-70000	Named *Bellevue* — Note 8.
13	4-4-0	Hinkley & Williams		1866	60-14x22-60000	Note 9.
14	4-4-0	Hinkley & Williams		1866	60-15x24-60000	Former 1st No. 20, sold Utah So. No. 1 (1871).
15	4-4-0	Hinkley & Williams		1866	60-14x22-60000	Sold to Utah Central No. 1 (10-14-69) Ex 1st No. 21.
16	4-4-0	Grant		1866	61-16x24-68600	Sold to Oregon Short Line No. 3(11-1882).
17	4-4-0	Grant		1866	61-16x24-68600	Renumbered to No. 595.
18	4-4-0	Grant		1866	61-16x24-68600	Sold to O.S.L. No. 10 on 11-1882.
19	4-4-0	Grant		1866	61-16x24-68600	Sold to O.S.L. No. 1 on 11-1882.
20	4-4-0	Grant		1886	61-16x24-68600	Sold to O.S.L. No. 2 on 11-1882.
21	4-4-0	Schenectady	486	6-1868	60-16x24-68600	Renumbered No. 576. Retired 3-1905.
22	4-4-0	Schenectady	436	3-1867	60-16x24-68600	Renumbered No. 577. Retired 6-1903.
23	4-4-0	Schenectady	440	3-1867	60-16x24-68600	Renumbered No. 578. Retired 1-1897.
24	4-4-0	Schenectady	442	4-1867	60-16x24-68600	Renumbered No. 579. Retired 3-1905.
25	4-4-0	Schenectady	456	7-1867	60-16x24-68600	Renumbered No. 580. Retired 12-1898.
26	4-4-0	Schenectady	457	8-1867	60-16x24-68600	Renumbered No. 581. Sold to F. M. Hicks 10-1899.
27	4-4-0	Schenectady	458	8-1867	60-16x24-68600	Renumbered No. 582. Retired 1895.
28	4-4-0	Rogers	1464	6-1867	60-16x24-70680	Renumbered No. 562. Retired 6-1900.
29	4-4-0	Rogers	1469	7-1867	60-16x24-70680	Sold to Colo. Cent., Julesburg Br. No. 8 — 1882.
30	4-4-0	Rogers	1470	8-1867	60-16x24-70680	Sold to Colo. Cent., Julesburg Br. No. 9 — 1882.
31	4-4-0	Rogers	1471	8-1867	60-16x24-70680	Sold to Colo. Cent., Julesburg Br., No. 10 — 1882.
32	4-4-0	Rogers	1472	8-1867	60-16x24-70680	Sold to Colo. Cent., Julesburg Br. No. 11 — 1882.
33	4-4-0	Hinkley & Williams		1867	60-16x24-66120	Sold to O.S.L. No. 25 on 11-1882.
34	4-4-0	Hinkley & Williams		1867	60-16x24-66120	Sold to O.S.L. No. 19 on 11-1882.
35	4-4-0	Hinkley & Williams		1867	60-16x24-66120	Sold to O.S.L. No. 20 on 11-1882.
36	4-4-0	Hinkley & Williams		1867	60-16x24-66120	Sold to Omaha & Repub. Vall. No. 36. Later UP No. 393.
37	4-4-0	Hinkley & Williams		1867	60-16x24-66120	Renumbered No. 650, later No. 482. Sold F. M. Hicks 8-02.
38	4-4-0	Taunton	408	5-1867	60-16x24-62800	Renumbered No. 700. Rebuilt to No. 823. Retired 1899.
39	4-4-0	Taunton	410	6-1867	60-16x24-62800	Renumbered No. 805. Retired 6-1901.
40	4-4-0	Taunton	412	7-1867	60-16x24-62800	Renumbered No. 391. Sold in 1886.
41	4-4-0	Taunton	414	8-1867	60-16x24-62800	Renumbered No. 567. Retired 10-1899.
42	4-4-0	Taunton	416	8-1867	60-16x24-62800	Renumbered No. 701. Sold to F. M. Hicks 11-1902.
43	4-4-0	Grant		1867	61-17x24-68600	Sold to O.S.L. No. 4 on 11-1882.
44	4-4-0	Grant		1867	61-17x24-68600	Sold to O.S.L. No. 5 on 11-1882.
45	4-4-0	Grant		1867	61-17x24-68600	Sold to O.S.L. No. 6 on 11-1882.
46	4-4-0	Grant		1867	61-17x24-68600	Renumbered No. 596. Retired 3-1905.
47	4-4-0	Grant		1867	61-17x24-68600	Sold to O.S.L. No. 9 on 11-1882.
48	4-4-0	Grant		1867	61-17x24-68600	Renumbered No. 597. Retired 1898.
49	4-4-0	Grant		1867	61-17x24-68600	Sold to Utah Sou. No. 2 — 1873.
50	4-4-0	Grant		1867	61-17x24-68600	Renumbered No. 598. Retired 1902.
51	4-6-0	Moore & Richardson		* 1867	55-18x24-	2nd hand from contractors. Retired 1881.
52	4-6-0	Moore & Richardson		* 1867	55-18x24-79450	2nd hand. Renumbered No. 908. Retired 10-1898. Rebuilt 1872.
53	4-4-0	R. Norris & Son		* 1867	56-15x22-59500	2nd hand. Renumbered No. 302. Rebuilt to No. 826 on 4-86.
54	4-6-0	Moore & Richardson		* 1867	55-18x24-	2nd hand. Not in list after 1-1870.
55	4-6-0	Moore & Richardson		* 1867	55-18x24-	2nd hand. Retired 1881.
56	4-4-0	Rogers		* 1867	56-16x24-80594	Note 10.
57	4-4-0	Grant		1867	61-17x24-68600	Renumbered No. 599. Sold to F. M. Hicks 9-1901.
58	4-4-0	Grant		1867	61-17x24-68600	Sold to O.S.L. No. 23 on 11-1882.
59	4-4-0	Schenectady	487	6-1868	60-16x24-68600	Renumbered No. 511. Retired 1898.
60	4-4-0	Schenectady	496	6-1868	60-16x24-68600	Sold to Colo. Central No. 4 — 1874.

* — Date locomotive acquired by Union Pacific   *All renumberings in the "Remarks" effective June 1885.*

No.	Type	Builder and Construction No.		Date Built	Dimensions Dr.—Cyls.—Wt.	Remarks
61	4-4-0	Schenectady	497	6-1868	60-16x24-68600	Renumbered No. 583. Retired 6-1898.
62	4-4-0	Schenectady	500	7-1868	60-16x24-68600	Renumbered No. 512. Retired 1896.
63	4-4-0	Schenectady	501	8-1868	60-16x24-68600	Renumbered No. 513. Retired 1898.
64	4-4-0	Schenectady	502	8-1868	60-16x24-68600	Renumbered No. 514. Retired 10-1899.
65	4-4-0	Schenectady	503	8-1868	60-16x24-68600	Sold to Utah Sou. No. 8 – 1879.
66	4-4-0	Schenectady	508	8-1868	60-16x24-68600	Renumbered No. 515. Retired 1898.
67	4-4-0	Schenectady	509	9-1868	60-16x24-68600	Renumbered No. 516. Retired 10-1899.
68	4-4-0	Rogers	1502	2-1868	54-16x24-68600	Renumbered No. 500. Sold to F. M. Hicks 1-1901.
69	4-4-0	Rogers	1503	2-1868	54-16x24-68600	Renumbered No. 338. Retired 9-1899.
70	4-4-0	Rogers	1506	3-1868	54-16x24-68600	Renumbered No. 339. Rebuilt to 824 on 2-1886.
71	4-4-0	Rogers	1507	3-1868	54-16x24-68600	Renumbered No. 340. Retired 1892.
72	4-4-0	Rogers	1508	3-1868	54-16x24-68600	Renumbered No. 341. Retired 1892.
73	4-4-0	Rogers	1505	3-1868	66-17x24-76100	Renumbered No. 657, later No. 489. Retired 7-1901.
74	4-4-0	Rogers	1509	3-1868	66-17x24-76100	Renumbered No. 658, later No. 490. Retired 7-1905.
75	4-4-0	Rogers	1510	4-1868	66-17x24-76100	Renumbered No. 659, later No. 491. Retired 3-1905.
76	4-4-0	Rogers	1511	4-1868	66-17x24-76100	Renumbered No. 660, later No. 492. Sold F. M. Hicks 12-01.
77	4-4-0	Rogers	1512	4-1868	66-17x24-76100	Renumbered No. 661, later No. 493. Retired 10-1899.
78	4-4-0	Hinkley & Williams		6-1868	56-16x24-65800	Renumbered No. 801. Retired 1898.
79	4-4-0	Hinkley & Williams		6-1868	56-16x24-65800	Sold to Omaha & Rep. Val. No. 5. Later UP No. 502.
80	4-4-0	Hinkley & Williams		6-1868	56-16x24-65800	Renumbered No. 802. Retired 8-1899.
81	4-4-0	Hinkley & Williams		6-1868	56-16x24-65800	Renumbered No. 503. Retired 1898.
82	4-4-0	Hinkley & Williams		6-1868	56-16x24-65800	Renumbered No. 330. Sold to F. M. Hicks 1-1903.
83	4-4-0	Danforth L&M		1868	56-17x24-73600	Sold prior 1885.
84	4-4-0	Danforth L&M		1868	56-17x24-73600	Renumbered No. 504. Retired 5-1900.
85	4-4-0	Danforth L&M		1868	56-17x24-73600	Renumbered No. 332. Rebuilt to 821 on 3-1885.
86	4-4-0	Danforth L&M		1868	56-17x24-73600	Renumbered No. 505. Retired 9-1899.
87	4-4-0	Danforth L&M		1868	56-17x24-73600	Renumbered No. 800. Retired 9-1899.
88	4-6-0	Baldwin	1707	3-1868	54-18x22-79450	Renumbered No. 909. Retired 6-1914.
89	4-6-0	Baldwin	1708	3-1868	54-18x22-79450	Renumbered No. 910. Retired 1896.
90	4-6-0	Baldwin	1710	4-1868	54-18x22-79450	Renumbered No. 911. Retired 10-1899.
91	4-6-0	Baldwin	1715	4-1868	54-18x22-79450	Note 11.
92	4-6-0	Baldwin	1716	4-1868	54-18x22-74950	Note 12.
93	4-6-0	Taunton	430	5-1868	54-18x24-75952	Renumbered No. 919. Retired 1898.
94	4-6-0	Taunton	432	5-1868	54-18x24-75952	Renumbered No. 920. Retired 6-1914.
95	4-6-0	Taunton	433	6-1868	54-18x24-75952	Renumbered No. 921. Rebuilt to No. 1701 on 10-1892.
96	4-6-0	Taunton	434	6-1868	54-18x24-75952	Renumbered No. 922. Rebuilt to No. 1700 on 6-1892.
97	4-6-0	Taunton	436	7-1868	54-18x24-75952	Renumbered No. 923. Sold to F. M. Hicks 8-1901.
98	4-6-0	Taunton	437	7-1868	54-18x24-75952	Renumbered No. 924, later No. 1202 (1915). Retired 4-1923.
99	4-6-0	Taunton	439	8-1868	54-18x24-75952	Renumbered No. 925. Rebuilt to 4-4-0 No. 844 on 3-1893.
100	4-6-0	Rhode Island	54	5-1868	54-18x24-81300	Renumbered No. 900. Retired 1898.
101	4-6-0	Rhode Island	55	5-1868	54-18x24-81300	Renumbered No. 901. Retired 1898.
102	4-6-0	Rhode Island	61	7-1868	54-18x24-81300	Renumbered No. 902. Retired 1896.
103	4-6-0	Rhode Island	62	8-1868	54-18x24-81300	Renumbered No. 903. Retired 12-1899.
104	4-6-0	Rhode Island	63	8-1868	54-18x24-81300	Renumbered No. 904. Retired 4-1900.
105	4-6-0	Rhode Island	64	8-1868	54-18x24-81300	Renumbered No. 905, later No. 1200 (1915). Retired 2-1924.
106	4-6-0	Rhode Island	65	8-1868	54-18x24-81300	Renumbered No. 906, later No. 1201 (1915). Retired 2-1924.
107	4-6-0	Rhode Island	66	9-1868	54-18x24-81300	Renumbered No. 907. No record of disposal.
108	4-6-0	Baldwin	1764	9-1868	54-18x24-79450	Renumbered No. 914. Retired 7-1899.
109	4-6-0	Baldwin	1765	9-1868	54-18x24-79450	Renumbered No. 915. Retired 1898.
110	4-6-0	Baldwin	1768	9-1868	54-18x24-79450	Renumbered No. 916. Rebuilt to 4-4-0 No. 847 on 12-1893.
111	4-6-0	Baldwin	1770	9-1868	54-18x24-79450	Renumbered No. 917. Retired 10-1899.
112	4-6-0	Baldwin	1774	10-1868	54-18x24-79450	Note 13.
113	2-8-0	Baldwin	1783	10-1868	49-20x24-93300	Renumbered No. 1250. Retired 11-1904.
114	2-8-0	Baldwin	1804	12-1868	49-20x24-93300	Renumbered No. 1251. Sold to Mt. Hood R.R. No. 1 on 2-1902.
115	2-8-0	Baldwin	1802	12-1868	49-20x24-93300	Renumbered No. 1252. Sold to Mt. Hood R.R. No. 2 on 11-1904.
116	4-4-0	Rogers	1556	10-1868	54-16x24-68400	Renumbered No. 803. Retired 8-1899.
117	4-4-0	Rogers	1557	10-1868	54-16x24-68400	Renumbered No. 342. Retired 8-1899.
118	4-4-0	Rogers	1563	11-1868	54-16x24-68400	Renumbered No. 804. Sold To F. M. Hicks 8-1902.
119	4-4-0	Rogers	1564	11-1868	54-16x24-68400	Renumbered No. 343. Retired 4-1903.
120	4-4-0	Rogers	1565	11-1868	54-16x24-68400	Renumbered No. 344, later No. 480. Sold to F. M. Hicks 4-1903.

In the scene above, Union Pacific No. 82 built by Hinkley & Williams in 1868. (RIGHT) No. 86 built by Danforth in 1868 on a construction train at Green River. — BOTH UNION PACIFIC MUSEUM

Locomotive No. 90 was one of the first Baldwin Locomotive Works engines on the Union Pacific. This ornate 4-6-0 photographed at the works in Philadelphia, was delivered in April 1868. — GERALD M. BEST COLLECTION

No.	Type	Builder and Construction No.		Date Built	Dimensions Dr.—Cyls.—Wt.	Remarks
121	4-4-0	Schenectady	523	11-1868	54-16x24-68600	Renumbered No. 517. Sold to F. M. Hicks 11-1901.
122	4-4-0	Schenectady	524	12-1868	54-16x24-68600	Renumbered No. 518. Retired 1898.
123	4-4-0	Schenectady	525	12-1868	54-16x24-68600	Sold to Utah Sou. No. 9 — 1879.
124	4-4-0	Schenectady	527	12-1868	54-16x24-68600	Note 14.
125	4-4-0	Schenectady	529	12-1868	54-16x24-68600	Sold to Utah Sou. No. 10 — 1879.
126	4-4-0	Taunton	445	11-1868	54-16x24-62600	Renumbered No. 702. Sold to Sou. Pac. No. 1481 — 1901.
127	4-4-0	Taunton	446	11-1868	54-16x24-62600	Renumbered No. 709. Sold to F. M. Hicks 5-1901.
128	4-4-0	Taunton	449	12-1868	54-16x24-62600	Renumbered No. 806. Retired 6-1900.
129	4-4-0	Taunton	450	12-1868	54-16x24-62600	Note 15.
130	4-4-0	Taunton	451	12-1868	54-16x24-62600	Renumbered No. 334. Retired 1890.
131	4-4-0	Rogers	1495	2-1868	60-16x24-69700	Renumbered No. 394. Retired 4-1902.
132	4-4-0	Rogers	1496	2-1868	60-16x24-69700	Renumbered No. 566. Sold to F. M. Hicks 1-1903.
133-140		Rogers 1518-21, 1524-25, 1528-29 5 & 6-1868, ordered with Nos. 131 and 132. Not delivered. Believed diverted to some other railroad. Not in 1-1870 Union Pacific locomotive list.				
141	4-4-0	Schenectady	544	3-1869	54-16x24-68600	Renumbered No. 519. Retired 7-1901.
142	4-4-0	Schenectady	545	3-1869	54-16x24-68600	Renumbered No. 520. Retired 10-1899.
143	4-4-0	Schenectady	546	3-1869	54-16x24-68600	Renumbered No. 335. Retired 5-1900.
144	4-4-0	Schenectady	547	3-1869	54-16x24-68600	Sold to Utah Sou. No. 3 — 1873.
145	4-4-0	Schenectady	548	3-1869	54-16x24-68600	Sold to Utah Sou. No. 11 — 1879.
146	4-4-0	Schenectady	557	5-1869	66-16x24-68600	Renumbered No. 653, later No. 485. Retired 4-1902.
147	4-6-0	Taunton	649	12-1874	54-18x24-78300	Renumbered No. 928, later No. 1203. Retired 2-1924.
148	4-6-0	Taunton	650	12-1874	54-18x24-78300	Renumbered No. 929. Retired 1896.
149	4-4-0	Taunton	657	9-1875	66-18x24-70300	Renumbered No. 807, later No. 931. Retired 11-1926.
150	4-4-0	Taunton	658	9-1875	66-18x24-70300	Renumbered No. 808, later No. 932. Retired 12-1933.
151	4-4-0	Taunton	659	9-1875	66-18x24-70300	Renumbered No. 809. Sold to F. M. Hicks 5-1901.
152	4-4-0	Taunton	660	9-1875	66-18x24-70300	Renumbered No. 810. Retired 1898.
153	4-4-0	Taunton	661	10-1875	66-18x24-70300	Renumbered No. 811. Retired 11-1899.
154	4-4-0	Taunton	662	10-1875	66-18x24-70300	Renumbered No. 812, later No. 933. Retired 12-1926.
155	4-4-0	Taunton	663	10-1875	66-18x24-70300	Renumbered No. 813. Retired 9-1900.
156	4-4-0	Hinkley & Williams		1869	68-17x24-76033	Renumbered No. 654, later No. 486. Sold to F. M. Hicks 9-1902.
157	4-4-0	Hinkley & Williams		1869	68-17x24-76033	Renumbered No. 561. Retired 1896.
158	4-4-0	Hinkley & Williams		1869	68-17x24-76033	Renumbered No. 655, later No. 487. Retired 11-1899.
159	4-4-0	Taunton	461	5-1869	66-16x24-74300	Renumbered No. 814. Retired 11-1899.
160	4-4-0	Taunton	462	5-1869	66-16x24-74300	Note 16.
161	4-4-0	Taunton	463	5-1869	66-16x24-74300	Note 17.
162	4-4-0	Taunton	495	5-1870	60-17x24-70680	Renumbered No. 570. Retired 10-1899.
163	4-4-0	Taunton	496	5-1870	60-17x24-70680	Renumbered No. 571. Sold to F. M. Hicks 5-1902.
164	4-4-0	Taunton	502	7-1870	60-17x24-70680	Renumbered No. 572. Retired 1897.
165	4-4-0	Taunton	503	7-1870	60-17x24-70680	Renumbered No. 573. Sold to F. M. Hicks 10-1901.
166	4-4-0	Taunton	664	11-1875	66-18x24-74300	Renumbered No. 815, later No. 934. Retired 4-1923.
167	4-4-0	Taunton	665	12-1875	66-18x24-74300	Renumbered No. 816, later No. 935. Retired 12-1933.
168	4-4-0	Taunton	666	12-1875	66-18x24-74300	Renumbered No. 817. Sold to S.P. No. 1482-1901.
169	4-4-0	Taunton	667	12-1875	66-18x24-74300	Renumbered No. 818, later No. 936. Retired 1-1916.
170	4-4-0	Taunton	668	12-1875	66-18x24-74300	Renumbered No. 819, later No. 937. Retired 10-1925.
171	4-6-0	Taunton	679	3-1878	60-18x24-77100	Renumbered No. 930. Retired 1-1901.
172	4-6-0	Taunton	680	3-1878	60-18x24-77100	Renumbered No. 931, later No. 1204. Retired 2-1924.
173	4-6-0	Taunton	681	4-1878	60-18x24-77100	Renumbered No. 932. Sold to F. M. Hicks 1-1902.
174	4-6-0	Taunton	682	4-1878	60-18x24-77100	Renumbered No. 933. Retired 9-1900.
175	4-6-0	Taunton	683	5-1878	60-18x24-77100	Renumbered No. 934. Retired 1915.
176	4-6-0	Taunton	684	5-1878	60-18x24-77100	Renumbered No. 935. Sold to F. M. Hicks 7-1901.
177	4-6-0	Taunton	685	6-1878	60-18x24-77100	Renumbered No. 936, later No. 1205. Retired 4-1923.
178	4-6-0	Taunton	686	6-1878	60-18x24-77100	Renumbered No. 937, later No. 1206. Retired 4-1923.
179	4-6-0	Taunton	687	6-1878	60-18x24-77100	Renumbered No. 938, 1104(1887), 1036(1890). Retired 1900.
180	4-6-0	Taunton	688	6-1878	60-18x24-77100	Renumbered No. 939. Retired 1896.
181	4-6-0	Taunton	700	6-1879	55-18x24-77100	Renumbered No. 940. Retired 1896.
182	4-6-0	Taunton	701	6-1879	55-18x24-77100	Renumbered No. 941, later No. 1207. Retired 2-1924.
183	4-6-0	Taunton	702	6-1879	55-18x24-77100	Renumbered No. 942, later No. 1208. Retired 2-1924.
184	4-6-0	Taunton	703	6-1879	55-18x24-77100	Sold to O.S.L. No. 22 on 11-1882.
185	4-6-0	Taunton	706	7-1879	55-18x24-77100	Renumbered No. 943, later No. 1209. Retired 4-1923.

In the top scene, Union Pacific No. 368, former No. 125 preserved its original appearance past 1885. (LEFT) No. 566, former No. 132 shows the results of rebuilding. — BOTH UNION PACIFIC MUSEUM (BELOW) No. 131, the mate to No 132, except for added air brakes is "as built" by Rogers in 1868. — E. L. DE GOLYER, JR. COLLECTION

A page of Taunton engines. At the left, No. 235 at the factory in 1881. (BELOW) An earlier Taunton engine No. 155 after 1875. — BOTH GERALD M. BEST COLLECTION (LOWER) No. 573, former No. 165 built in 1870, has survived to 1885 with few changes. — UNION PACIFIC MUSEUM

No.	Type	Builder and Construction No.		Date Built	Dimensions Dr.—Cyls.—Wt.	Remarks
186	4-6-0	Taunton	707	7-1879	55-18x24-77100	Renumbered No. 944. Sold to F. M. Hicks 11-1900.
187	4-6-0	Taunton	710	9-1879	55-18x24-77100	Renumbered No. 945. Sold to Leavenworth, Kan. & Wn. 10-01.
188	4-6-0	Taunton	712	9-1879	55-18x24-77100	Renumbered No. 946. Retired 11-1899.
189	4-6-0	Taunton	714	10-1879	55-18x24-77100	Renumbered No. 947. Sold to F. M. Hicks 12-1901.
190	4-6-0	Taunton	715	10-1879	55-18x24-77100	Renumbered No. 1103, 1035(1890), 1216(1915). Retired 6-1925.
191	4-6-0	Taunton	722	1-1880	55-18x24-77100	Renumbered No. 949. Retired 6-1900.
192	4-6-0	Taunton	723	1-1880	55-18x24-77100	Renumbered No. 950, later No. 1210. Retired 10-1923.
193	4-6-0	Taunton	724	1-1880	55-18x24-77100	Renumbered No. 951. Retired 1896.
194	4-6-0	Taunton	725	1-1880	55-18x24-77100	Renumbered No. 952. Sold to Block-Pollock Co. 1-1900.
195	4-6-0	Taunton	726	2-1880	55-18x24-77100	Renumbered No. 953. Sold to F. M. Hicks 3-1901.
196	4-6-0	Taunton	727	2-1880	55-18x24-77100	Renumbered No. 954. Retired 9-1900.
197	4-6-0	Taunton	728	3-1880	55-18x24-77100	Renumbered No. 955. Sold to Block-Pollock Co. 1-1900.
198	4-6-0	Taunton	729	3-1880	55-18x24-77100	Renumbered No. 956. Retired 9-1900.
199	4-6-0	Taunton	732	4-1880	55-18x24-77100	Sold to O.S.L. No. 28 on 11-1882.
200	4-6-0	Taunton	733	4-1880	55-18x24-77100	Renumbered No. 957, later No. 1211. Retired 10-1925.
201	4-6-0	Danforth L&M	1113	1-1880	55-18x24-85950	Renumbered No. 1004. Sold to Salt Lake & Wn. 1902.
202	4-6-0	Danforth L&M	1114	1-1880	55-18x24-85950	Renumbered No. 1005. Sold to F. M. Hicks 1-1902.
203	4-6-0	Danforth L&M	1115	1-1880	55-18x24-85950	Renumbered No. 1006. Retired 1896.
204	4-6-0	Danforth L&M	1116	1-1880	55-18x24-85950	Renumbered No. 1007. Sold to Block-Pollock Co. 1-1900.
205	4-6-0	Danforth L&M	1117	1-1880	55-18x24-83110	Renumbered No. 1008. Retired 1888.
206	4-6-0	Danforth L&M	1118	1-1880	55-18x24-83110	Renumbered No. 1009, later No. 1214. Retired 2-1924.
207	4-6-0	Danforth L&M	1119	1-1880	55-18x24-83110	Renumbered No. 1010. Retired 6-1914.
208	4-6-0	Danforth L&M	1120	1-1880	55-18x24-83110	Renumbered No. 1011. Retired 9-1899.
209	4-6-0	Danforth L&M	1121	1-1880	55-18x24-83110	Renumbered No. 1012. Retired 10-1900.
210	4-6-0	Danforth L&M	1122	1-1880	55-18x24-83110	Renumbered No. 1013. Retired 1896.
211	4-6-0	Danforth L&M	1123	1-1880	55-18x24-83110	Renumbered No. 1014. Retired 8-1900.
212	4-6-0	Danforth L&M	1124	1-1880	55-18x24-83110	Renumbered No. 1015. Sold to Block-Pollock Co. 1-1900.
213	4-6-0	Danforth L&M	1130	2-1880	55-18x24-83110	Renumbered No. 1016. Sold to Block-Pollock Co. 1-1900.
214	4-6-0	Danforth L&M	1131	2-1880	55-18x24-83110	Renumbered No. 1017. Retired 1-1900.
215	2-6-0	Danforth L&M	1168	3-1880	50-18x22-81500	Renumbered No. 1200. Retired 1899.
216	2-6-0	Danforth L&M	1169	3-1880	50-18x22-81500	Renumbered No. 1201. Retired 1899.
217	2-6-0	Danforth L&M	1170	3-1880	50-18x22-81500	Renumbered No. 1202. Retired 1899.
218	2-6-0	Danforth L&M	1171	3-1880	50-18x22-81500	Renumbered No. 1203. Retired 1901.
219	2-8-0	Baldwin	5606	4-1881	50-20x24-102200	Renumbered No. 1253. Retired 7-1900.
220	2-8-0	Baldwin	5607	4-1881	50-20x24-102200	Renumbered No. 1254. Retired 1-1905.
221	2-8-0	Baldwin	5621	5-1881	50-20x24-102200	Renumbered No. 1255. Retired 8-1900.
222	2-8-0	Baldwin	5623	5-1881	50-20x24-102200	Renumbered No. 1256. Sold Atl. Equip. Co. 1-05.
223	2-8-0	Baldwin	5656	6-1881	50-20x24-102200	Renumbered No. 1257. Sold Atl. Equip. Co. 2-05.
224	2-8-0	Baldwin	5657	6-1881	50-20x24-102200	Renumbered No. 1258. Sold to F. M. Hicks 3-1901.
225	2-8-0	Baldwin	5792	8-1881	50-20x24-102200	Renumbered No. 1259. Retired 10-1900.
226	2-8-0	Baldwin	5793	8-1881	50-20x24-102200	Renumbered No. 1260. Sold 8-1900. Later Ironton R.R. No. 24.
227	2-8-0	Baldwin	5806	9-1881	50-20x24-102200	Renumbered No. 1261. Retired 10-1900.
228	2-8-0	Baldwin	5816	9-1881	50-20x24-102200	Renumbered No. 1262. Sold to Atl. Equip. Co. 1-1906.
229	2-8-0	Baldwin	5937	12-1881	50-20x24-102200	Renumbered No. 1263. Sold to Atl. Equip. Co. 2-1905.
230	2-8-0	Baldwin	5939	12-1881	50-20x24-102200	Renumbered No. 1264. Retired 11-1899.
231	2-8-0	Baldwin	5943	12-1881	50-20x24-102200	Renumbered No. 1265. Sold 7-1900. Later BB&BC No. 5.
232	2-8-0	Baldwin	5961	12-1881	50-20x24-102200	Renumbered No. 1266. Sold to F. M. Hicks 1-1901.
233	2-8-0	Baldwin	5962	12-1881	50-20x24-102200	Renumbered No. 1267. Sold 8-1900. Later Ches. Wn. No. 103.
234	4-6-0	Taunton	775	3-1881	54-18x24-86350	Sold to O.S.L. No. 17 on 11-1882.
235	4-6-0	Taunton	776	3-1881	54-18x24-86350	Sold to O.S.L. No. 11 on 11-1882.
236	4-6-0	Taunton	777	3-1881	54-18x24-86350	Sold to Colo. Cent., Julesburg Br. No. 12 – 1882.
237	4-6-0	Taunton	778	4-1881	54-18x24-86350	Sold to Colo. Cent., Julesburg Br. No. 13 – 1882.
238	4-6-0	Taunton	783	4-1881	54-18x24-86350	Renumbered No. 985. Retired 1915.
239	4-6-0	Taunton	784	5-1881	54-18x24-86350	Renumbered No. 1101, later No. 1033. Retired 1915.
240	4-6-0	Taunton	785	5-1881	54-18x24-86350	Renumbered No. 1102, later No. 1034. Retired 1900.
241	4-6-0	Taunton	786	5-1881	54-18x24-86350	Sold to Colo. Cent., J.B. No. 14 – 1882.
242	4-6-0	Taunton	787	5-1881	54-18x24-86350	Renumbered No. 986. Retired 11-1899.
243	4-6-0	Taunton	788	6-1881	54-18x24-86350	Renumbered No. 987. Retired 11-1912.
244	4-6-0	Taunton	789	6-1881	54-18x24-86350	Renumbered No. 988, later No. 1212. Retired 5-1915.
245	4-6-0	Taunton	790	6-1881	54-18x24-86350	Renumbered No. 989. Sold to F. M. Hicks 2-1901.

No.	Type	Builder and Construction No.		Date Built	Dimensions Dr.—Cyls.—Wt.	Remarks
246	4-6-0	Taunton	792	6-1881	54-18x24-86350	Sold to O.S.L. No. 18 on 11-1882.
247	4-6-0	Taunton	793	7-1881	54-18x24-86350	Renumbered No. 991. Sold to F. M. Hicks on 7-1901.
248	4-6-0	Taunton	794	7-1881	54-18x24-86350	Renumbered No. 992. Retired 10-1900.
249	4-6-0	Taunton	795	7-1881	54-18x24-86350	Renumbered No. 993. Sold to Block-Pollock Co. 1-1900.
250	4-6-0	Taunton	796	7-1881	54-18x24-86350	Renumbered No. 994. Retired 11-1899.
251	4-6-0	Taunton	797	8-1881	54-18x24-86350	Sold to Colo. Cent. J. B. No. 15 — 1882.
252	4-6-0	Taunton	798	8-1881	54-18x24-86350	Renumbered No. 996. Sold to F. M. Hicks 3-1901.
253	4-6-0	Taunton	799	8-1881	54-18x24-86350	Renumbered No. 997. Sold to Block-Pollock Co. 1-1900.
254	4-6-0	Taunton	800	8-1881	54-18x24-86350	Renumbered No. 998. Sold to F. M. Hicks 1-1901.
255	4-6-0	Taunton	801	8-1881	54-18x24-86350	Renumbered No. 999. Sold to F. M. Hicks 10-1903.
256	4-6-0	Taunton	802	8-1881	54-18x24-86350	Renumbered No. 1000, later No. 1213. Retired 2-1924.
257	4-6-0	Taunton	803	9-1881	54-18x24-86350	Sold to Colo. Cent. J. B. No. 16 — 1882.
258	4-6-0	Taunton	804	9-1881	54-18x24-86350	Sold to Colo. Cent. J. B. No. 17 — 1882.
259	4-6-0	Taunton	774	3-1881	54-18x24-86350	Note 18.
260	2-8-0	Cooke L&M	1371	10-1882	50-20x24-103550	Renumbered No. 1271. Sold to F. M. Hicks 3-1901.
261	2-8-0	Cooke L&M	1372	10-1882	50-20x24-103550	Renumbered No. 1272. Sold to F. M. Hicks 1-1902.
262	2-8-0	Taunton	875	12-1882	50-20x24-104300	Renumbered No. 1278. Retired 9-1906.
263	2-8-0	Taunton	876	12-1882	50-20x24-104300	Renumbered No. 1279. Retired 5-1901.
264	2-8-0	Taunton	879	1-1883	50-20x24-104180	Renumbered No. 1280. Retired 1-1905.
265	2-8-0	Taunton	880	1-1883	50-20x24-104180	Renumbered No. 1281. Retired 1-1905.
266	2-8-0	Taunton	881	2-1883	50-20x24-104180	Renumbered No. 1282. Retired 8-1900.
267	2-8-0	Taunton	882	2-1883	50-20x24-104180	Renumbered No. 1283. Sold to O.R. & N. No. 170 8-1900.
268	2-8-0	Taunton	883	2-1883	50-20x24-104180	Renumbered No. 1284. Sold to F. M. Hicks 4-1901.
269	2-8-0	Taunton	884	2-1883	50-20x24-104180	Renumbered No. 1285. Sold to F. M. Hicks 4-1901.
270	2-8-0	Taunton	885	3-1883	50-20x24-104180	Renumbered No. 1286. Retired 7-1905.
271	2-8-0	Taunton	886	3-1883	50-20x24-104180	Renumbered No. 1287. Retired 2-1905.
272	2-8-0	Taunton	887	4-1883	50-20x24-104180	Renumbered No. 1288. Retired 6-1913.
273	2-8-0	Taunton	888	4-1883	50-20x24-104180	Renumbered No. 1289. Sold to F. M. Hicks 11-1900.
274	2-8-0	Cooke L&M	1536	11-1883	50-20x24-103550	Renumbered No. 1273. Retired 7-1900.
275	2-8-0	Cooke L&M	1537	11-1883	50-20x24-103550	Renumbered No. 1274. Sold to Atl. Equip. Co. 3-1906.
276	2-8-0	Cooke L&M	1538	11-1883	50-20x24-103550	Renumbered No. 1275. Sold to Atl. Equip. Co. 3-1906.
277	2-8-0	Cooke L&M	1539	11-1883	50-20x24-103550	Renumbered No. 1276. Sold to F. M. Hicks 3-1901.
278	2-8-0	Cooke L&M	1540	11-1883	50-20x24-103550	Renumbered No. 1277. Sold to B. Ry. & Coal Co. 10-1906.

REPLACEMENT OR SECOND NUMBERS

No.	Type	Builder and Construction No.		Date Built	Dimensions Dr.—Cyls.—Wt.	Remarks
49	4-6-0	Taunton	861	8-1882	54-18x24-71900	Sold to O.S.L. No. 12 on 11-1882.
51	4-6-0	Taunton	862	8-1882	54-18x24-71900	Sold to O.S.L. No. 8 on 11-1882.
54	4-6-0	Taunton	863	8-1882	54-18x24-71900	Sold to Salt Lake & Western No. 1 — 1882.
55	4-6-0	Taunton	864	8-1882	54-18x24-71900	Sold to O.S.L. No. 7 11-1882.
65	4-6-0	Taunton	865	8-1882	54-18x24-71900	Sold to Utah Central No. 6 — 1883.
123	4-6-0	Taunton	866	8-1882	54-18x24-71900	Sold to O.S.L. No. 13(11-1882).
125	2-8-0	Cooke L&M	1368	10-1882	50-20x24-103550	Renumbered No. 1268. Retired 1900.
133	4-6-0	Taunton	639	7-1874	54-18x24-78300	Sold to O.S.L. No. 21(11-1882).
134	4-6-0	Taunton	640	7-1874	54-18x24-78300	Sold to O.S.L. No. 16 (11-1882).
135	4-6-0	Taunton	641	7-1874	54-18x24-78300	Renumbered No. 926. Retired 1890.
136	4-6-0	Taunton	644	9-1874	54-18x24-78300	Sold to O.S.L. No. 27(11-1882).
137	4-6-0	Taunton	645	10-1874	54-18x24-78300	Note 19.
138	4-6-0	Taunton	646	10-1874	54-18x24-78300	Renumbered No. 927. Retired 1896.
139	4-6-0	Taunton	647	11-1874	54-18x24-78300	Sold to O.S.L. No. 15(11-1882).
140	4-6-0	Taunton	648	11-1874	54-18x24-78300	Sold to O.S.L. No. 14(11-1882).
144	2-8-0	Cooke L&M	1369	10-1882	50-20x24-103550	Note 20.
145	2-8-0	Cooke L&M	1370	10-1882	50-20x24-103550	Renumbered No. 1270. Sold 8-1900.
246	4-6-0	Taunton	903	1-1884	56-18x24-86350	Renumbered No. 990. Retired 10-1900.
251	4-6-0	Taunton	904	1-1884	56-18x24-86350	Renumbered No. 995. Sold to F. M. Hicks 10-1901.
257	4-6-0	Taunton	905	1-1884	56-18x24-86350	Renumbered No. 1001. Sold to Block-Pollock Co. 1-1900.
258	4-6-0	Taunton	906	1-1884	56-18x24-86350	Renumbered No. 1002. Retired 10-1899.

No.	Type	Builder and Construction No.		Date Built	Dimensions Dr.—Cyls.—Wt.	Remarks
1	0-4-0T	Danforth L&M		1866	14x22	Named *Utah*. Renumbered No. 1397. Retired 1886.
2	0-4-0T	Grant	535	6-1868	50-15x24	Renumbered No. 1394. Retired 1890.
3	0-4-0T	Grant	575	7-1868	50-14x24	Renumbered No. 1396. Retired 1889.
4	0-4-0T	Grant		6-1868	50-15x24	Renumbered No. 1395. Retired 1888.
5	4-4-0T	Schenectady	535	1-1869	56-16x24-62600	Retired prior 1885.
6	0-4-0T	U. P. Shops			10x16	Renumbered No. 1399. Retired 1886.

Note 1 — The *Major General Sherman* No. 1 was sold to the Omaha & Republican Valley in 1880.

Note 2 — The *Major General McPherson* No. 2 was sold to the Colorado Central No. 2 in 1872.

Note 3 — The *Major General Sheridan* No. 4 was sold to the Oregon Short Line No. 29 (11-1882).

Note 4 — The *Vice Admiral Farragut* No. 5 was sold to the Oregon Short Line No. 24 (11-1882).

Note 5 — The *Black Hawk* No. 6 was sold to the Colorado Central No. 3 in 1871.

Note 6 — The *Osceola* No. 9 probably Ex U.S. Military Railroad *Osceola*, renumbered No. 300.

Note 7 — The *Colorado* No. 11 was sold to the Oregon Short Line No. 26 (11-1882).

Note 8 — The *Bellevue* No. 12 was sold to the Utah Southern No. 12 in 1880.

Note 9 — Sold to the Omaha & Republican Valley No. 1 in 1873.

Note 10 — Acquired secondhand. Sold to Omaha, Niobrara & Black Hills RR as No. 56. Became Union Pacific No. 337, retired in 1890.

Note 11 — Sold to Colorado Central No. 91 in 1878. Later became Union Pacific No. 912, Colorado & Southern No. 308.

Note 12 — Sold to Colorado Central No. 92 in 1878. Later became Union Pacific No. 913, Colorado & Southern No. 304.

Note 13 — Renumbered No. 918. Sold to Block-Pollock Co. 1-1900. Blew up at Rawlins 2-18-1869. Rebuilt 3-1870.

Note 14 — Sold to the Omaha, Niobrara & Black Hills RR as No. 124. Renumbered Union Pacific No. 336.

Note 15 — Sold to Marysville & Blue Valley RR as No. 129. Renumbered Union Pacific No. 501.

Note 16 — Sold to Colorado Central No. 5 in 1878. Later Union Pacific No. 568, Colorado & Southern No. 104.

Note 17 — Sold to Colorado Central No. 6 in 1878. Later Union Pacific No. 569, Colorado & Southern No. 105.

Note 18 — Was No. 233, 3-1881 to 12-1881. Renumbered No. 1003, retired 7-1900.

Note 19 — Renumbered No. 1100, later No. 1032. Sold to Salt Lake & Western 10-1901.

Note 20 — Renumbered No. 1269. Sold to Laramie, Hahns Peak & Western No. 4, 10-1906.

Notes

The report of the U.S. Railroad Commission on the Union Pacific R.R. released October 5, 1865, gives the following interesting information about the first five locomotives. One locomotive working at Omaha, arrived there July, 1865. One stored at St. Joseph, Missouri, awaiting shipment up the river to Omaha. One working on the Hannibal & St. Joseph R.R. hauling cars of rail destined for the Union Pacific. Two working on the Chicago, Alton & St. Louis, hauling rail for the Union Pacific, using 20 platform cars belonging to that company.

Names of railroads which purchased Union Pacific locomotives, 1863-1885:

Bellingham Bay & British Columbia
Birmingham Railway & Coal Co.
Colorado Central
Colorado Central, Julesburg Branch
Laramie, Hahn's Peak & Western
Leavenworth, Kansas & Western
Marysville & Blue Valley
Omaha, Niobrara & Black Hills
Omaha & Pleasant Valley
Oregon Short Line
Salt Lake & Western
Utah Central
Utah Southern

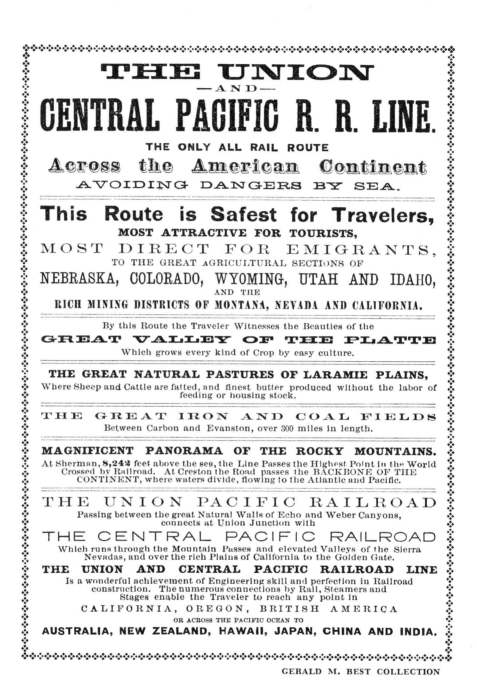

THE UNION
—AND—
CENTRAL PACIFIC R. R. LINE.

THE ONLY ALL RAIL ROUTE

Across the American Continent

AVOIDING DANGERS BY SEA.

This Route is Safest for Travelers,
MOST ATTRACTIVE FOR TOURISTS,

MOST DIRECT FOR EMIGRANTS,

TO THE GREAT AGRICULTURAL SECTIONS OF

NEBRASKA, COLORADO, WYOMING, UTAH AND IDAHO,

AND THE

RICH MINING DISTRICTS OF MONTANA, NEVADA AND CALIFORNIA.

By this Route the Traveler Witnesses the Beauties of the

GREAT VALLEY OF THE PLATTE

Which grows every kind of Crop by easy culture.

THE GREAT NATURAL PASTURES OF LARAMIE PLAINS,

Where Sheep and Cattle are fatted, and finest butter produced without the labor of
feeding or housing stock.

THE GREAT IRON AND COAL FIELDS

Between Carbon and Evanston, over 300 miles in length.

MAGNIFICENT PANORAMA OF THE ROCKY MOUNTAINS.

At Sherman, **8,242** feet above the sea, the Line Passes the Highest Point in the World
Crossed by Railroad. At Creston the Road passes the BACKBONE OF THE
CONTINENT, where waters divide, flowing to the Atlantic and Pacific.

THE UNION PACIFIC RAILROAD

Passing between the great Natural Walls of Echo and Weber Canyons,
connects at Union Junction with

THE CENTRAL PACIFIC RAILROAD

Which runs through the Mountain Passes and elevated Valleys of the Sierra
Nevadas, and over the rich Plains of California to the Golden Gate.

THE UNION AND CENTRAL PACIFIC RAILROAD LINE

Is a wonderful achievement of Engineering skill and perfection in Railroad
construction. The numerous connections by Rail, Steamers and
Stages enable the Traveler to reach any point in

CALIFORNIA, OREGON, BRITISH AMERICA

OR ACROSS THE PACIFIC OCEAN TO

AUSTRALIA, NEW ZEALAND, HAWAII, JAPAN, CHINA AND INDIA.

Pacific Railroad
Potpourri

TIME TABLES-TICKETS-BROADSIDES

BRIDGES-TOWNS-PROFILES

CENTRAL PACIFIC RAILROAD.

PRINCIPAL OFFICES:

422 California street, San Francisco,   **56 and 58 K street, Sacramento.**

54 William street, New York City,   **303 Broadway, New York City.**

LELAND STANFORD, President.
C. P. HUNTINGTON, First Vice-President.
CHARLES CROCKER, Second Vice-President.
MARK HOPKINS, Treasurer.
E. B. CROCKER, Att'y and General Agent.
CHARLES W. SMITH, General Freight Agent.

E. H. MILLER, Jr., Secretary.
W. H. PORTER, Auditor.
S. S. MONTAGUE, Chief Engineer.
B. B. REDDING, Land Commissioner.
J. R. WATSON, General Supply Agent.

A. N. TOWNE, General Superintendent.
JNO. CORNING, Ass't Gen'l Superintendent.
E. C. FELLOWS, Sup't Western Division.
F. W. BOWEN, Sup't Sacramento Division.
C. D. MONTANYE, Sup't Truckee Division.
T. H. GOODMAN, General Passenger and Ticket Agent.

C. E. GILLETT, Sup't Humboldt Division.
JAS. CAMPBELL, Sup't Salt Lake Division.
F. L. VANDENBURGH, Sup't Telegraph.
FR. KNOWLAND, New York Agent.
HENRY STARRING, General Baggage Agent.

EASTWARD.				Miles fm San F'co	Local coin rates from San Francisco.	Divisions and Stations.	Miles from Omaha.	Elevations.	WESTWARD.			
Passenger.	Mixed.	Passenger.	Express.						Express.	Passenger.	Mixed.	Passenger.
No. 9.	No. 5.	No. 3.	No. 1.						No. 2.	No. 4.	No. 6.	No. 10.
P.M.	P.M.	P.M.	A.M.						P.M.	P.M	A.M	A.M
3.00	6.45	4.00	8.00	0	$ .00	Lv. **San Francisco.** Ar.	1,913	0	5.45	12.30	8.30	9.40
......	......	......	......	5	.25	Alameda Wharf........	1,908	0	......	......	......	......
......	......	......	......	8	.25	Alameda........	1,905	0	......	......	......	......
3.15	8.10	4.25	8.25	3	.25	Oakland Wharf........	1,810	0	5.30	12.15	8.00	9.25
3.32	8.35	4.42	8.40	6	.25	Oakland........	1,907	11	5.12	11.58	7.35	9.08
3.38	8.45	4.50	8.48	8	.25	Brooklyn........	1,905	12	5.06	11.50	7.25	9.01
3.45	8.55	5.00	8.55	11	.50	Simpson's........	1,902	18	5.00	11.42	7.13	8.55
3.55	9.15	5.09	9.05	15	.75	San Leandro........	1,898	49	4.50	11.34	6.55	8.45
4.05	9.35	5.15	9.13	18	1.00	Lorenzo........	1,895	33	4.42	11.25	6.35	8.36
4.25	10.10	5.28	9.28	26	1.52	Decoto........	1,887	72	4.25	11.12	6.00	8.20
4.40	10.25	5.35	9.35	29	1.25	Niles........	1,844	87	4.20	11.05	5 45	8.15
5.40				47	2.00	**San Jose**........	1,000	91				7.30

(Western Division, E. C. Fellows, Sup't.)

Nos. 3 and 10 run daily. Nos. 5 and 6 (East of Sacramento) daily. Nos. 3 and 4 daily, (Sundays excepted). †Meals. *All Trains west of Ogden are run by Sacramento time.*

EASTWARD.			Miles fm San F'co	Local coin rates from San Francisco.	Divisions and Stations.	Miles from Omaha.	Elevations.	WESTWARD.		
Mixed.	Passenger.	Express.						Express.	Passenger.	Mixed.
No. 5.	No. 3.	No. 1.						No. 2.	No. 4.	No. 6.
P.M.	P.M.	A.M.						P.M.	P.M.	A.M.
10.25	5.35	9.35	29	$1.50	Lv. Niles........	1,884	87	4.20	11.05	5.45
......	......	......	36	1.75	Sunol........	1,877	200	......	......	......
11.40	6.00	10.07	41	2.00	Pleasanton........	1,872	351	3.52	10.38	4.40
12.15 AM	6.13	10.23	47	2.00	Livermore........	1,866	485	3.39	10.23	4.05
1.20	6.32	10.43	55	2.00	Altamont........	1,858	740	3.20	10.00	3.15
2.15	6 55	11.06	63	2.00	Midway........	1,850	357	2.55	9.38	2.15
2.40	7.07	11.18	69	2.00	Ellis........	1,844	76	2.40	9.24	1.30
3.00	7.17	11.28	74	2.00	Bantas........	1,839	30	2.30	9.14	12.55
3.20	7.28	11.40	78	2.00	San Joaquin Bridge........	1,835	36	2.19	9.04	12.20
3.32	7.36	11.48	81	2.00	*Lathrop*........	1,832	26	2.10	8.55	12.00
4.10	7.58	12.10 PM	91	2.00	**Stockton.**........	1,822	23	1.46	8.35	11.20
5.02	8.25	12.42	103	2.50	Mokelumne........	1,810	55	1.17	8.10	10.28
5.35	8.41	1.00	112	2.50	Galt........	1,801	50	1.00	7.55	9.52
6.08	8.55	1.15	119	2.50	McConnell's........	1,794	49	12.40	7.41	9.20
6.23	9.03	1.23	123	2.50	Elk Grove........	1,790	53	12.30	7.35	9.03
6.50	9.15	1.36	129	2.50	Florin........	1,784	42	12.11	7.23	8.15
7.15	9.22	1.45	133	2.50	Brighton........	1,780	51	12.00	7.15	7.55
7.40 AM	9.35	2.00	138	2.50	**Sacramento**........ Lv.	1,775	30	11.45 AM	7.00 AM	7.30 PM

(Western Division, E. C. Fellows, Sup't.)

EASTWARD.			Miles fm San F'co	Local coin rates from San Francisco.	Divisions and Stations.	Miles from Omaha.	Elevations.	WESTWARD.		
Mixed,	Passenger.	Express.						Express.	Passenger.	Freight.
No. 7.	No. 5.	No. 1.						No. 2.	No. 6.	No. 8.
P.M.	A.M.	P.M.						A.M.	P.M.	A.M.
9.00	9.00	2.20	138	$ 2.50	Lv. **Sacramento**........ Ar.	1,775	30	11.25	5.15	7.45
9 15	9.15	2.29	141	2.75	American River Bridge........	1,772	52	11.16	5.00	7.28
9.36	9.35	2.41	146	3.00	Arcade........	1,767	55	11.03	4.40	7.06
10.12	10.05	3.00	153	3.00	Antelope........	1,760	154	10.41	4.05	6.35
10.30	10.30	3.09	156	3.00	Junction........	1,757	163	10.30	3.50	6.20

(Sac'to T'n'l Div'n.)

Nos. 1 and 2 run daily. Nos. 5 and 6 (East of Sacramento), daily. Nos. 3 and 4 daily (Sundays excepted). † Meals. *All Trains west of Ogden are run by Sacramento time.*

188

EASTWARD.						Divisions and Stations.			WESTWARD.		
Mixed.	Passenger.	Express.	Miles fm San F'co	Local coin rates from San Francisco.			Miles from Omaha.	Eleva-tions.	Express.	Passenger.	Freight.
No. 7.	No. 5.	No. 1.							No. 2.	No. 6.	No. 8.
P.M.	A.M.	P.M.							A.M.	P.M.	A.M.
11.15	11.15	3.25	160	$ 3.25	Lv.	Rocklin...............Ar.	1,753	249	10.20	3.00	5.45
11.36	11.35	3.35	162	3.50		Pino........................	1,751	403	10.10	2.35	5.25
....	....	....	166	3.75		Penryn....................	1,747	500	....	....	....
12.15	12.20 PM	3.56	169	4.00		Newcastle...............	1,744	970	9.52	1.50	4.55
12.50 AM	1.15	4.13	174	4.50		Auburn....................	1,739	1,363	9.37	1.15	4.30
1.35	2.00	4.35	180	5.00		Clipper Gap............	1,733	1,759	9.18	12.35	3.55
2.15	2.40	4.55	187	5.50		N. E. Mills..............	1,726	2,209	9.06	12.05	3.20
2.55	3.30	5.25	192	5.75		**Colfax**...................	1,721	2,421	† 8.45 8.20	11.35	2.55
3.25	4.05	5.44	196	6.25		Cape Horn..............	1,717	2,692	8.00	11.10	2.30
4.00	4.45	6.05	202	6.75		Gold Run................	1,711	3,206	7.40	10.41	1.55
4.15	5.05	6.15	205	7.00		Dutch Flat..............	1,708	3,403	7.30	10.30	1.42
4.30	5.25	† 6.25 6.45	207	7.25		Alta.......................	1,706	3,612	7.21	10.20	1.30
5.00	6.00	7.15	211	7.75		Shady Run..............	1,702	4,154	7.00	9.55	1.03
5.15	6.20	7.30	213	8.00		China Ranch............	1,700	4,411	6.50	9.42	12.50 PM
5.30	6.40	7.41	216	8.25		Blue Canyon...........	1,697	4,678	6.40	9.30	12.35
6.10	7.25	8.10	222	8.75		Emigrant Gap..........	1,691	5,230	6.10	9.00	12.03
7.05	8.20	8.50	230	9.75		Cisco......................	1,683	5,939	5.35	8.15	11.15
7.30	8.40	9.05	233	10.15		Tamarack................	1,680	6,191	5.20	7.30	10.55
↓7.55	9.07	9.21	237	10.25		Cascade..................	1,676	6,520	5.05	7.06	10.35
....	....	....	241	10.50		Summit Valley.........	1,672	6,900	....	....	....
8.30	9.50	9.50	243	10.75		Summit...................	1,670	7,017	4.40	6.33	10.00
8.45	10.20	10.00	246	11.25		Strong's.................	1,667	6,781	4.30	6.15	9.25
9.45	11.20	10.50	258	12.25		**Truckee**............Lv.	1,655	5,846	3.40	5.15	8.15
12.30 PM	2.05 AM	11.15	258	12.25		**Truckee**............Ar.	1,655	5,846	3.30	3.55	2.15
1.20	2.55	11.40	266	12.75		Boca.......................	1,647	5,533	2.55	2.55	1.20 PM
....	....	....	276	13.75		State Line................	1,637	5,138	....	....	....
2.55	4.25	12.25 AM	282	14.00		Verdi......................	1,631	4,927	1.45	12.25 AM	11.15
4.30	5.45	1.15	292	15.00		**Reno**...................	1,621	4,507	1.00	11.10	9.50
5.10	6.26	1.37	300	15.50		Camp Thirty-seven...	1,613	4,404	12.18	10.25	8.35
6.05	7.30	2.10	312	16.50		Clark's...................	1,601	4,263	11.35	9.15	7.30
9.05	9.45	3.00	327	17.50		**Wadsworth**..........	1,586	4,077	10:45	7.45	6.00
9.15	10.00	3.07	329	17.75		Two-mlie Station......	1,584	4,155	10.22	7.00	5.15

Nos. 1 and 2 run daily. Nos. 5 and 6 (East of Sacramento), daily. Nos. 7 and 8 daily (Sundays excepted). †Meals *All Trains west of Ogden are run by Sacramento time.*

EASTWARD.						Divisions and Stations.			WESTWARD.		
Mixed.	Passenger.	Express.	Miles fm San F'co	Local coin rates from San Francisco.			Miles from Omaha.	Eleva-tions.	Express.	Passenger.	Freight.
No. 7.	No. 5.	No. 1.							No. 2.	No. 6.	No. 8.
P.M.	A.M.	A.M.							A.M.	A.M.	P.M.
10.05	10.35	3.25	335	$18.25	Lv.	Desert....................	1,578	4,017	10.05	6.25	4.42
11.00	11.35	3.55	346	19.00		Hot Springs............	1,567	4,070	9.35	5.40	3.55
11.40	12.20 PM	4.15	354	19.50		Mirage...................	1,559	4,199	9.15	5.00	3.00
12.15 AM	1.00	4.30	361	20.00		White Plains...........	1,552	3,894	8.57	4.20	2.25
1.25	2.07	4.58	373	21.00		Brown's..................	1,540	3,925	8.27	3.25	1.25
2.00	2.50	5.15	379	21.50		Granite Point..........	1,534	3,918	8.05	2.50	12.50
2.40	3.30	5.34	389	22.25		Lovelock's..............	1,524	3,977	7.45	2.11	12.10 AM
....	....	....	393	22.50		Bridge....................	1,520	4,009	....	....	....
3.35	4.25	6.00	400	23.00		Oreana...................	1,515	4,183	7.15	1.25	11.20
4.25	5.15	6.23	411	23.75		Rye Patch..............	1,502	4,257	6.46	12:37 PM	10.25
5.20	6.15	6.50 †7.15	422	24.75		Humboldt................	1,491	4,234	† 6.15 5.50	11.50	9.30
6.15	7.15	7.45	434	25.50		Mill City.................	1,479	4,228	5.20	11 00	8.30
6.50	7.50	8.05	441	26.00		Raspberry...............	1,472	4,327	5.00	10.30	7.50
7.40	8.40	8.32	451	26.75		Rose Creek..............	1,462	4,322	4.33	9.45	6.50
8.30	9.35	9.00	462	27.75	Ar.	**Winnemucca**.....Lv.	1,451	4,332	4.05	9.00	5.45
9.30	10.15	9.10	462	27.75	Lv.	**Winnemucca**.....Ar.	1,451	4,332	4.00	8.00	5.00
10.05	10.45	9.27	468	28.00		Tule.......................	1,445	4,315	3.43	7.32	4.25
11.03	11.40	9.54	479	29.00		Golconda.................	1,434	4,387	3.15	6.40	3.15
12.03 PM	12.35 AM	10.23	490	29.75		Iron Point...............	1,423	4,375	2.45	5.45	2.05
1.15	1.35	10.55	503	30.75		Stone House............	1,410	4,422	2.12	4.45	1.15 PM
3.00	3.10 †	11.45 12.00	522	32.25		**Battle Mountain**...	1,391	4,504	† 1.25 1.05	3.10	12.00
4.00	4.10	12.35 PM	534	33.00		Argenta..................	1,379	4,548	12.35	2.07	10.30
4.55	5.00	1.05	545	33.75		Shoshone................	1,361	4,636	12.05 PM	1.10	9.40
6.00	6.00	1.30	555	34.50		Be-o-wa-we.............	1,358	4,690	11.37	12.20 AM	8.55
6.40	6.40	1.52	563	35.25		Cluro......................	1,350	4,766	11.15	11.20	8.20
7.35	7.30	2.23	573	36.00		Palisade.................	1,340	4,841	10 45	10.50	7.30
9.15	10.00	2.50 3.10	583	36.75		**Carlin**.................	1,330	4,903	10.15	10.00	6.45
10.25	11.00	3.47	594	37.50		Moleen...................	1,319	4,982	9.20	8.15	4.50
11.50	12.30 PM	†4.20 4.40	606	38.50		**Elko**...................	1,307	5,065	† 8.45 8.25	7.15	3.55
12.40 AM	1.20	5.05	616	39.25		Osino......................	1,297	5,135	7.57	6.26	3.00
1.40	2.07	5.35	626	40.00		Peko.......................	1,287	5,204	7.30	5.35	2.15
2.00	2.25	5.43	630	40.25		Halleck...................	1,283	5,228	7.21	5.00	2.00

Nos. 1 and 2 run daily. Nos. 5 and 6 (East of Sacramento)), daily. Nos. 7 and 8 daily (Sundays excepted). † Meals. *All Trains west of Ogden are run by Sacramento time.*

CENTRAL PACIFIC RAILROAD. [CONTINUED.]

EASTWARD.					Divisions and Stations.			WESTWARD.		
Mixed.	Passenger.	Express.	Miles fm San F'co	Local coin rates from San Francisco.		Miles from Omaha.	Eleva-tions.	Express.	Passenger.	Freight.
No. 7.	No. 5.	No. 1.						No. 2.	No. 6.	No. 8.
A.M.	P.M.	P.M.						P.M.	A.M.	P.M.
3.00	3.30	6.18	642	$41.25	Lv. Deeth	1,271	5,340	6.50	3.30	1.15
3.55	4.30	6.53	655	42.00	Tulasco	1,258	5,484	6.15	2.30	12.30
4.30	5.20	7 15	663	42.50	Wells	1,250	5,629	5.55	1.55	12.05 AM
5.30	6.10	7.42	669	43.25	Moore's	1,244	6,118	5.30	1.08	11.35
6.07	6.50	8.05	677	43.75	Independence	1,236	6,007	5.07	12.30 PM	11.02
6.40	7.25	8.25	686	44.50	Otego	1,227	6,154	4.47	12.00	10.30
7.10	8.00	8.45	689	44.75	Pequop	1,224	6,184	4.30	11.30	10.03
8.00	8.50	9.15	699	45.25	Ar. **Toano** Lv.	1,214	5,970	4.00	10.40	9.15
8.35	9.45	9.20	699	45.25	Lv. **Toano** Ar.	1,214	5,970	3.50	10.10	8.40
9.20	10.45	9.43	706	46 00	Loray	1,207	5,555	3.15	9.20	7.40
10 15	11.40	10.07	715	46.50	Montello	1,198	4,999	2.40	8.25	6.45
11.15	12.45	10.31	725	47.25	Tecoma	1,188	4,812	2.13	7.35	6.00
12.15 PM	1.45 AM	10.56	734	48.00	Lucin	1,179	4,495	1.45	6.45	5.20
1.35	3.00	11.30	747	49.00	Bovine	1,166	4,347	1.02	5.40	4.20
3.30	4.45	12.10	758	49.75	Terrace	1,155	4,619	12.25 AM	4.45	3.30
5.10	6.10	12.55	774	51.00	Matlin	1,139	4,630	11.07	3.00	2.00
6.40	7.30	1.35	790	52.25	**Kelton**	1,123	4,222	10.10	1.35 AM	12.40 PM
8.00	8.40	2.06	804	53.00	Monument	1,109	4,223	9.20	12.20	11.30
8.45	9.20	2.25	812	53.00	Lake	1,101	4,222	8.45	11.37	10.45
9.30	10.10	2.55	820	53.00	Rozel	1,093	4,589	8.15	10.55	10.10
10.10	11.00	3.25	828	53.00	Promontory	1,085	4,905	7.45	10.10	9.30
1.10	2.00	4.55	857	53.00	Corinne	1,056	4,230	6.05	7.35	7.05
1.36	2.20	5.10	862	53.00	Brigham	1,051	4,220	5.52	6.35	6.22
2.35	3.10	5.40 AM	872	53.00	Bonneville	1,041	4,300	5.25	5.50	5.40
3.30 AM	4.00 PM	†6.10	881	53 00	Ar. **Ogden** Lv.	1,032	4,301	†5.00 PM	5.10 PM	4.45 AM

Nos. 1 and 2 run daily. Nos. 5 and 6 (East of Sacramento), daily. Nos. 7 and 8 daily (Sundays excepted). † Meals. *All Trains west of Ogden are run by Sacramento time.*

UNION PACIFIC RAILROAD.

PRINCIPAL OFFICES:

Railroad Building, Omaha, Nebraska. **Sears' Building, Boston, Mass.**

OLIVER AMES.
    President.
JOHN DUFF,
    Vice-President.
J. M. S. WILLIAMS,
    Treasurer.
E. H. ROLLINS,
    Secretary.
T. E. SICKLES,
    General Superintendent.

....
    Ass't Gen'l Sup't.
S. H. H. CLARK,
    Sup't Platte Division.
C. H. CHAPPEL,
    Sup't Lodge Pole Division.
L. FILLMORE,
    Sup't Laramie Division.
H. H. GIVEN,
    Acting Sup't Utah Div'n.

F. COLTON,
    Gen'l Passenger Agent.
....
    Ass't Passenger Agent.
H. BROWNSON,
    Gen'l Freight Agent.
J, J. DICKEY,
    Sup't Telegraph.
G. F. DAVIS,
    Land Commssssioner.

HENRY STARRING, General Baggage Agent, Chicago.

EASTWARD				Divisions and Stations.	Miles from Omaha.	Eleva-tions.	WESTWARD	
Mixed.	Express.	Miles fm San F'co					Express.	Mixed.
No. 6.	No. 4.						No. 3.	No. 7.
P.M.	A M.						P.M.	M
6.30	†8.30	881	Lv.	**Ogden**	1,032	4,332	†5.30	12.00
7.05	8.50	888		Uintah	1,025	4,550	5.08	11.20 AM
7.35	9.15	895		Devil's Gate	1,014	4,870	4.50	10.55
8.35	9.50	907		Weber	1,006	5,130	4.10	9.50
9.55	10.35	923		Echo	990	5,540	3.25	8.25
11.25	11.30	939		Castle Rock	974	6,290	2.30	7.05
12.30	†12.10 PM	948		**Wahsatch**	965	6,879	†1.35	2.20
1.20	1.10	957		Evanston	956	....	1.10	1.20
3.55	2.45	977		Piedmont	936	6,540	11.25 AM	10.40 PM
4.45	3,10	986		Leroy	927	7.123	10.45	9.40
5.10	3.25	1,001		Bridger	912	6,780	10.32	9.15
7.35	4.35	1,027		Church Buttes	886	6,317	9.25	7.00
8.55	5.00	1,038		Granger	875	6,270	8.55	6 05
10.45 PM	†6.00	1,056		**Bryan**	857	6,340	†8.15	4.45
12.00	6.45	1,069		Green River	844	6,140	7.00	2.20
1.10	7.25	1,082		Rock Springs	830	6,280	6.20	1.10
2.30	8.05	1,097		Salt Wells	816	6,360	5.40	11.30 AM
3.30	8.37	1,109		Point of Rocks	804	6,490	5.10	10.30
4.10	8.58	1,116		Hallville	797	6,500	4.47	9.45
4.40	9.10	1,120		Black Buttes	790	6,600	4.35	9.25
5.30	9.35	1,129		**Bitter Creek**	784	6,686	4.05	8.00
6.30	10.05	1,139		Table Rock	773	6,8.0	3.35	7.10
7.35	10.45	1,153		Red Desert	760	6,710	2.55	6.05
8.15	11.15	1,162		Wash-a-kie	751	6,697	2.30	5.25
9.45	12.05 AM	1,177		Creston	736	7,030	1.40	4.15
10.50	12.55	1,191		Separation	722	6,900	12.55	3.05
12.00	1.30	1,205		**Rawlins**	708	6,732	12.00 n't	10.50 PM
1.55	2.30	1,218		Fort Steele	695	6,840	11.05 PM	9.25
3.15	3.15	1,234		St. Mary's	679	6,751	10.20	8.15
4,35	3.55	1,245		Percy	668	6,950	9.40	7.05
5.40	4.30	1,258		Carbon	655	6,750	9.05	5.30
6.45	5.00	1,269		Medicine Row	644	6,550	8.30	4.45
7.15	5.22	1,276		Como	639	6,680	8.10	4.10
7.55	6.32	1,291		Rock Creek	612	6,690	7.30	3.00
9.30 AM	7.28	1,308		Lookout	605	7,169	6.45	1.25
10.55	8.15	1,327		Wyoming	586	7,068	5.50	11.50 AM
11.50	8.30	1,333		Howell's	580	7,100	5.30	11.25
12.30 PM	†1.10	1,341		**Laramie**	572	7,123	†5.10	11.40

Trains are run between Ogden and Laramie by Laramie time.
Trains are run between Laramie and Omaha by Omaha time.   † Meals.

UNION PACIFIC RAILROAD. [CONTINUED.]

EASTWARD			Divisions and Stations.	Miles from Omaha.	Elevations.	WESTWARD	
Mixed.	Express.	Miles fm San F'co				Express.	Mixed.
No. 6.	No. 4.					No. 3.	No. 7.
P.M.	A.M.					A.M.	P.M.
3.00	9.30	1,350	Red Buttes	563	....	4.08	9.30
3.40	9.55	1,356	Harney	557	7,857	3.40	8.50
4.40	10.35	1,365	Sherman	548	8,242	3.05	7.25
6.15	11.20	1,378	Granite Canyon	535	7,298	2.05	6.00
6.50	11.45	1,383	Otto	550	6,724	1.30	5.30
†9.15	†1.40 PM	1,398	**Cheyenne**	515	6,041	†12.40 PM	4.10
10.50	2.35	1,418	Hillsdale	495	5'591	11.45	2.40
11.50	3.05	1,430	Egbert	483	5'272	11.05	1.35
12.40 AM	3.33	1,441	Pine Bluffs	472	5,026	10.35	12.40 AM
1.30	3.58	1,451	Bushnell	462	4,860	10.05	11 35
2.30	4.28	1,463	Antelope	450	4.712	9 35	10.25
3.20	4.53	1,472	Bennett	441	....	9.05	9.30
4.00	5.15	1,481	Potter	432	4,370	8.43	8.45
4.45	5.40	1,491	Brownson	422	....	8.15	7.55
†5.30	6.05	1,500	**Sidney**	413	4,073	†7.25	6.25
7.00	6.45	1,506	Colton	407	4,000	7.00	5.40
7.50	7.10	1,517	Lodge Pole	396	3,800	6.33	4.45
8.05	7,38	1,527	Chappel	386	3,700	6.05	3.55
9 25	8.02	1,537	Julesburg	376	3.500	5.35	3.05
10.45	8.50	1,553	Big Springs	360	3,325	4.50	1.45
11.30	9.15	1,563	Brule	350	3'266	4.20	1.05
1.05	10.05	1,582	Roscoe	331	3,105	3.30	11.30 AM
1.50	10.30	1,592	Alkali	321	3,038	3.03	10.40
3.00	11.10	1,606	O'Fallon's	307	2,976	2.25	9.25
4.15	11.55	1,623	**North Platte**	290	2,789	1.40 AM	8.00
6.20	12.40	1,637	McPherson	276	2,695	12.40	5.50
7.05	1.07	1,646	Brady Island	267	2,637	12.13	5.00
7.50	1.52	1,654	Warren	259	2,570	11.47	4.10
8.35	2.00	1,664	Willow Island	249	2,511	11.20	3.20
9.20	2.55	1,674	Coyote	239	2,440	10.52	2.28
10.10	2.23	1,684	Plum Creek	229	2,370	10.25	1.35
11.15	3.50	1,693	Overton	220	2,305	10.00	12.45
12.00	4.13	1,702	Elm Creek	211	2,241	9.35	12.00
12.50	4.43	1,713	Stevenson	200	2,170	9.10	11.15
1.40	4.45	1,723	Kearny	190	2,106	8.42	10.25 PM
2.25	5.10	1,731	Gibbon	181	2,046	8.20	9.45
3.15	5.40	1,742	Wood River	171	1,974	7.50	8.55
6.05	6.08	1,752	Pawnee	161	1,907	6.55	7.10
†5.20	7.00	1,760	**Grand Island**	153	1,850	†6 30	6.30
6.10	7.30	1,772	Chapman's	141	1,760	5.57	5.40
7.00	7.55	1,782	Lone Tree	131	1,686	5.35	4.50
7 55	8.25	1,793	Clark's	120	1,610	5 05	3.55
8.55	8 55	1,805	Silver Creek	108	1,534	4.35	3.00
9 40	9 25	1,815	Jackson	98	1,470	4.07	2.05
10.30	9.45	1,822	Columbus	91	1,432	3.47	1.30
....	....	1,830	Cooper	83			
12.10 AM	10.25	1,838	Schuyler	75	1,335	3.05	12.10
1.20	11.05	1,852	North Bend	61	1,259	2.25	11.05 AM
2.00	11.25	1,850	Ketchum	53	1,200	1.35	10.05
†3.20	12.10 PM	1.867	Fremont	46	1,176	1.15	9.35
4.15	12.45	1,879	Valley	34	1.120	12.45 PM	8.40
5.00	1.05	1,885	Elk Horn	28	1,150	12.25	8.00
5.25	1.20	1,899	Papillion	14	972	11.45	6.50
6.55	2.00	1,905	Gilmore	9	976	11.30	6 25
8.00 PM	3.00	1,913	Ar. **Omaha** .... Lv.	0	966	†10.00 AM	5.30

Lodge Pole Division, C. H. Chappel, Superintendent.

Platte Division, S. H. H. Clark, Superintendent.

Trains are run between Ogden and Laramie by Laramie time.
Trains are run between Laramie and Omaha by Omaha time.   † Meals.

Dale Creek Bridge

The largest trestle on the Union Pacific was across Dale Creek, west of Sherman Summit where the railroad crossed a ravine on a timber trestle 560 feet long, with the center 130 feet above the inconsequential stream below. An early transcontinental guide classified the structure as an engineering marvel. "Dale Creek Bridge comes into sight. There is a rush to the platform to enjoy the sensation of crossing the abyss. Seen from a distance, this marvel of wood spanning the deep, rocky bed of the stream has the airiest and most gossamer-like effect; but it is a substantial structure over which our long train goes roaring in safety, though not without a few shrieks from those on the platforms who are averse to seeing a 130 feet of empty space yawning below them."

Due to the ever increasing weight of motive power and trains, plus the great fire hazard, the wooden structure was soon replaced by an iron trestle of equal dimension in 1876. This was replaced by one with iron girder spans in 1885; it was dismantled in 1901 when the line was relocated and the crossing made on an earth and rock fill.

Dale Creek Bridge as seen from the north side a few days before it was completed in 1868, had a foundation on solid rock. In the foreground is a crude log shelter for the workmen. (BELOW) The second Dale Creek Bridge, known as the "Spider Web" was completed in 1876. Nine years later an iron girder span was to replace this structure.

UNION PACIFIC MUSEUM

CENTRAL PACIFIC-UNION PACIFIC

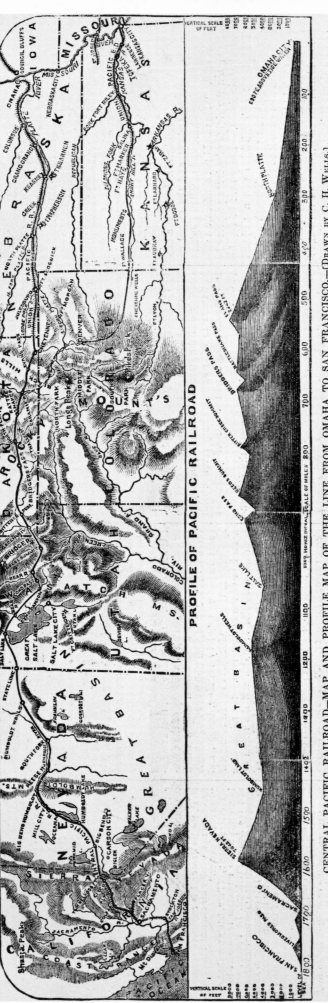

CENTRAL PACIFIC RAILROAD—MAP AND PROFILE MAP OF THE LINE FROM OMAHA TO SAN FRANCISCO.—[DRAWN BY C. H. WELLS.]

In 1868 *Harpers Weekly* published this interesting map and profile of the Pacific Railroad. The crosshatched lines indicate completed sections, but the cartographer used stage names for many of the towns in the unfinished territory. The steep grade from Cheyenne to Sherman Summit is not shown on the profile.

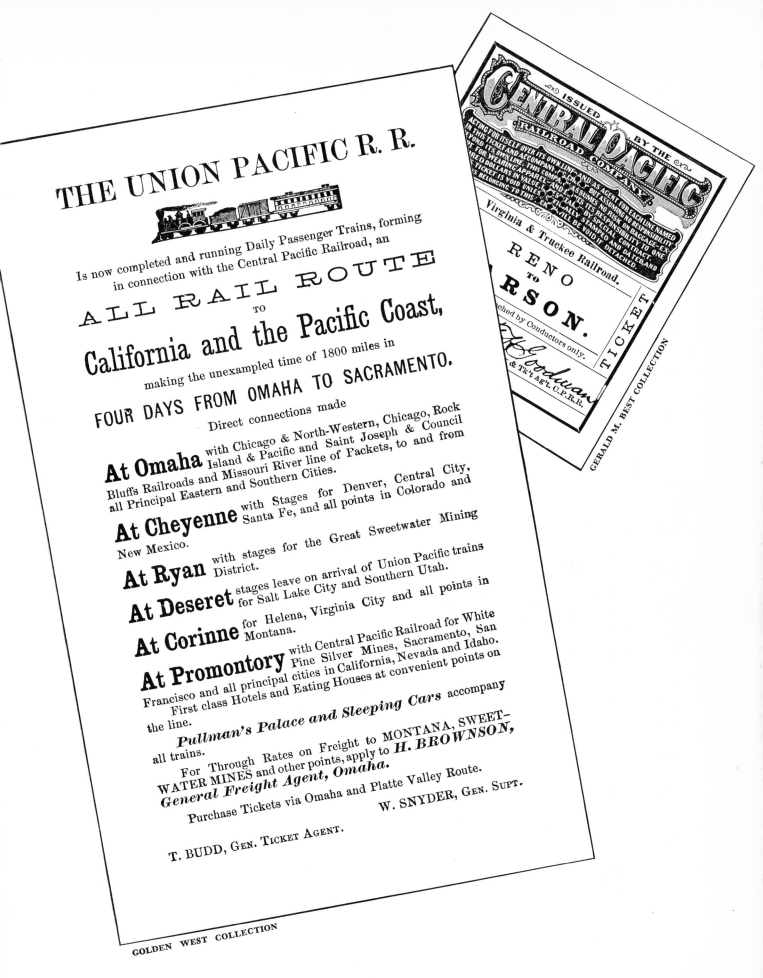

THE UNION PACIFIC R. R.

Is now completed and running Daily Passenger Trains, forming in connection with the Central Pacific Railroad, an

ALL RAIL ROUTE

TO

California and the Pacific Coast,

making the unexampled time of 1800 miles in

FOUR DAYS FROM OMAHA TO SACRAMENTO.

Direct connections made

At Omaha with Chicago & North-Western, Chicago, Rock Island & Pacific and Saint Joseph & Council Bluffs Railroads and Missouri River line of Packets, to and from all Principal Eastern and Southern Cities.

At Cheyenne with Stages for Denver, Central City, Santa Fe, and all points in Colorado and New Mexico.

At Ryan with stages for the Great Sweetwater Mining District.

At Deseret stages leave on arrival of Union Pacific trains for Salt Lake City and Southern Utah.

At Corinne for Helena, Virginia City and all points in Montana.

At Promontory with Central Pacific Railroad for White Pine Silver Mines, Sacramento, San Francisco and all principal cities in California, Nevada and Idaho. First class Hotels and Eating Houses at convenient points on the line.

Pullman's Palace and Sleeping Cars accompany all trains.

For Through Rates on Freight to MONTANA, SWEET–WATER MINES and other points, apply to **H. BROWNSON,** *General Freight Agent, Omaha.*

Purchase Tickets via Omaha and Platte Valley Route.

W. SNYDER, Gen. Supt.

T. BUDD, Gen. Ticket Agent.

CENTRAL PACIFIC RAILROAD COMPANY.

Virginia & Truckee Railroad.

RENO TO CARSON.

TICKET

Punched by Conductors only.

Goodman G. Tk't Ag't. C.P.R.R.

Corinne-Queen City of the Valley

By March 1869, Corinne, Utah, was flourishing around an advance base for grading crews of the Union Pacific. Early citizens classed it the first gentile town in Utah Territory, and had high hopes of its becoming the major city of the Salt Lake Basin. The town was laid out and lots sold in March 1869, under the Union Pacific regime, by General James A. Williamson, their land agent. The town derived its name from his daughter Corinna.

Corinne became a focal point to the untapped territories of Montana and Idaho with the new Pacific Railroad forming a connection east and west, it was the proud possessor of destiny unlimited. As the railroad neared completion, thousands of freight handlers and miners swarmed in, looking for excitement, and turned the primitive "Queen City of the Great Basin" into a rakehell metropolis for prostitutes and professional gamblers. The well-known Salt Lake photographer, Colonel Charles R. Savage, had been engaged by the Union Pacific to take additional photographs of the meeting of the rails. While roaming Corinne, he reported drunken men being heaped aboard flatcars and run out of town. He stated that all of Corinne was "on the wrong side of the tracks." Englishman W. F. Rae in his book *Westward By Rail*, reported one gallant little custom of the gambling sharks who plied their trade during the brief stop there. Having stripped the unwary greenhorn, he wrote, they were wont to give him a gold piece so that be need not go hungry during the remainder of his trip. With the construction of Southern Pacific's Lucin Cutoff across Great Salt Lake in 1903, Corinne lost what little importance it had in the valley.

Corinne appeared to be more permanent than Promontory when the Union Pacific rails reached town. At the end of Corinne's main street was the Uintah House which served a full course meal for $1.00. — WILLIAM HENRY JACKSON — U.S. GEOLOGICAL SURVEY

Promontory's principal thoroughfare in early 1869 during its raffish year of whiskey, gambling tents, meals at all hours, and cheap hotels. This vanished overnight when the junction of the railroads was shifted to Ogden where no such liberal philosophy was tolerated. — SOUTHERN PACIFIC

Promontory

Promontory became the meeting place of the Union Pacific and Central Pacific more by luck rather than design. Since various junctions were unsatisfactory to one railroad or the other, Congress in 1866 decided to allow the lines to build until they met. Promontory became a compromise meeting point. Waterless Promontory never thrived except prior to and shortly after the "meeting of the rails." By the time trains were rolling through Promontory on regular schedules, pausing often for several hours to transfer mail and baggage from the cars of one railroad to the other, the shack and tent town took on the overtones of a fast place.

Passengers descending from the steamcars were warned by train crews against the card tables, the prostitutes and wild ways. The Golden Spike Hotel where the train paused for meals in the seventies, advertised that the table was top notch, but accounts differ. The town of Promontory was partly built of wood, and of canvas; it boasted of but one main street. After many passenger complaints, the railroads ran off most of the gamblers and women of sin. With the construction of Lucin Cutoff, Promontory vanished from the countryside.

Handbill passed out on all transcontinental trains announcing the cuisine of the Golden Spike Hotel. — WARD KIMBALL COLLECTION

197

Governor Stanford-No. 1

The first locomotive to run on the Central Pacific was the *Governor Stanford* No. 1 built by Richard Norris & Son of Philadelphia in 1862. The locomotive arrived in Sacramento October 6, 1863, after a long voyage on a sailing vessel around Cape Horn. It made its trial run on November 10, 1863, and was put to work hauling the construction train.

The *Governor Stanford* held the honor of handling the first Central Pacific revenue freight train, the first scheduled passenger train, and was veritably a pioneer.

Delegated to the unglamorous work of yard engine in later years, it also served as a fire engine. It was retired in 1894 and presented to Leland Stanford Junior University at Palo Alto, California, where it was stored in a shed until 1916 when it was moved into the Leland Stanford Junior Museum.

In 1963 the space the locomotive occupied became more important to the museum for other purposes, and the engine was loaned to the Pacific Coast Chapter-Railway & Locomotive Historical Society to be exhibited in a proposed transportation museum. The engine has been stored in Richmond and Oakland since removed from the museum and will go to Sacramento where it first operated, in time for the Centennial of the Golden Spike, May 10, 1969.

The *Governor Stanford* being moved into the Leland Stanford Jr. Museum in 1916. Donated earlier, it had been in storage in a nearby shed. — SOUTHERN PACIFIC

Framed in the arched entrance to the museum rotunda, No. 1 was viewed by many visitors. (TOP RIGHT) Behind the engine pilot, the sign which had been removed from the western end of the "10 Miles Of Track Laid In One Day." (ABOVE-LEFT) The fenders below the cab and running board went out of style 70 years ago. (ABOVE-RIGHT) High angle view showing steam dome, sand dome, bell and headlight. — ALL ROGER BROGGIE (BELOW) Outside the museum the *Governor Stanford* leaves its home for half a century. — SOUTHERN PACIFIC

With the grade excavated and hand-hewn ties in place, the men in the foreground lay out the exact amount of spikes on each tie, soon to be followed by the tracklayers. Note Andrew J. Russell in the center as he prepares one of his famous photographs. This illustration is from the great film classic "Union Pacific", produced and directed by Cecil B. DeMille. — PARAMOUNT PICTURES

Bibliography

BOOKS

Beebe, Lucius, *The Central Pacific & The Southern Pacific Railroads.* Berkeley, Howell-North Books, 1963.

Block, Eugene B., *Great Train Robberies of the West.* New York, Coward-McCann, Inc., 1959.

Crofutt, George A., *New Overland Tours and Pacific Coast Guide.* Chicago, The Overland Publishing Co., 1878.

Daggett, Stuart, *History of the Southern Pacific.* New York, The Ronald Press, 1922.

Dodge, Major General Grenville M., *How We Built the Union Pacific Railway.* Washington, U. S. Government Printing Office, 1910.

Duke, Donald, *Southern Pacific Steam Locomotives.* San Marino, Golden West Books, 1962.

Dunscomb, Guy L., *A Century of Southern Pacific Steam Locomotives.* Modesto, Dunscomb Press, 1963.

Evans, Cerinda W., *Collis Potter Huntington.* Volumes 1-2, Newport News, The Mariner's Museum, 1954.

Fergusson, J. C., *The Alta California Pacific Coast and Transcontinental Railroad Guide.* San Francisco, Fred MacCrellish & Co., 1871.

Galloway, John D., *The First Transcontinental Railroad.* New York, Simmons-Boardman, 1950.

Griswold, Wesley S., *The Work of Giants.* New York, McGraw-Hill Book Co., 1962.

Halley, William, *Centennial Yearbook of Alameda County-California.* 1876.

Hayes, William E., *Iron Road to Empire.* New York, Simmons-Boardman, 1953.

Howard, Robert West, *The Great Iron Trail.* New York, G. P. Putnam's Sons, 1962.

Kneiss, Gilbert H., *Bonanza Railroads.* Stanford, Stanford University Press, 1941.

Leonard, Levi O., and Johnson, Jack T., *A Railroad to the Sea.* Iowa City, Midland House, 1939.

Lewis, Oscar, *The Big Four.* New York, Alfred A. Knopf, Inc., 1938.

Leslie, Frank, and Reinhardt, Richard, *Out West on the Overland Train (1877-1967).* Palo Alto, American West Publishing Co., 1967.

Lyles, James A., *Manual of the Railroads of North America.* Volumes 1-3, New York, Lindsay, Walton & Co., 1869-1871.

Mauck, G. P., *Grenville Mellen Dodge — Soldier — Engineer.* Iowa City, State Historical Society of Iowa, 1966.

McCague, James, *Moguls and Iron Men.* New York, Harper & Row, 1964.

Myrick, David F., *The Railroads of Nevada.* Volume 1., Berkeley, Howell-North Books, 1962.

Nathan, Adele, *The Building of the First Transcontinental Railroad.* New York, Random House, 1950.

Nelson, T., *Nelson's Pictorial Guide Book to The Central Pacific Railroad — A Trip Across the North American Continent from Ogden to San Francisco.* New York, T. Nelson & Sons, 1869.

————., *Nelson's Pictorial Guide Book to The Union Pacific Railroad — A Trip Across the North American Continent from Omaha to Ogden.* New York, T. Nelson & Sons, 1869.

Poor, Henry V., *Manual of the Railroads of the United States.* Volumes 1-25, New York, H. V. and H. W. Poor, 1868-1892.

Rae, W. F., *Westward By Rail.* New York, D. Appleton & Co., 1871.

Richmond, Robert W., and Mardock, Robert W., *A Nation Moving West.* Lincoln, University of Nebraska Press, 1966.

Riegel, Robert Edgar, *The Story of Western Railroads.* New York, The Macmillan Co., 1926.

Russell, A. J., *The Great West — Photo Views Across the Continent Taken Along the Lines of the Union Pacific Railroad.* New York, Union Pacific Railroad Co., 1869.

Russell, Charles Edward, *Stories of the Great Railroads.* Chicago, Charles H. Kerr & Co., 1912.

Sabin, Edwin L., *Building the Pacific Railway.* Philadelphia, J. B. Lippincott Co., 1919.

Sedgwick, S. J., *Illustrated Course of Lectures — Across the Continent.* Newton, S. J. Sedgwick Co., 1869.

The Biographical Directory of The Railway Officials of America. Volumes 1-3, Chicago, Railway Age Publishing Co., 1885-1887.

Warman, Cy, *The Story of the Railroad.* New York, D. Appleton & Co., 1898.

White, Henry Kirke, *History of the Union Pacific Railway.* Chicago, University of Chicago Press, 1895.

Winther, Oscar D., *The Transportation Frontier 1865-1890.* New York, Holt, Rinehart & Winston, 1964.

PERIODICALS AND MAGAZINES

Best, Gerald M., *Locomotives of the Southern Pacific.* Railway & Locomotive Historical Society—Bulletin 94, Boston, 1956.

Bowman, Jacob N., *Driving the Last Spike.* California Historical Society Quarterly, San Francisco, Volume 36, No. 2 (June 1957), Volume 36, No. 3 (September 1957).

Frank Leslie's Illustrated Newspaper. New York, May 29, 1869; June 5, 1869.

Harper's Weekly. New York, June 5, 1869.

Harris, Daniel L., *Memorandum Concerning the Union Pacific Railroad, a Diary, March 18 to August 31, 1869.* Railway & Locomotive Historical Society — Bulletin 32. Boston, 1933.

Joslyn, David L., *Railroads of the West.* Railway & Locomotive Historical Society—Bulletin 5. Boston, 1923.

————, *Locomotives Built at the Sacramento Shops.* Railway & Locomotive Historical Society — Bulletin 6. Boston, 1923.

————, *A Trip Across the Sierra Nevada Mountains in 1868.* Railway & Locomotive Historical Society — Bulletin 29. Boston, 1932.

————, *Hoisting Engine Hauled to Summit of Sierra Nevada Mountains in 1866.* Railway & Locomotive Historical Society — Bulletin 32. Boston, 1933.

————, *Romance of the Railroads Entering Sacramento.* Railway & Locomotive Historical Society — Bulletin 48. Boston, 1939.

————, *Andrew Jackson Stevens — A Biography.* Railway & Locomotive Historical Society — Bulletin 65. Boston, 1944.

Jukes, Fred, *Smokestacks: Ours' and Others.* Railway & Locomotive Historical Society — Bulletin 112. Boston, 1965.

Kneiss, Gilbert H., *The Sacramento Valley Railroad.* Railway & Locomotive Historical Society — Bulletin 29. Boston, 1932.

————, *History of the Union Iron Works.* Railway & Locomotive Historical Society — Bulletin 68. Boston, 1946.

"Locomotive Smokestacks of the Union Pacific." *American Engineer and Railroad Journal,* May 1899.

Nordhoff, Charles, *California — How to go there, and what to see by the way.* Harper's New Monthly Magazine, Volume XLIV (May 1872).

Official Guide of the Railroads of the United States. New York, Volumes 1-25 (1868-1892).

Railroad Gazette. New York, Volumes 5-23 (1873-1891).

The Railway Review. Chicago, Volumes 1-10 (1868-1875).

Southern Pacific's First Century. San Francisco, Southern Pacific Company, 1955.

Stillman, J. D. B., *The Last Tie.* The Overland Monthly, Volume 3, No. 1 (July 1869).

Wheat, Carl I., *A Sketch of the Life of Theodore D.*

Judah. California Historical Society, Volume 4, No. 3 (September 1925).

Wooster, Clarence M., *Reminiscences of Railroading in California in the 1870's.* California Historical Society Quarterly, Volume 18, No. 4 (December 1939).

COMPANY RECORDS

CENTRAL PACIFIC RAILROAD — Annual reports to the stockholders; *Locomotive Engines—June 1869; Locomotive Engines — January 1871; Locomotive Engines and Rolling Stock — June 1878;* The Log Books of the Shop Foreman, 1870-1874, Sacramento Shops. SOUTHERN PACIFIC RAILROAD—*Classification, Renumbering and Assignment of Locomotives and Rolling Stock, January 1, 1891; Classification of Locomotives, Pacific System, January 1, 1893; Classification of Locomotives, Pacific System, August 26, 1896.* UNION PACIFIC RAILROAD — Annual reports to the stockholders 1866 to 1885; *Classification and Renumbering of Locomotives, July 1, 1885.*

LOCOMOTIVE MANUFACTURER RECORDS

Lists of the locomotives built by the following companies in the Library — Railway & Locomotive Historical Society, Inc., Charles E. Fisher, President, Boston, Massachusetts: Baldwin Locomotive Works; Danforth, Cooke & Co.; Danforth Locomotive & Machine Co.; Hinkley & Williams (Boston Locomotive Works); Manchester Locomotive Works; William Mason (Mason Machine Works); Rhode Island Locomotive Works; Rogers Locomotive & Machine Works; Schenectady Locomotive Works; Taunton Locomotive Works.

NEWSPAPERS

Alta California, San Francisco, California, 1863-1869.

Bee, Sacramento, California, 1863-1870.

Chronicle, San Francisco, California, 1863-1869.

Crescent, Reno, Nevada, 1869.

Daily Transcript, Nevada City, California, 1863-1891.

Daily Republican, Omaha, Nebraska, 1862-1869.

Deseret News, Salt Lake City, Utah, 1868-1869.

Republican, Truckee, California, 1869-1877.

Telegraph, Salt Lake City, Utah, 1868-1869.

Times, New York, New York, 1869.

Tribune, New York, New York, 1869.

Union, Sacramento, California, 1858, 1861-1877.

Weekly Republican, Omaha, Nebraska, 1862-1869.

"ALL HAIL AND FAREWELL TO THE PACIFIC RAILROAD."
WENDELL PHILLIPS.

Index